WatchKit App Development Essentials

WatchKit App Development Essentials – First Edition

ISBN-13: 978-1512302578

Rev 1.0

 eBookFrenzy

Table of Contents

1. Start Here 1
   1.1 Source Code Download... 1
   1.2 Download the eBook 1
   1.3 Feedback 2
   1.4 Errata 2

2. WatchKit Apps – An Overview 3
   2.1 What is a WatchKit App? 3
   2.2 WatchKit and iOS Apps 3
   2.3 The WatchKit Framework 4
   2.4 Understanding iOS Extensions 4
   2.5 Basic WatchKit App/Extension Structure 5
   2.6 WatchKit App Entry Points... 5
   2.7 Summary 6

3. Building an Example WatchKit App 7
   3.1 Creating the WatchKit App Project 7
   3.2 Designing the iOS App User Interface 7
   3.3 Adding the WatchKit Extension and App 9
   3.4 Designing the WatchKit App Storyboard 10
   3.5 Running the WatchKit App 13
   3.6 Running the App on a Physical Apple Watch Device 14
   3.7 Setting the Scene Title and Key Color 16
   3.8 Adding App Icons to the Project 17
   3.9 Summary.. 20

4. An Overview of the WatchKit App Architecture 21
   4.1 Basic WatchKit App Architecture 21
   4.2 WatchKit Interface Controllers 21
   4.3 WatchKit Action Methods.. 22
   4.4 WatchKit Outlets 23
   4.5 The Lifecycle of a WatchKit App 24
   4.6 WatchKit Extension Guidelines 25
   4.7 Summary.. 25

5. An Example Interactive WatchKit App 27

5.1 About the Example App 27

5.2 Creating the TipCalcApp Project 27

5.3 Adding the WatchKit App Target 27

5.4 Designing the WatchKit App User Interface 28

5.5 Reviewing the Interface Controller Class 30

5.6 Establishing Outlet Connections 31

5.7 Establishing Action Connections 34

5.8 Implementing the sliderChange Action Method 36

5.9 Implementing the calculateTip Action Method 37

5.10 Hiding the Tip Label 38

5.11 Removing the WatchKit App 39

5.12 Summary 39

6. An Overview of WatchKit Tables **41**

6.1 The WatchKit Table 41

6.2 Table Row Controller 41

6.3 Row Controller Type 42

6.4 Table Row Initialization 42

6.5 Implementing a Table in a WatchKit App Scene 42

6.6 Adding the Row Controller Class to the Extension 44

6.7 Associating a Row Controller with a Row Controller Class 44

6.8 Creating Table Rows at Runtime 45

6.9 Inserting Table Rows 46

6.10 Removing Table Rows 47

6.11 Scrolling to a Specific Table Row 47

6.12 Summary 47

7. A WatchKit Table Tutorial **49**

7.1 About the Table Example 49

7.2 Creating the Table Project 49

7.3 Adding the WatchKit App Target 49

7.4 Adding the Table to the Scene 50

7.5 Creating the Row Controller Class 51

7.6 Establishing the Outlets 52

7.7 Connecting the Table Outlet 54

7.8 Creating the Data 54

7.9 Adding the Image Files to the Project 56

7.10 Testing the WatchKit App 57

7.11 Adding a Title Row to the Table 58

7.12 Connecting the Outlet and Initializing the Second Table Row 59

7.13 Summary 60

8. Implementing WatchKit Table Navigation..**63**

8.1 Table Navigation in WatchKit Apps.. 63

8.2 Performing a Scene Transition... 63

8.3 Extending the TableDemoApp Project.. 64

8.4 Adding the Detail Scene to the Storyboard 65

8.5 Adding the Detail Interface Controller.. 66

8.6 Adding the Detail Data Array 67

8.7 Implementing the didSelectRow Method.. 68

8.8 Modifying the awakeWithContext Method 69

8.9 Adjusting the Interface Controller Insets 69

8.10 Summary... 70

9. WatchKit Page-based User Interfaces and Modal Interface Controllers **71**

9.1 The Elements of a Page-based WatchKit Interface.. 71

9.2 Associating Page Scenes 72

9.3 Managing Pages at Runtime 73

9.4 Modal Presentation of Interface Controllers... 73

9.5 Modal Presentation in Code 74

9.6 Modal Presentation using Storyboard Segues.. 74

9.7 Passing Context Data During a Modal Segue 75

9.8 Summary... 76

10. A WatchKit Page-based Interface Tutorial..**77**

10.1 Creating the Page Example Project.. 77

10.2 Adding the WatchKit App Target 77

10.3 Adding the Image Files to the Project.. 78

10.4 Designing the First Interface Controller Scene 78

10.5 Adding More Interface Controllers 79

10.6 Establishing the Segues.. 80

10.7 Assigning Interface Controllers 81

10.8 Adding the Timer Interface Controller.. 82

10.9 Adding the Modal Segues 84

10.10 Configuring the Context Data 85

10.11 Configuring the Timer 87

10.12 Playing the Alert Sound... 88

10.13 Summary.. 90

11. Handling User Input in a WatchKit App **91**

11.1 Getting User Input 91

11.2 Displaying the Text Input Controller 92

11.3 Detecting if Input is a String or NSData Object 93

11.4 Direct Dictation Input 93

11.5 Creating the User Input Example Project 93

11.6 Adding the WatchKit App Target 93

11.7 Designing the WatchKit App Main Scene 94

11.8 Getting the User Input 94

11.9 Testing the Application 95

11.10 Summary 95

12. WatchKit App and Parent iOS App Communication 97

12.1 Parent iOS App Communication 97

12.2 The openParentApplication Method 98

12.3 The handleWatchKitExtensionRequest Method 99

12.4 Understanding iOS Background Modes 99

12.4.1 Using the beginBackgroundTaskWithName Method 99

12.4.2 Using Background Modes 100

12.5 Summary 101

13. A WatchKit openParentApplication Example Project 103

13.1 About the Project 103

13.2 Creating the Project 103

13.3 Enabling Audio Background Mode 103

13.4 Designing the iOS App User Interface 104

13.5 Establishing Outlets and Actions 105

13.6 Initializing Audio Playback 106

13.7 Implementing the Audio Control Methods 108

13.8 Adding the WatchKit App Target 109

13.9 Designing the WatchKit App Scene 109

13.10 Opening the Parent Application 111

13.11 Handling the WatchKit Extension Request 112

13.12 Testing the Application 113

13.13 Summary 114

14. Sharing Data Between a WatchKit App and the Containing iOS App 115

14.1 Sandboxes, Containers and User Defaults 115

14.2 Sharing Data Using App Groups 116

14.3 Adding an App or Extension to an App Group 116

14.4 App Group File Sharing 119

14.5 App Group User Default Sharing 120

14.6 Summary 120

15. WatchKit Extension and iOS App File and Data Sharing - A Tutorial 121

15.1 About the App Group Sharing Example 121

15.2 Creating the Sharing Project 121

15.3 Designing the iOS App User Interface 121

15.4 Connecting Actions and Outlets 123

15.5 Creating the App Group 123

15.6 Performing Initialization Tasks 124

15.7 Saving the Data 126

15.8 Adding the WatchKit App Target 126

15.9 Adding the WatchKit App to the App Group 127

15.10 Designing the WatchKit App Scene 127

15.11 Adding the WatchKit App Actions and Outlets 128

15.12 Performing the WatchKit App Initialization 128

15.13 Implementing the switchChanged Method 130

15.14 Testing the Project 131

15.15 Summary 131

16. Configuring Preferences with the WatchKit Settings Bundle 133

16.1 An Overview of the WatchKit Settings Bundle 133

16.2 Adding a WatchKit Settings Bundle to a Project 134

16.3 WatchKit Bundle Settings Controls 135

16.4 Accessing WatchKit Bundle Settings from Code 137

16.5 Registering Default Preference Values 138

16.6 Configuring a Settings Icon 139

16.7 Summary 140

17. A WatchKit Settings Bundle Tutorial 141

17.1 About the WatchKit Settings Bundle Example 141

17.2 Creating the WatchKit Settings Bundle Project 141

17.3 Adding the WatchKit App Target 141

17.4 Designing the WatchKit App Scene 142

17.5 Adding the WatchKit Settings Bundle 142

17.6 Adding a Switch Control to the Settings Bundle 144

17.7 Adding a Slider Control to the Settings Bundle 145

17.8 Adding a Multi Value Control to the Settings Bundle 146

17.9 Setting Up the App Group 149

17.10 Adding the App Group to the Settings Bundle 150

17.11 Accessing Preference Settings from the WatchKit Extension 150

17.12 Registering the Default Preference Settings 153

17.13 Adding the Companion Settings Icons 153

17.14 Testing the Settings Bundle Project 154

17.15 Summary 155

18. An Overview of WatchKit Glances **157**

18.1 WatchKit Glances... 157

18.2 The Architecture of a WatchKit Glance 157

18.3 Adding a Glance During WatchKit App Creation... 158

18.4 Adding a Glance to an Existing WatchKit App 159

18.5 WatchKit Glance Scene Layout Templates 161

18.6 Passing Context Data to the WatchKit App 163

18.7 Summary... 163

19. A WatchKit Glance Tutorial...**165**

19.1 About the Glance Scene 165

19.2 Adding the Glance to the Project... 165

19.3 Designing the Glance Scene Layout.. 167

19.4 Establishing Outlet Connections.. 168

19.5 Adding Data to the Glance Interface Controller 169

19.6 Creating an App Group 170

19.7 Storing and Retrieving the Currently Selected Table Row............................... 171

19.8 Passing Context Data to the WatchKit App 172

19.9 Summary... 174

20. A WatchKit Context Menu Tutorial **175**

20.1 An Overview of WatchKit Context Menus 175

20.2 Designing Menu Item Images 176

20.3 Creating a Context Menu in Interface Builder 177

20.4 Adding and Removing Menu Items in Code 179

20.5 Creating the Context Menu Example Project 180

20.6 Adding the WatchKit App Target 180

20.7 Designing the WatchKit App User Interface 181

20.8 Designing the Context Menu 181

20.9 Establishing the Action Connections 182

20.10 Testing the Context Menu App.. 183

20.11 Summary... 183

21. Working with Images in WatchKit...**185**

21.1 Displaying Images in WatchKit Apps.. 185

21.2 Images Originating in the WatchKit Extension 185

21.3 Understanding Named Images 186

21.4 Adding Images to a WatchKit App 186

21.5 Caching Extension-based Images on the Watch Device 189

21.6 Compressing Large Images 190

21.7 Specifying the WKInterfaceImage Object Dimensions in Code 191

21.8 Displaying Animated Images 191

21.9 Template Images and Tinting 193

21.10 Summary 194

22. A WatchKit Animated Image Tutorial 195

22.1 Creating the Animation Example Project 195

22.2 Adding the WatchKit App Target 195

22.3 Designing the Main Scene Layout 195

22.4 Adding the Animation Sequence Images 196

22.5 Creating and Starting the Animated Image 197

22.6 Summary 198

23. Working with Fonts and Attributed Strings in WatchKit 201

23.1 Dynamic Text and Text Style Fonts 201

23.2 Using Text Style Fonts in Code 203

23.3 Understanding Attributed Strings 203

23.4 Using System Fonts 205

23.5 Summary 207

24. A WatchKit App Custom Font Tutorial 209

24.1 Using Custom Fonts in WatchKit 209

24.2 Downloading a Custom Font 210

24.3 Creating the Custom Font Project 211

24.4 Adding the WatchKit App Target 211

24.5 Designing the WatchKit App Scene 211

24.6 Adding the Custom Font to the Project 212

24.7 Selecting Custom Fonts in Interface Builder 214

24.8 Using Custom Fonts in Code 215

24.9 Summary 217

25. Supporting Different Apple Watch Display Sizes 219

25.1 Screen Size Customization Attributes 219

25.2 Working with Screen Sizes in Interface Builder 221

25.3 Identifying the Screen Size at Runtime 223

25.4 Summary 223

26. A WatchKit Map Tutorial 225

26.1 Creating the Example Map Project 225

26.2 Adding the WatchKit App Target to the Project 225

26.3 Designing the WatchKit App User Interface 225

26.4 Configuring the Containing iOS App 226

26.5 Enabling Background Location Updates 228

26.6 Handling the Open Parent App Request 229

26.7 Getting the Current Location 231

26.8 Implementing the WatchKit Extension Map Code 232

26.9 Adding Zooming Support 235

26.10 Summary 235

27. An Overview of Notifications in WatchKit **237**

27.1 Default WatchKit Notification Handling 237

27.2 Creating Notification Actions 238

27.3 Handling Notification Actions 240

27.4 Custom Notifications 241

27.5 Dynamic and Static Notifications 241

27.6 Adding a Custom Notification to a WatchKit App 242

27.7 Configuring the Notification Category 243

27.8 Updating the Dynamic Notification Scene 244

27.9 Summary 245

28. A WatchKit Notification Tutorial **247**

28.1 About the Example Project 247

28.2 Creating the Xcode Project 247

28.3 Designing the iOS App User Interface 247

28.4 Establishing Outlets and Actions 249

28.5 Creating and Joining an App Group 249

28.6 Initializing the iOS App 250

28.7 Updating the Time Delay 251

28.8 Setting the Notification 251

28.9 Adding the Notification Action 252

28.10 Implementing the handleActionWithIdentifier Method 254

28.11 Adding the WatchKit App to the Project 255

28.12 Adding Notification Icons to the WatchKit App 255

28.13 Testing the Notification on the Apple Watch 256

28.14 Adding the WatchKit App to the App Group 257

28.15 Designing the WatchKit App User Interface 258

28.16 Testing the App 259

28.17 Summary 259

29. A WatchKit Custom Notification Tutorial **261**

29.1 About the WatchKit Custom Notification Example 261

29.2 Creating the Custom Notification Project 261

29.3 Designing the iOS App User Interface 261

29.4 Registering and Setting the Notifications 262

29.5 Adding the WatchKit App to the Project.. 264

29.6 Configuring the Custom Notification 264

29.7 Designing the Dynamic Notification Scene 266

29.8 Configuring the didReceiveLocalNotification method 267

29.9 Adding the Images to the WatchKit App Bundle 267

29.10 Testing the Custom Notification 268

29.11 Summary... 269

Index **271**

1. Start Here

Announced in September 2014, the Apple Watch family of devices is Apple's first foray into the market of wearable technology. The introduction of this new device category was accompanied by the release of the WatchKit framework designed specifically to allow developers to build Apple Watch app extensions to iPhone-based iOS apps.

WatchKit App Development Essentials is intended for readers with some existing experience of iOS development using Xcode and the Swift programming language. Beginning with the basics, this book provides an introduction to WatchKit apps and the WatchKit app development architecture before covering topics such as tables, navigation, user input handling, working with images, maps and menus.

More advanced topics are also covered throughout the book, including communication and data sharing between a WatchKit app and the parent iOS app, working with custom fonts and the design and implementation of custom notifications.

As with all the books in the "Development Essentials" series, WatchKit App Development Essentials takes a modular approach to the subject of WatchKit app development for the Apple Watch, with each chapter covering a self-contained topic area consisting of detailed explanations, examples and step-by-step tutorials. This makes the book both an easy to follow learning aid and an excellent reference resource.

1.1 Source Code Download

The source code and Xcode project files for the examples contained in this book are available for download at:

http://www.ebookfrenzy.com/print/watchkit/

1.2 Download the eBook

Thank you for purchasing the print edition of this book. If you would like to download the eBook version of this book, please email proof of purchase to *feedback@ebookfrenzy.com* and we will provide you with a download link for the book in PDF, ePub and MOBI formats.

1.3 **Feedback**

We want you to be satisfied with your purchase of this book. If you find any errors in the book, or have any comments, questions or concerns please contact us at *feedback@ebookfrenzy.com*.

1.4 **Errata**

Whilst we make every effort to ensure the accuracy of the content of this book, it is inevitable that a book covering a subject area of this size and complexity may include some errors and oversights. Any known issues with the book will be outlined together with solutions at the following URL:

http://www.ebookfrenzy.com/errata/watchkit.html

In the event that you find an error not listed in the errata, please let us know by emailing our technical support team at *feedback@ebookfrenzy.com*.

2. WatchKit Apps – An Overview

Before embarking on the creation of a WatchKit app it is important to gain a basic understanding of what a WatchKit app consists of and, more importantly, how it fits into the existing iOS application ecosystem. Within this chapter, a high level overview of WatchKit apps will be provided, together with an outline of how these apps are structured and delivered to the customer.

2.1 What is a WatchKit App?

Prior to the introduction of the Apple Watch family of devices, it was only possible to develop mobile applications for iPhone, iPad and iPod Touch devices running the iOS operating system. With the introduction of the Apple Watch, however, it is now possible for iOS developers to also create WatchKit apps.

In simplistic terms, WatchKit apps are launched on an Apple Watch device either as the result of an action by the user or in response to some form of local or remote notification. Once launched, the WatchKit app presents a user interface on the watch screen displaying information and controls with which the user can interact to perform tasks.

2.2 WatchKit and iOS Apps

It is important to understand that WatchKit apps are not standalone entities. A WatchKit app can only be created as an *extension* to an existing iOS app. It is not, therefore, possible to create a WatchKit app that is not bundled as part of a new or existing iOS application.

Consider, for example, an iPhone iOS application designed to provide the user with detailed weather information. Prior to the introduction of the Apple Watch, the only way for the user to access the information provided by the app would have been to pick up the iPhone, unlock the device, launch the iOS app and view the information on the iPhone display. Now that information can be made available via the user's Apple Watch device.

In order to make the information provided by the iOS app available via the user's Apple Watch, the developer of the weather app would add a WatchKit app extension to the iOS app, design a suitable user interface to display the information on the watch display and implement the logic to display the appropriate weather information and respond to any user interaction. Instead of having to launch the iOS app from the iPhone device to check the weather, the user can now launch the WatchKit app from the Apple Watch and view and interact with the information.

Clearly, the display size of an Apple Watch is considerably smaller than that of even the smallest of iPhone models. As such, a WatchKit app will typically display only a subset of the content available on the larger iPhone screen. For more detailed information, the user would still need to make use of the iOS application.

2.3 **The WatchKit Framework**

WatchKit apps are made possible by the WatchKit framework which is included as part of the iOS SDK and embedded into both Watch OS (the operating system installed on the Apple Watch) and iOS. The WatchKit framework contains a set of classes that provide the underlying functionality of both the WatchKit extension and WatchKit app. WatchKit, for example, provides the classes that can be used to construct a WatchKit app user interface (such as Button, Label and Slider classes).

WatchKit is also responsible for handling the communication between the iPhone device on which the WatchKit extension is running and the corresponding WatchKit app installed on the Apple Watch.

2.4 **Understanding iOS Extensions**

Extensions are a feature introduced as part of the iOS 8 SDK release and were originally intended solely to allow certain capabilities of an application to be made available for use within other applications running on the same device. The developer of a photo editing application might, for example, have devised some unique image filtering capabilities and decide that those features would be particularly useful to users of the iOS Photos app. To achieve this, the developer would implement these features in a Photo Editing extension which would then appear as an option to users when editing an image within the Photos app. Other extension types are also available for performing document storage, creating custom keyboards and embedding information from an application into the iOS notification panel.

With the introduction of the Apple Watch and WatchKit, however, the concept of extensions has now been extended to make the functionality of an iOS app available in the form of a WatchKit app.

Extensions are separate executable binaries that run independently of the corresponding iOS application. Although extensions take the form of an individual binary, they must be supplied and installed as part of an iOS application bundle. The application with which an extension is bundled is referred to as the *containing app* or *parent app*. The containing app must provide useful functionality and must not be an empty application provided solely for the purpose of delivering an extension to the user.

Once an iOS application containing a WatchKit extension has been installed on an iPhone device, it will be accessible from the Apple Watch device paired with that iPhone. When the user launches a WatchKit app on a watch device, the WatchKit framework will launch the corresponding WatchKit extension on the paired iPhone device, establish communication between the two entities and then begin the app initialization process.

2.5 Basic WatchKit App/Extension Structure

Simply by the nature of its physical size, an Apple Watch is always going to be resource constrained in terms of storage and processing power when compared to an iPhone. As previously outlined, the implementation of a WatchKit app is divided between the WatchKit app installed on the watch and the WatchKit extension bundled with the iOS app on the iPhone device. This raises the question of how the responsibilities of providing the functionality of the WatchKit app are divided between the app and the extension.

By necessity, the WatchKit app needs to be small and efficient. In fact, the WatchKit app bundle installed on the Apple Watch device consists solely of the storyboard file containing the user interface and corresponding resources (such as image and configuration files).

All of the code for providing the functionality of the WatchKit app and responding to user interaction is contained within the WatchKit extension and executed on the iPhone, with the WatchKit framework handling the communication between the app and the extension. This communication primarily takes the form of responding to user interactions (for example notifying the extension that a button was pressed in the user interface), making changes to the user interface on the watch (such as changing the text displayed on a label) and transferring data.

This separation ensures that WatchKit apps remain small and that the resource intensive code execution is performed almost entirely on the iPhone device.

2.6 WatchKit App Entry Points

There are number of different ways in which the user may enter a WatchKit app, each of which will be detailed in later chapters and can be summarized as follows:

- **Home Screen** – Once installed, the WatchKit app will be represented by an icon on the home screen of the Apple Watch display. When this icon is selected by the user the app will load and display the main user interface scene.
- **Glance** – When developing a WatchKit app, the option is available to add a *Glance* interface to the app. This is a single, non-scrollable, read-only scene that can be used to display a quick-look summary of the information normally presented by the full version of the app. Glances are accessed when the user performs an upward swiping motion on the watch display and, when tapped by the user, launch the corresponding WatchKit app.
- **Notifications** – When a notification for a WatchKit app appears on the Apple Watch device, the app will be launched when the notification is tapped.

2.7 **Summary**

A WatchKit app is an application designed to run on the Apple Watch family of devices. A WatchKit app cannot be a standalone application and must instead be created as an extension of an existing iOS application. WatchKit apps and extensions are built in Xcode using the WatchKit framework which, in turn, provides the classes necessary to build WatchKit apps. The WatchKit app is installed on the Apple Watch device and consists of a storyboard file containing the user interface of the app together with a set of resource files. The WatchKit extension, on the other hand, is bundled with the corresponding iOS app and resides and executes on the iPhone device. The extension is a separate binary from the main iOS app and contains all of the code logic to implement the behavior of the WatchKit app. When the app is launched on the Apple Watch, the WatchKit framework launches the corresponding extension on the iPhone device and handles the communication between the app and extension.

3. Building an Example WatchKit App

Having outlined the basic architecture for a WatchKit app in the previous chapter, it is now time to start putting some of this knowledge to practical use through the creation of a simple example app.

The project created in this chapter will work through the creation of a basic WatchKit app that does nothing more than display a message and an image on an Apple Watch display.

3.1 Creating the WatchKit App Project

Start Xcode and, on the Welcome screen, select the *Create a new Xcode project* option. On the template screen choose the *Application* option located under *iOS* in the left hand panel and select *Single View Application*. Click *Next,* set the product name to *WatchKitSample,* enter your organization identifier and make sure that the *Devices* menu is set to *Universal* so that the user interface will be suitable for deployment on all iPhone and iPad screen sizes. Before clicking *Next*, change the *Language* menu to *Swift*. On the final screen, choose a file system location in which to store the project files and click on the *Create* button to proceed to the main Xcode project window.

3.2 Designing the iOS App User Interface

The next step in the project is to design the user interface for the iOS app. This layout is contained within the *Main.storyboard* file and is listed in the Project Navigator panel on the left hand side of the main Xcode window. Locate and click on this file to load it into the Interface Builder environment. Once loaded, locate the Label view object in the Object Library panel and drag and drop it so that it is centered in the layout canvas. Once positioncd, double-click on the label and change the text so that it reads "Welcome to WatchKit" as illustrated in Figure 3-1:

Figure 3-1

Select the new label in the layout canvas and display the *Resolve Auto Layout Issues* menu by clicking on the button in the lower right hand corner of the Interface Builder panel as indicated in Figure 3-2:

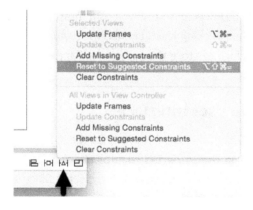

Figure 3-2

From the resulting menu, select the *Reset to Suggested Constraints* option. This will set up recommended layout constraints so that the label remains centered both horizontally and vertically within the screen regardless of whether the application is running on an iPhone or iPad display.

The user interface for the iOS application is now complete. Verify this by running the application on an iPhone device or iOS Simulator session before continuing.

3.3 **Adding the WatchKit Extension and App**

With a rudimentary iOS application created the next step is to add the WatchKit extension and WatchKit app to the project. This is achieved by selecting the Xcode *New -> File -> Target...* menu option. From within the resulting panel, select the *Apple Watch* option listed under *iOS* in the left hand panel as outlined in Figure 3-3:

Figure 3-3

With the WatchKit App option selected, click on the *Next* button to proceed to the options screen shown in Figure 3-4. The product name will be preset based on the name of the containing app and cannot be changed. Before clicking on the *Finish* button, make sure that the Include Notification Scene and Include Glance Scene options are switched off (Glances and Notifications will be introduced in later chapters) and that the language menu is set to *Swift*.

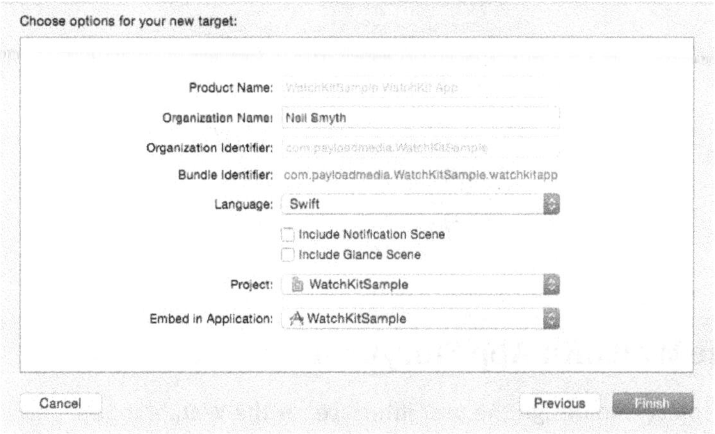

Figure 3-4

As soon as the extension target has been created, a new panel will appear requesting permission to activate the new scheme for the extension target. Every target within an Xcode project has associated with it a scheme which defines how that target is to be built. When an extension target is added to a project, Xcode automatically creates a corresponding scheme so that the extension can be built and run. Activate this scheme now by clicking on the *Activate* button in the request panel:

Figure 3-5

A review of the project files within the Project Navigator panel will reveal that new folders have been added for the WatchKit Extension and the WatchKit App (Figure 3-6), each of which contains the files that will need to be modified to implement the appearance and behavior of the WatchKit app:

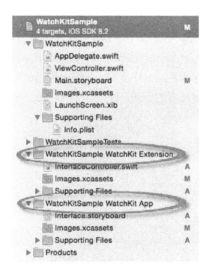

Figure 3-6

3.4 Designing the WatchKit App Storyboard

The next step in the project is to design the user interface for the WatchKit app. This is contained within the *Interface.storyboard* file located under the *WatchKitSample WatchKit App* folder within the Project

Navigator. Locate and select this file to load it into the Interface Builder tool where the scene will appear as illustrated in Figure 3-7:

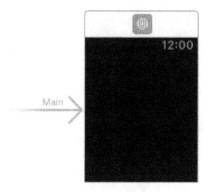

Figure 3-7

Designing the user interface for a WatchKit app involves dragging objects from the Object Library panel onto the layout canvas. When user interface objects are added to the layout canvas they are stacked vertically. These elements are then positioned at runtime by WatchKit based on the available display space combined with any sizing and positioning attributes declared during the storyboard design phase.

For the purposes of this example, the user interface will be required to display an image and a label. Locate the Image object in the Object Library panel and drag and drop it onto the scene layout. Repeat this step to position a Label object immediately beneath the Image object. Double click on the newly added Label object and change the text so that it reads "Hello WatchKit" such that the layout matches that of Figure 3-8:

Figure 3-8

Before testing the app, some additional attributes need to be set on the objects in the user interface. The first step is to configure the Image object to display an image. Before this can be configured, however, the image file needs to be added to the project. The image file is named *watch_image@2x.png* and can be found in the *sample_images* folder of the sample code archive which can be downloaded from the following URL:

http://www.ebookfrenzy.com/print/watchkit/index.php

Within the Project Navigator panel, select the *Images.xcassets* entry listed under *WatchKitSample WatchKit App* so that the image asset catalog loads into the main panel. Locate the *watch_image@2x.png* image file in a Finder window and drag and drop it onto the left hand panel in the asset catalog as illustrated in Figure 3-9:

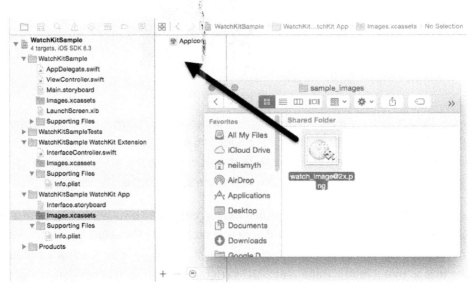

Figure 3-9

With the image file added to the project, the Image object needs to be configured to display the image when the app runs. Select the Image object in the storyboard scene and display the Attributes Inspector in the utilities panel (*View -> Utilities -> Show Attributes Inspector*). Within the inspector panel, use the drop down menu for the Image attribute to select the *watch_image* option:

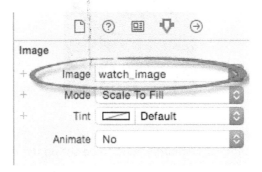

Figure 3-10

Finally, select the Label object in the scene and use the Attribute Inspector panel to change the *Alignment* attribute so that the text is centered within the label. Having set this attribute, a review of the scene will show that the text is still positioned on the left of the layout. The reason for this is that the text has been centered within the label but the Label object itself is still positioned on the left side of the display. To correct this, locate the *Position* section in the Attributes Inspector panel and change the *Horizontal* attribute from *Left* to *Center*. Figure 3-11 shows the Attributes Inspector panel with these attributes set:

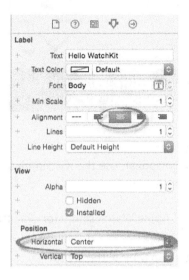

Figure 3-11

3.5 Running the WatchKit App

All that remains is to run the WatchKit app and make sure that it appears as expected. For the purposes of this example this will be performed using the simulator environment. In order to test the WatchKit app, the run target may need to be changed in the Xcode toolbar. Select the current scheme in the toolbar and use the drop down menu (Figure 3-12) to select the *WatchKitSample WatchKit App -> iPhone 6* option:

Figure 3-12

With the WatchKit app selected, click on the run button. Once the simulator has loaded, two windows should appear, one representing the iPhone 6 device and the other the Apple Watch device. After a short delay, the WatchKit app should appear on the watch simulator display as illustrated in Figure 3-13:

Figure 3-13

If the WatchKit simulator window fails to appear, use the iOS Simulator *Hardware -> External Displays* menu option to select one of the Apple Watch options.

By default Xcode will launch the 42mm Apple Watch simulator. To also test the layout on the 38mm Apple Watch model, select the iOS Simulator *Hardware -> External Displays -> Apple Watch – 38 mm* menu option and then stop and restart the WatchKit app from within Xcode.

3.6 **Running the App on a Physical Apple Watch Device**

In order to test the app on a physical Apple Watch device, connect the iPhone with which the Apple Watch is paired to the development system and select it as the target device within the Xcode toolbar panel (Figure 3-14).

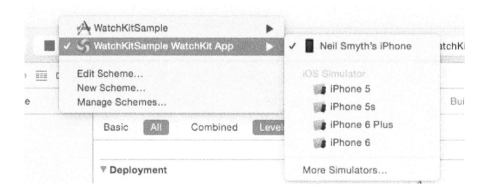

Figure 3-14

With *WatchKitSample WatchKit App* still selected as the run target, click on the run button and wait for the app icon to appear on the Apple Watch home screen. Once the icon appears, tap on it to launch the app.

Depending on the version of Xcode that you are using, the following error may occur when attempting to run the app on a watch device:

```
Embedded Binary Validation Utility error: WatchKit apps must have a
deployment target equal to iOS 8.2 (was 8.3).
```

If this error appears in Xcode, select the WatchKitSample target entry at the top of the Project Navigator panel to display the target settings. Within the settings panel, select the *Build Settings* screen as highlighted in Figure 3-15:

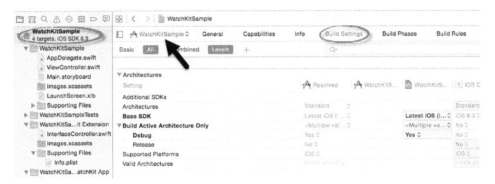

Figure 3-15

By default, the build settings for the iOS app will be displayed. Using the menu in the upper left hand corner of the settings panel (indicated by the arrow in Figure 3-15 above), select the *WatchKitSample WatchKit App* option as highlighted in Figure 3-16:

Figure 3-16

With the WatchKit app build settings displayed, enter *iOS Deployment Target* into the search box and change the deployment target settings to *iOS 8.2*:

Figure 3-17

Having changed the deployment target the app should compile and run on the Apple Watch device.

3.7 Setting the Scene Title and Key Color

The area at the top of the Apple Watch display containing the current time is the *status bar* and the area to the left of the time is available to display a title string. To set this property, click on the scene within the storyboard so that it highlights in blue, display the Attributes Inspector panel and enter a title for the scene into the *Title* field:

Figure 3-18

The foreground color of all of the scene titles in a WatchKit app may be configured by setting the *global tint* attribute for the storyboard file. To set this property, select the *Interface.storyboard* file in the Project Navigator panel and display the File Inspector panel (*View -> Utilities -> Show File Inspector*). Within the File Inspector panel change the color setting for the *Global Tint* attribute (Figure 3-19) to a different color.

Figure 3-19

Next time the app runs, all of the titles in the scenes that make up the storyboard will be rendered using the selected foreground color.

The global tint color is also adopted by the app name when it is displayed in the short look notification panel, a topic area that will be covered in detail in the chapter entitled *An Overview of Notifications in WatchKit.*

3.8 Adding App Icons to the Project

Every WatchKit app must have associated with it an icon. This icon represents the app on the Apple Watch Home screen and identifies the app in notifications and within the iPhone-based Apple Watch app. A variety of icon sizes may need to be created depending on where the icon is displayed and the size of Apple Watch on which the app is running. The various icon size requirements are as outlined in Table 3-1:

Icon	38mm Watch	42mm Watch
Home Screen	80 x 80 pixels	80 x 80 pixels
Long Look Notification	80 x 80 pixels	88 x 88 pixels
Short Look Notification	172 x 172 pixels	196 x 196 pixels
Notification Center	48 x 48 pixels	55 x 55 pixels

Table 3-1

In addition to the icons in Table 3-1, icons are also required for the Apple Watch app on the paired iPhone device (a topic outlined in the chapter entitled *Configuring Preferences with the WatchKit Settings Bundle*).

Two versions of the icon are required for this purpose so that the icon can be represented on both iPhone (@2x) and iPhone Plus (@3x) size models:

Icon	iPhone @2x	iPhone Plus @3x
Apple Watch App	58 x 58 pixels	87 x 87 pixels

Table 3-2

Since the app created in this chapter does not make use of notifications, only Home Screen and Apple Watch app icons need to be added to the project. The topic of notification icons will be addressed in greater detail in the chapter entitled *A WatchKit Notification Tutorial*.

The home screen icon needs to be circular and 80x80 pixels in size with a 24-bit color depth. The image must be in PNG format with a file name ending with "@2x", for example *homeicon@2x.png*.

Icons are stored in the image asset catalog of the WatchKit app target. Access the image set in the asset catalog by selecting the *Images.xcassets* file listed under the *WatchKitSample WatchKit App* folder in the project navigator panel. Within the asset catalog panel (Figure 3-20), select the *AppIcon* image set:

Figure 3-20

To add icons, locate them in a Finder window and drag and drop them onto the corresponding location within the image set. For the purposes of this example, app icons can be found in the *app_icons* folder of the sample code download.

Once the icons have been located, drag and drop the icon file named *HomeIcon@2x.png* onto the *Apple Watch Home Screen (All)* image location within the image asset catalog as shown in Figure 3-21:

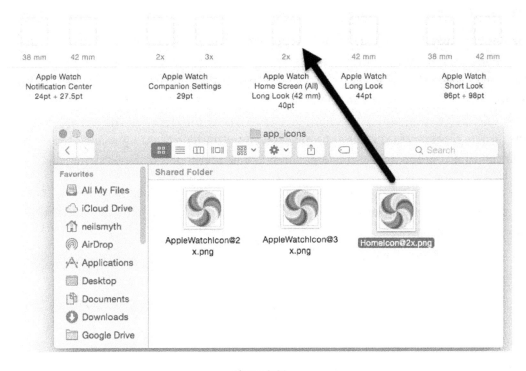

Figure 3-21

The two Apple Watch app icons are named *AppleWatchIcon@2x.png* and *AppleWatchIcon@3x.png* and should be placed in the *Apple Watch Companion Settings* 2x and 3x image locations respectively. Once these icons have been added the three icon categories in the AppIcon image set should resemble Figure 3-22:

Figure 3-22

When the sample WatchKit app is now compiled and run on a physical Apple Watch device the app will be represented on the device Home Screen by the provided icon.

3.9 **Summary**

This chapter has worked through the steps involved in creating a simple WatchKit app and running it within the simulator environment. A WatchKit app is added as a target to an existing iOS app project. When a WatchKit target is added, Xcode creates an initial storyboard for the WatchKit app user interface and the basic code for the WatchKit Extension template. The user interface for the WatchKit app is designed in the storyboard file by selecting and positioning UI objects in the Interface Builder environment and setting attributes where necessary to configure the appearance and position of the visual elements. In order to test run a WatchKit app, the appropriate run target must first be selected from the Xcode toolbar.

Before a WatchKit app can be published, app icons must be added to the image asset catalog of the WatchKit App target. These icons must meet strict requirements in terms of size and format, details of which have also been covered in this chapter.

Chapter 4

4. An Overview of the WatchKit App Architecture

The previous chapters have explained that a WatchKit app consists of two main components, the WatchKit app itself residing on the Apple Watch and the WatchKit extension installed on the iPhone device. We have also established that the wireless communication between the WatchKit app and the WatchKit extension is handled transparently by the WatchKit framework.

It has also been established that the WatchKit app is primarily responsible for displaying the user interface while the programming logic of the app resides within the WatchKit extension.

It is less clear at this point, however, how the user interface elements in the app are connected to the code in the extension. In other words, how the project is structured such that tapping on a button in a scene causes a specific method in the extension to be called. Similarly, we need to understand how the code within the extension can manipulate the properties of a visual element in a storyboard scene, for example changing the text displayed on a Label interface object. These topics will be covered in this chapter and then put into practice in the next chapter entitled *An Example Interactive WatchKit App*.

This chapter will also provide an overview of the lifecycle of a WatchKit app and outline the ways in which this can be used to perform certain initialization tasks when a WatchKit app is launched.

4.1 Basic WatchKit App Architecture

As discussed in previous chapters, the WatchKit app itself consists only of the storyboard file and a set of resource files. The storyboard contains one or more scenes, each of which represents a different screen within the app and may, optionally, provide mechanisms for the user to transition from one scene to another. Clearly this does not provide any functionality beyond presenting user interfaces to the user. The responsibility of providing the behavior behind a user interface scene so that the app actually does something useful belongs to the *interface controller*.

4.2 WatchKit Interface Controllers

Each scene within a storyboard must have associated with it an interface controller instance. Interface controllers are subclassed from the WatchKit framework WKInterfaceController class and contain the code that allows the WatchKit app to perform tasks beyond simply presenting a user interface to the user. This provides a separation between the user interfaces (the storyboard) and the logic code (the interface controllers). In fact, interface controllers are similar to view controllers in iOS applications.

The interface controllers for a WatchKit app reside within the WatchKit extension associated with the app and are installed and executed on the iPhone device with which the Apple Watch is paired. It is the responsibility of the interface controller to respond to user interactions in the corresponding user interface scene and to make changes to the visual elements that make up the user interface. When a user taps a button in a WatchKit scene, for example, a method in the interface controller will be called by the WatchKit framework in order to perform some form of action. In the event that a change needs to be made to a user interface element, for example to change the text displayed on a label, the interface controller will make the necessary changes and the WatchKit framework will transmit those changes to the WatchKit app where the update will be performed.

This sounds good in theory but does not explain how the connections between the elements in the user interface on the watch device and the interface controller on the iPhone are established. This requires an understanding of the concepts of *outlets* and *action methods*.

4.3 **WatchKit Action Methods**

Creation of a WatchKit app typically involves designing the user interface scenes using the Interface Builder tool and writing the code that provides the logic for the app in the source code files of the interface controller classes. In this section we will begin to look at how the user interface scene elements and the interface controller code interact with each other.

When a user interacts with objects in a scene of a WatchKit app, for example touching a button control, an *event* is triggered. In order for that event to achieve anything, it needs to trigger a method call on the interface controller class. Use of a technique known as *target-action* provides a way to specify what happens when such events are triggered. In other words, this is how you connect the objects in the user interface you have designed in the Interface Builder tool to the back end Swift code you have implemented in the corresponding interface controller class. Specifically, this allows you to define which method of the interface controller gets called when a user interacts in a certain way with a user interface object.

The process of wiring up a user interface object to call a specific method on an interface controller is achieved using something called an *Action*. Similarly, the target method is referred to as an *action method*. Action methods are declared within the interface controller class using the IBAction keyword, for example:

```
@IBAction func buttonPress() {
    println("Button Pressed")
    // Perform tasks in response to a button press
}
```

4.4 **WatchKit Outlets**

The opposite of an *Action* is an *Outlet*. As previously described, an Action allows a method in an interface controller instance to be called in response to a user interaction with a user interface element. An Outlet, on the other hand, allows an interface controller to make changes to the properties of a user interface element. An interface controller might, for example, need to set the text on a Label object. In order to do so an Outlet must first have been defined using the *IBOutlet* keyword. In programming terms, an *IBOutlet* is simply an instance variable that references the user interface object to which access is required. The following line demonstrates an outlet declaration for a label:

```
@IBOutlet weak var myLabel: WKInterfaceLabel!
```

Once outlets and actions have been implemented and connected, all of the communication required to make these connections work is handled transparently by WatchKit. Figure 4-1 provides a visual representation of actions and outlets:

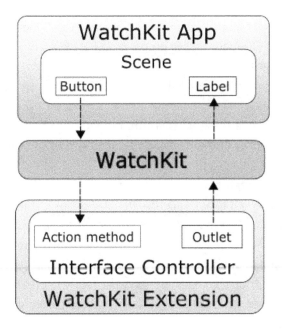

Figure 4-1

Outlets and actions can be created visually with just a few mouse clicks from within Xcode using the Interface Builder tool in conjunction with the Assistant Editor panel, a topic which will be covered in detail in the chapter entitled *An Example Interactive WatchKit App*.

4.5 **The Lifecycle of a WatchKit App**

The lifecycle of a WatchKit app and the corresponding WatchKit extension is actually very simple. When a WatchKit app is launched on the device, a scene will be loaded from within the storyboard file. When the scene has loaded, the WatchKit framework will request that the extension corresponding to the app be launched on the iPhone device (or woken up if it is currently suspended). The extension is then instructed to create the interface controller associated with the scene that was loaded.

As long as the user is interacting with the WatchKit app the extension will continue to run on the iPhone. When the system detects that the user is no longer interacting with the watch, or the user exits the app, the interface controller is deactivated and the extension suspended.

At various points during this initialization and de-initialization cycle, calls will be made to specific lifecycle methods declared within the interface controller class where code can be added to perform initialization and clean up tasks. These methods are as follows:

- **init()** - The first method called on the interface controller when the scene is to be displayed. This method can be used to perform initialization tasks in preparation for the scene being displayed to the user. It is also possible to make changes to user interface objects via outlets from within this method.
- **awakeWithContext()** - This method is called after the call to the init() method and may optionally be passed additional context data. This is typically used when navigating from one scene to another in a multi-scene app and allows data to be passed from the interface controller of the currently displayed scene to the interface controller of the destination scene. Access to user interface objects is available from within this method.
- **willActivate()** – Called immediately before the scene is presented to the user on the Apple Watch device. This is the recommended method for making final minor changes to the elements in the user interface. Access to user interface objects is available from within this method.
- **didDeactivate()** – The last method called when the user exits the current scene or the system detects that, although the app is still running, the user is no longer interacting with the Apple Watch device. This method should be used to perform any cleanup tasks necessary to ensure a smooth return to the scene at a later time. Access to user interface objects is not available from within this method. Calls to this method may be triggered for testing purposes from within the WatchKit simulator environment by locking the simulator via the *Hardware -> Lock* menu option.

The diagram in Figure 4-2 illustrates the WatchKit app lifecycle as it corresponds to the WatchKit extension and interface controller:

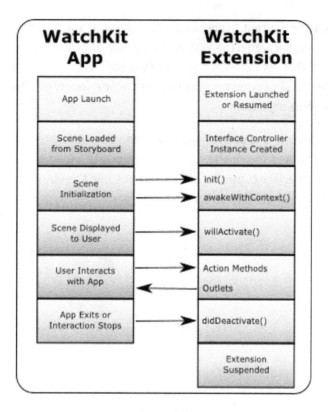

Figure 4-2

It should be noted that, with the exception of the app launch and extension suspension phases in the above diagram, the same lifecycle sequence is performed each time a scene is loaded within a running WatchKit app.

4.6 WatchKit Extension Guidelines

A key point to note from the lifecycle description is that the WatchKit extension is suspended when the user either exits or stops interacting with the WatchKit app. It is important, therefore, to avoid performing any long term tasks within the extension. Any tasks that need to continue executing after the extension has been suspended should be passed to the containing iOS app to be handled. Details of how this can be achieved are outlined in the *WatchKit App and Parent iOS App Communication* chapter of this book.

4.7 Summary

Each scene within a WatchKit app has associated with it an interface controller within the WatchKit extension. The interface controller contains the code that provides the underlying logic and behavior of the WatchKit app.

An Overview of the WatchKit App Architecture

The interactions between the current scene of a WatchKit app running on an Apple Watch and the corresponding interface controller within the WatchKit extension are implemented using actions and outlets. Actions define the methods that get called in response to specific actions performed by the user within the scene. Outlets, on the other hand, provide a mechanism for the interface controller code to access and modify the properties of user interface objects.

When a WatchKit app is launched, and each time a new scene is loaded, the app has a lifecycle consisting of initialization, user interaction and termination. At multiple points within this lifecycle, calls are made to specific methods within the interface controller of the current scene thereby providing points within the code where initialization and de-initialization tasks can be performed.

5. An Example Interactive WatchKit App

Having covered actions and outlets in the previous chapter, it is now time to make practical use of these concepts. With this goal in mind, this chapter will work through the creation of a WatchKit app intended to demonstrate the way in which the Interface Builder and Assistant Editor features of Xcode work together to simplify the creation of actions and outlets to implement interactive behavior within a WatchKit app.

5.1 About the Example App

The purpose of the WatchKit app created in this chapter is to calculate a recommended gratuity amount when dining at a restaurant. A mechanism will be provided for the user to select the amount of the bill and then tap a button to display the recommended tip amount (assuming a percentage of 20%).

5.2 Creating the TipCalcApp Project

Start Xcode and, on the Welcome screen, select the *Create a new Xcode project* option. On the template screen choose the *Application* option located under *iOS* in the left hand panel followed by *Single View Application* in the main panel. Click *Next,* set the product name to *TipCalcApp,* enter your organization identifier and make sure that the *Devices* menu is set to *Universal.* Before clicking *Next*, change the *Language* menu to Swift if necessary. On the final screen, choose a location in which to store the project files and click on the *Create* button to proceed to the main Xcode project window.

5.3 Adding the WatchKit App Target

For the purposes of this example we will assume that the iOS app has already been implemented. The next step, therefore, is to add the WatchKit app target to the project. Within Xcode, select the *File -> New -> Target...* menu option. In the target template dialog, select the *Apple Watch* option listed beneath the *iOS* heading. In the main panel, select the *WatchKit App* icon and click on *Next.* On the subsequent screen (Figure 5-1) turn off the *Include Glance Scene* and *Include Notification Scene* options before clicking on the *Finish* button:

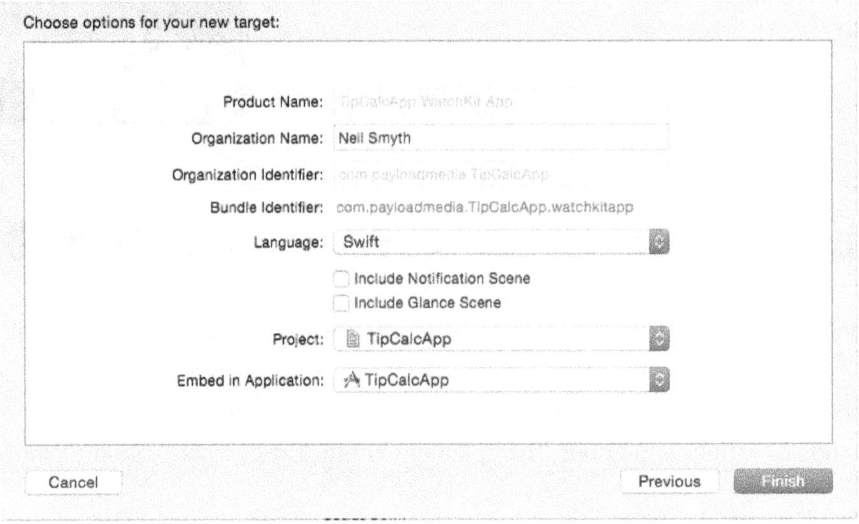

Figure 5-1

As soon as the extension target has been created, a new panel will appear requesting permission to activate the new scheme for the extension target. Activate this scheme now by clicking on the *Activate* button in the request panel.

5.4 Designing the WatchKit App User Interface

Within the Xcode Project Navigator panel unfold the *TipCalcApp WatchKit App* folder entry and select the *Interface.storyboard* file to load it into the Interface Builder tool.

The user interface for the app is going to consist of two Label objects, a Slider and a Button. Begin the design by locating the Label object in the Object Library panel and dragging and dropping it onto the scene so that it appears at the top of the scene layout. Select the newly added label and display the Attributes Inspector in the utilities panel (*View -> Utilities -> Show Attributes Inspector*). Within the inspector panel, change the text so that it reads $0.00 and change the Alignment setting so that the text is positioned in the center of the label.

Remaining within the Attributes Inspector panel, click on the 'T' icon located in the far right of the *Font* attribute text field to display the font setting panel. Within this panel, change the *Font* setting to *System*, the *Style* to *Bold* and the *Size* value to 28 as shown in Figure 5-2. Once the font settings are complete, click on the *Done* button to commit the changes.

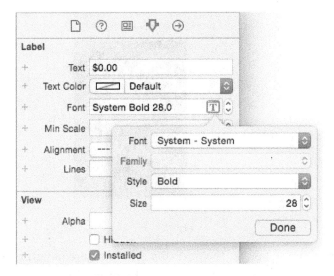

Figure 5-2

With the Label object still selected within the scene, locate the *Position* section within the Attribute Inspector panel and change the *Horizontal* property setting to *Center*.

Next, drag a Slider object from the library and drop it onto the scene so that it appears beneath the Label object. Select the Slider object in the scene and, within the Attributes Inspector, configure the *Minimum* and *Maximum* attributes to 0 and 100 respectively and enable the *Continuous* checkbox. Since we want the slider to adjust in $1 units the *Steps* value needs to be changed to 100.

Drag and drop a second Label object so that it is positioned beneath the slider. Select the new label and set the same alignment, font and positioning properties as those used for the first label. This time, however, change the *Text Color* attribute so that the text is displayed in green.

Finally, position a Button object beneath the second label. Double click on the button and change the text so it reads "Calculate Tip". With the button still selected, use the Attribute Inspector and change the *Vertical* property located in the *Position* section of the panel to *Bottom*.

At this point the scene layout should resemble that shown in Figure 5-3:

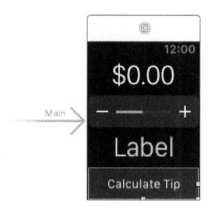

Figure 5-3

The user interface design is now complete. The next step is to configure outlets on the two Label objects so that the values displayed can be controlled from within the code of the interface controller class in the WatchKit extension. Before doing so, however, it is worth taking a look at the interface controller class file.

5.5 Reviewing the Interface Controller Class

As previously discussed, each scene within the storyboard of a WatchKit app has associated with it an interface controller class located within the WatchKit extension. By default, the Swift source code file for this class will be named *InterfaceController.swift* and will be located within the Project Navigator panel under the *<AppName> WatchKit Extension* folder where *<AppName>* is replaced by the name of the containing iOS app. Figure 5-4, for example, highlights the interface controller source file for the main scene of the TipCalcApp extension:

Figure 5-4

Locate and select this file so that it loads into the editing panel. Once loaded, the code should read as outlined in the following listing:

```
import WatchKit
import Foundation

class InterfaceController: WKInterfaceController {

    override func awakeWithContext(context: AnyObject?) {
        super.awakeWithContext(context)

        // Configure interface objects here.
    }

    override func willActivate() {
        // This method is called when watch view controller is about to be
visible to user
        super.willActivate()
    }

    override func didDeactivate() {
        // This method is called when watch view controller is no longer
visible
        super.didDeactivate()
    }

}
```

Xcode has created an interface controller class implementation that overrides a subset of the lifecycle methods outlined in the chapter entitled *An Overview of WatchKit App Architecture*. Later in this chapter some initialization code will be added to the *willActivate()* method. At this point, some outlets need to be configured so that changes can be made to the Label objects in the main WatchKit app scene.

5.6 Establishing Outlet Connections

Outlets provide the interface controller class with access to the interface objects within the corresponding storyboard scene. Outlets can be created visually within Xcode by using Interface Builder and the Assistant Editor panel.

To establish outlets, begin by loading the *Interface.storyboard* file into the Interface Builder tool. Within Interface Builder, click on the scene so that it is highlighted before displaying the Assistant Editor by selecting the *View -> Assistant Editor -> Show Assistant Editor* menu option. Alternatively, it may also be displayed by selecting the center button (the one containing an image of interlocking circles) of the row of Editor toolbar buttons in the top right hand corner of the main Xcode window as illustrated in the following figure:

Figure 5-5

In the event that multiple Assistant Editor panels are required, additional tiles may be added using the *View -> Assistant Editor -> Add Assistant Editor* menu option.

By default, the editor panel will appear to the right of the main editing panel in the Xcode window. For example, in Figure 5-6 the panel to the immediate right of the Interface Builder panel is the Assistant Editor (marked A):

Figure 5-6

By default, the Assistant Editor will be in *Automatic* mode, whereby it automatically attempts to display the correct source file based on the currently selected item in Interface Builder. If the correct file is not displayed, use the toolbar along the top of the editor panel to select the correct file. The small instance of the Assistant Editor icon in this toolbar can be used to switch to *Manual* mode allowing the file to be selected from a pull-right menu containing all the source files in the project:

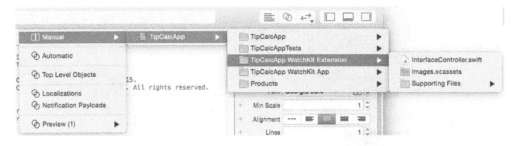

Figure 5-7

Make sure that the *InterfaceController.swift* file is displayed in the Assistant Editor and establish an outlet for the top-most label by Ctrl-clicking on the Label object in the scene and dragging the resulting line to the area immediately beneath the *class InterfaceController* declaration line in the Assistant Editor panel as shown in Figure 5-8:

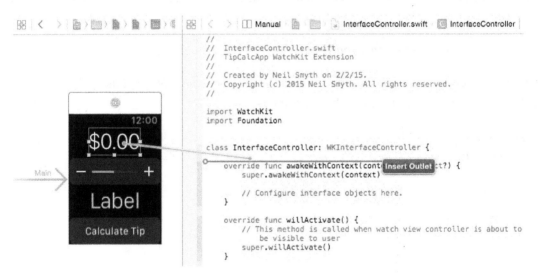

Figure 5-8

Upon releasing the line, the configuration panel illustrated in Figure 5-9 will appear requesting details about the outlet to be defined.

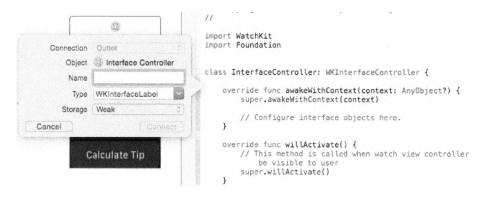

Figure 5-9

Since this is an outlet, the *Connection* menu should be set to *Outlet*. The type and storage values are also correct for this type of outlet. The only task that remains is to enter a name for the outlet, so in the *Name* field enter *amountLabel* before clicking on the *Connect* button.

Repeat the above steps to establish an outlet for the second Label object named *tipLabel*.

Once the connections have been established, review the *InterfaceController.swift* file and note that the outlet properties have been declared for us by the Assistant Editor:

```
import WatchKit
import Foundation

class InterfaceController: WKInterfaceController {

    @IBOutlet weak var amountLabel: WKInterfaceLabel!
    @IBOutlet weak var tipLabel: WKInterfaceLabel!
.
.
.
}
```

When we reference these outlet variables within the interface controller code we are essentially accessing the objects in the user interface.

5.7 Establishing Action Connections

Now that the outlets have been created, the next step is to connect the Slider and Button objects to action methods within the interface controller class. When the user increments or decrements the slider value the interface controller will need to change the value displayed on the *amountLabel* object to reflect the new value. This means that an action method will need to be implemented within the interface controller class and connected via an action to the Slider object in the storyboard scene.

With the scene displayed in Interface Builder and the *InterfaceController.swift* file loaded into the Assistant Editor panel, Ctrl-click on the Slider object in the storyboard scene and drag the resulting line to a position immediately beneath the *tipLabel* outlet as illustrated in Figure 5-10:

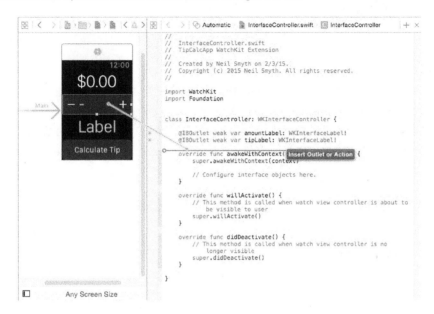

Figure 5-10

Once the line has been released, the connection configuration dialog will appear (Figure 5-11). Within the dialog, select *Action* from the *Connection* menu and enter *sliderChange* as the name of the action method to be called when the value of the slider is changed by the user:

Figure 5-11

Click on the *Connect* button to establish the action and note that Xcode has added a stub action method at the designated location within the *InterfaceController.swift* file:

```
import WatchKit
import Foundation

class InterfaceController: WKInterfaceController {

    @IBOutlet weak var amountLabel: WKInterfaceLabel!
```

```
    @IBOutlet weak var tipLabel: WKInterfaceLabel!

    @IBAction func sliderChange(value: Float) {
    }
    .
    .
    .
}
```

An action method will also need to be called when the user taps the Button object in the user interface. Ctrl-click on the Button object in the scene and drag the resulting line to a position beneath the *sliderChange* method. On releasing the line, the connection dialog will appear once again. Change the connection menu to *Action* and enter *calculateTip* as the method name before clicking on the *Connect* button to create the connection.

5.8 Implementing the sliderChange Action Method

The Slider object added to the scene layout is actually an instance of the WatchKit framework WKInterfaceSlider class. When the user adjusts the slider value, that value is passed to the action method assigned to the object, in this instance the *sliderChange* method created in the previous section.

It is the responsibility of this action method to display the current value on the amount label using the *amountLabel* outlet variable and to store the current amount locally within the interface controller object so that it can be accessed when the user requests that the tip amount be calculated. Select the *InterfaceController.swift* file and modify it to add a floating point variable in which to store the current slider value and to implement the code in the *sliderChange* method:

```
class InterfaceController: WKInterfaceController {

    @IBOutlet weak var amountLabel: WKInterfaceLabel!
    @IBOutlet weak var tipLabel: WKInterfaceLabel!

    var currentAmount: Float = 0.00

    @IBAction func sliderChange(value: Float) {
        let amountString = String(format: "%0.2f", value)
        amountLabel.setText("$\(amountString)")
        currentAmount = value
    }
    .
    .
    .
}
```

The code added to the action method performs a number of tasks. First a new String object is created based on the current floating point value passed to the action method from the Slider object. This is formatted to two decimal places to reflect dollars and cents. The *setText* method of the *amountLabel* outlet is then called to set the text displayed on the Label object in the user interface, prefixing the *amountString* with a dollar sign. Finally, the current value is assigned to the *currentAmount* variable where it can be accessed later from within the *calculateTip* action method.

Make sure that the run target in the Xcode toolbar is set to *TipCalcApp Watchkit App* and click on the run button to launch the app. Once it has loaded into the simulator, click on the – and + slider buttons to change the current value. Note that the amount label is updated each time the value changes:

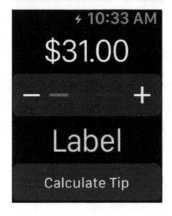

Figure 5-12

5.9 Implementing the calculateTip Action Method

The *calculateTip* action method will calculate 20% of the current amount and display the result to the user via the *tipAmount* outlet, once again using string formatting to display the result to two decimal places prefixed with a dollar sign:

```
@IBAction func calculateTip() {
    let tipAmount = currentAmount * 0.20
    let tipString = String(format: "%0.2f", tipAmount)
    tipLabel.setText("$\(tipString)")
}
```

Run the application once again, adjust the slider and click on the Calculate Tip button, verifying that the tip amount is displayed on the tip Label object as shown in Figure 5-13:

Figure 5-13

5.10 Hiding the Tip Label

Until the user taps the calculate button, the tip label is largely redundant. The final task for the project, therefore, is to hide the tip label until the app is ready to display the recommended tip amount. The Label object can be hidden by adding some code to the *willActivate* lifecycle method within the *InterfaceController.swift* class file as follows:

```
override func willActivate() {
    // This method is called when watch view controller is about to be
visible to user
    super.willActivate()
    tipLabel.setHidden(true)
}
```

This method uses the *tipLabel* outlet to call the *setHidden* method on the Label object so that it is hidden from the user. When an object is hidden it is invisible to the user and the user interface layout behaves as though the object no longer exists. As such, the layout will re-arrange to occupy the vacated space. To hide an object whilst retaining the occupied space, call the *setAlpha* method passing through a value of 0 to make the object transparent.

Having hidden the label during the initialization phase, a line of code needs to be added to the *calculateTip* method to reveal the Label object after the tip has been calculated:

```
@IBAction func calculateTip() {
    let tipAmount = currentAmount * 0.20
    let tipString = String(format: "%0.2f", tipAmount)
    tipLabel.setText("$\(tipString)")
    tipLabel.setHidden(false)
}
```

Run the app one last time and verify that the tip label remains hidden until the calculate button is pressed.

5.11 Removing the WatchKit App

To avoid cluttering the Apple Watch Home screen with all of the sample WatchKit apps created in this book, it is recommended that the apps be removed from the Apple Watch device at the end of each chapter.

One option is to delete the containing iOS app from the iPhone device by pressing and holding on the app icon on the iPhone screen until the "x" marker appears. Tapping the "x" to delete the iOS app will also remove the WatchKit app from the paired Apple Watch.

Another option is to hide the app using the Apple Watch app. This app is installed by default on iPhone devices and is the app that you used when pairing your iPhone with the Apple Watch. Within this app, select the *My Watch* option in the bottom tab bar and scroll down and select the *TipCalcApp* entry. On the resulting preferences screen (Figure 5-14) turn off the *Show App on Apple Watch* option:

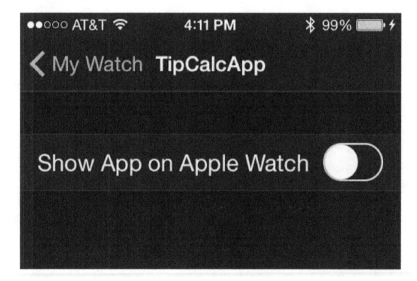

Figure 5-14

5.12 Summary

The Interface Builder tool and the Assistant Editor panel can be used together to quickly establish outlet and action connections between the user interface objects in a storyboard scene and the underlying interface controller scene in the WatchKit extension. This chapter has worked through the creation of a sample application project designed to demonstrate this technique. This chapter also made use of the *willActivate* lifecycle method to perform an initialization task and briefly covered the hiding and showing of objects in a WatchKit scene.

6. An Overview of WatchKit Tables

The WatchKit Table object allows content to be displayed within a WatchKit app scene in the form of a single vertical column of rows. Tables can be used purely as a mechanism for displaying lists of information, or to implement navigation whereby the selection of a particular row within a table triggers a transition to another scene within the storyboard.

This chapter will provide an overview of tables in WatchKit, exploring how tables are structured and explaining areas such as the WKInterfaceTable class, row controllers, row controller classes, row controller types and the steps necessary to initialize a WatchKit table at runtime. The next chapter, entitled *A WatchKit Table Tutorial*, will then work through the creation of an example WatchKit table scene. Table based navigation will then be explored in the *Implementing WatchKit Table Navigation* chapter of the book.

6.1 The WatchKit Table

WatchKit tables provide a way to display information to the user in the form of a single column of rows. If a table has too many rows to fit within the watch display the user can scroll up and down within the table using the touch screen or the digital crown. The individual rows in a table may also be configured to call action methods when tapped by the user.

Tables are represented by the WatchKit WKInterfaceTable class, with each row displayed within the table represented by a *table row controller* instance.

6.2 Table Row Controller

There are two parts to the table row controller. The first is the visual representation of the row within the table. This essentially defines which user interface objects are to be displayed in the row (for example a row might consist of an Image and a Label object).

The second component of a table row is a corresponding *row controller class* which resides within the WatchKit app extension. This class is created as a subclass of the NSObject class and, at a minimum, contains outlets to the user interface objects contained in the row controller. Once declared, these outlets are used by the scene's interface controller to configure the content displayed within each row. If the row controller in the scene contained two Label objects, for example, the outlets could be used to set the text on those labels for each row in the table.

6.3 **Row Controller Type**

The user interface objects defined within a row controller in the scene combined with the corresponding row controller class in the extension define the *row controller type*. A single table can consist of multiple row controller types. One row controller might, for example, contain a label and an image while another might contain two labels. The type of row controller used for each row within the table is controlled by the interface controller during the table row initialization process.

6.4 **Table Row Initialization**

When a scene containing a table is displayed within a WatchKit app, the table object will need a row controller instance for each row to be displayed to the user. The interface controller is responsible for performing the following initialization tasks:

1. Calculate the number of rows to be displayed in the table.
2. Request the creation of a row controller instance of a particular row controller type for each row in the table.
3. Configure the appearance of the user interface objects in each row using the outlets declared in the row controller class.

6.5 **Implementing a Table in a WatchKit App Scene**

A Table is added to a WatchKit scene by dragging and dropping a Table object from the Object Library onto the storyboard scene. By default, the table instance will contain a single row controller instance containing a Group object. A Group object is a single user interface element that can contain one or more interface objects in a horizontal or vertical arrangement. Figure 6-1 shows a scene with a newly added table with the default row controller:

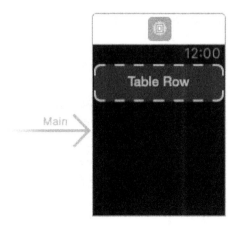

Figure 6-1

The hierarchical structure of the table and table row controller can be viewed within the Xcode *Document Outline* panel. This panel appears by default to the left of the Interface Builder panel and is controlled by the small button in the bottom left hand corner (indicated by the arrow in Figure 6-2) of the Interface Builder panel.

Figure 6-2

When displayed, the document outline shows a hierarchical overview of the elements that make up a user interface layout. This enables us, for example, to see that a scene consists of a Table, Table Row Controller and a Group object:

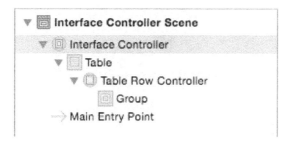

Figure 6-3

The row controller within the table is a template for the row controllers that will be created within the interface controller. To design the row, simply drag and drop user interface objects from the Object Library onto the row and resize the items to achieve the desired layout. In Figure 6-4, for example, the template row controller contains an image and label:

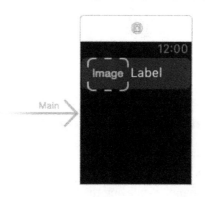

Figure 6-4

It is important to be aware that the appearance of the visual elements in a row is generally defined at runtime by the interface controller using the outlets declared in the row controller class. Any attributes set within the storyboard will serve as the default attributes for the visual elements and will appear in the app at runtime unless overridden in the interface controller.

The row controller template must also be assigned an identifier which will be referenced in the interface controller code when instances of that row type are created during initialization. The identifier is configured by selecting the row controller item in the Document Outline panel and entering a suitable identifier name into the Identifier field of the Attributes Inspector panel:

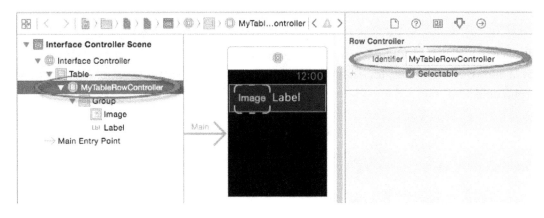

Figure 6-5

6.6 Adding the Row Controller Class to the Extension

As previously outlined, each row controller type must have a corresponding row controller class file within the app extension. This must be a subclass of NSObject and can be created using the following steps:

1. Locate the WatchKit Extension folder within the Project Navigator panel and Ctrl-click on it.
2. From the resulting menu select the *New File...* menu option.
3. In the new file template panel, select *Source* listed under *iOS* in the left hand panel and *Cocoa Touch Class* from the main panel before clicking *Next*.
4. Enter a name for the class into the *Class* field and select *NSObject* from the *Subclass of:* menu before clicking *Next*.
5. Click *Finish* to add the new class to the extension.

6.7 Associating a Row Controller with a Row Controller Class

Before the table can be displayed, the row controller in the scene needs to be associated with the corresponding row controller class residing within the extension. This is achieved by selecting the row controller in the Document Outline panel, displaying the Identity Inspector (*View -> Utilities -> Show Identity Inspector*) and selecting the row controller class name from the *Class* menu.

6.8 **Creating Table Rows at Runtime**

The interface controller class for the scene containing the table is responsible for configuring the table and creating the rows during the initialization phase of the WatchKit app launch process. The interface controller will need an outlet connected to the table instance in the scene on which it will call either the *setNumberOfRows(_:withRowType:)* or *setRowTypes(_:)* methods:

- **setNumberOfRows** – Used when all of the rows to be created in the table are of the same row type. This method takes as parameters the number of rows to be created and the Identifier string for the row controller type as defined in the Attributes Inspector.
- **setRowTypes** – Called when the table is to comprise rows of different types. This method takes as a parameter an array containing the Identifiers of the row controller types (as defined in the Attributes Inspector) in the order in which they are to appear in the table.

When the above methods are called they remove any existing rows from the table and create new rows based on the parameters provided. The methods also create an internal array containing an instance of the row controller class for each of the rows displayed in the table. These instances can then be accessed by calling the *rowControllerAtIndex* method of the table object. Once a reference to a row controller class instance has been obtained, the outlets declared in that instance can be used to set the attributes of the user interface objects in the row controller.

The following code listing, for example, displays a color name on each row of a table within a WatchKit app scene using the row type identified by "MyTableRowController":

```
import WatchKit
import Foundation

class InterfaceController: WKInterfaceController {

    // The outlet to the Table object in the scene
    @IBOutlet weak var myTable: WKInterfaceTable!

    // The data array
    let colorNames = ["Red", "Green", "Blue", "Yellow"]

    override init() {
        super.init()
        loadTable() // Call to initialize the table rows
    }

    func loadTable() {
        // Create the table row controller instances
```

```
            // based on the number of items in colorNames array
            myTable.setNumberOfRows(colorNames.count,
                withRowType: "MyTableRowController")

            // Iterate through each of the table row controller
            // class instances.
            for (index, labelText) in enumerate(colorNames)
            {
                // Get a reference to the current instance
                let row = myTable.rowControllerAtIndex(index)
                        as MyRowController
                // Set the text using the outlet in the row controller
                // class instance.
                row.myLabel.setText(labelText)
            }
        }
    .
    .
    .
}
```

This approach is not restricted to the initialization phase of a table. The same technique can be used to dynamically change the properties of the user interface objects in a table row at any point when a table is displayed during the lifecycle of an app. The following action method, for example, dynamically changes the text displayed on the label in row zero of the table initialized in the above code:

```
@IBAction func buttonTap() {
    let row = myTable.rowControllerAtIndex(0) as MyRowController
    row.myLabel.setText("Hello")
}
```

6.9 Inserting Table Rows

Additional rows may be added to a table at runtime using the *insertRowsAtTableIndexes* method of the table instance. This method takes as parameters an index set indicating the positions at which the rows are to be inserted and the identifier of the row controller type to be used. The following code, for example, inserts new rows of type "MyImageRowController" at row index positions 0, 2 and 4:

```
let indexSet = NSMutableIndexSet()
indexSet.addIndex(0)
indexSet.addIndex(2)
indexSet.addIndex(4)

myTable.insertRowsAtIndexes(indexSet,
```

```
withRowType: "MyImageRowController")
```

6.10 Removing Table Rows

Similarly, rows may be removed from a table using the *removeRowsAtIndexes* method of the table instance, once again passing through as a parameter an index set containing the rows to be removed. The following code, for example, removes the rows inserted in the above code fragment:

```
let indexSet = NSMutableIndexSet()
indexSet.addIndex(0)
indexSet.addIndex(2)
indexSet.addIndex(4)

myTable.removeRowsAtIndexes(indexSet)
```

6.11 Scrolling to a Specific Table Row

The table can be made to scroll to a specific row programmatically using the *scrollToRowAtIndex* method of the table instance, passing through as a parameter an integer value representing the index position of the destination row:

```
myTable.scrollToRowAtIndex(1)
```

A negative index value will scroll to the top of the table, while a value greater than the last index position will scroll to the end.

6.12 Summary

Tables are created in WatchKit using the WKInterfaceTable class which allows content to be presented to the user in the form of a single column of rows. Each row within a table is represented visually within a storyboard scene by a row controller which, in turn, has a corresponding row controller class residing in the app extension. A single table can display multiple row controller types so that individual rows in a table can comprise different user interface objects. Initialization and runtime configuration of the row controller instances is the responsibility of the interface controller for the scene in which the table appears. A variety of methods are available on the table class to dynamically insert and remove rows while the table is displayed to the user.

7. A WatchKit Table Tutorial

The previous chapter provided an overview of tables within WatchKit apps. Now that these basics have been covered, this chapter will provide a tutorial that implements a table-based user interface within a WatchKit app using the techniques outlined in the previous chapter.

7.1 About the Table Example

The WatchKit app created in this chapter will take the form of an extension to a hypothetical iOS-based physical fitness application. The main WatchKit app storyboard will use a table to provide a list of the different steps in a workout routine with each table row containing an image and a label.

Although no interactive features will be added to the app in this chapter, the example will be extended in the next chapter (*Implementing WatchKit Table Navigation*) so that selecting a row in the table navigates to a second scene providing more detail on the selected workout step.

7.2 Creating the Table Project

Start Xcode and create a new iOS project. On the template screen choose the *Application* option located under *iOS* in the left hand panel and select *Single View Application.* Click *Next,* set the product name to *TableDemoApp,* enter your organization identifier and make sure that the *Devices* menu is set to *Universal.* Before clicking *Next*, change the *Language* menu to Swift. On the final screen, choose a location in which to store the project files and click on *Create* to proceed to the main Xcode project window.

7.3 Adding the WatchKit App Target

For the purposes of this example we will assume that the iOS app has already been implemented. The next step, therefore, is to add the WatchKit app target to the project. Within Xcode, select the *File -> New -> Target...* menu option. In the target template dialog, select the *Apple Watch* option listed beneath the *iOS* heading. In the main panel, select the *WatchKit App* icon and click on *Next.* On the subsequent screen turn off the *Include Glance Scene* and *Include Notification Scene* options before clicking on the *Finish* button.

As soon as the extension target has been created, a new panel will appear requesting permission to activate the new scheme for the extension target. Activate this scheme now by clicking on the *Activate* button in the request panel.

7.4 **Adding the Table to the Scene**

Navigate to and select the storyboard file for the WatchKit app (*TableDemoApp WatchKit App ->
Interface.storyboard*) so that it appears in the Interface Builder tool. Within the Object Library panel, locate
the Table object and drag and drop it onto the scene layout so that it appears as shown in Figure 7-1:

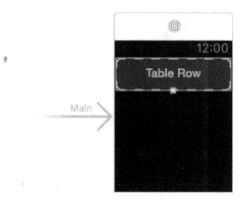

Figure 7-1

Drag an Image object from the Object Library panel and drop it onto the table row in the storyboard scene
so that it is positioned on the left hand side of the row. Repeat this step, this time selecting a Label object
and positioning it to the right of the Image object. Select the label and, using the Attributes Inspector panel,
set the *Vertical* position menu to *Center*.

Select the Image object and make the following changes within the Attributes Inspector panel:

1. Set the *Mode* menu to *Aspect Fit* so that images are not distorted when displayed.
2. In the Position section of the panel change the *Vertical* menu to *Center* so that the image is in alignment
    with the label object.
3. Within the Size section of the panel set both the *Height* and *Width* attributes to be *Fixed* at 25 points.

On completion of these steps, the layout of the scene should resemble that of Figure 7-2:

Figure 7-2

Display the Document Outline panel, select the Table Row Controller object from the hierarchy, display the Attributes Inspector panel and enter "MyRowController" into the *Identifier* field (Figure 7-3):

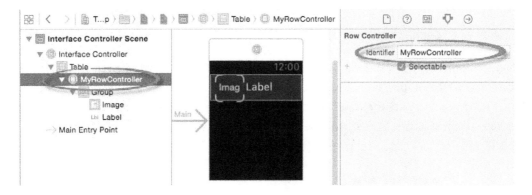

Figure 7-3

7.5 Creating the Row Controller Class

As discussed in the chapter entitled *An Overview of WatchKit Tables*, each row controller in the table must have associated with it a row controller class within the app extension. The next step, therefore, is to add this class. Locate the *TableDemoApp WatchKit Extension* entry with in the Project Navigator panel and Ctrl-click on it to display the context menu. From this menu, select the *New File...* menu option and, in the template selection panel, click on the *Source* entry listed under *iOS* in the left hand panel and *Cocoa Touch Class* from the main panel. Click *Next* to proceed to the next screen, enter MyRowController into the *Class* field and select *NSObject* from the *Subclass of:* menu as outlined in Figure 7-4:

Choose options for your new file:

Class: MyRowController

Subclass of: NSObject

☐ Also create XIB file

iPhone

Language: Swift

Cancel   Previous   Next

Figure 7-4

Click *Next* followed by *Create* to generate the source file for the class into the WatchKit app extension folder.

Before connecting outlets from the storyboard scene to the new row controller class, the row controller needs to be configured as a subclass of MyRowController. With the *Interface.storyboard* file selected and the Document Outline visible select the row controller object and display the Identity Inspector panel (*View -> Utilities -> Show Identity Inspector*). Within the Identity Inspector panel, use the *Class* drop down menu to select the *MyRowController* class as shown in Figure 7-5:

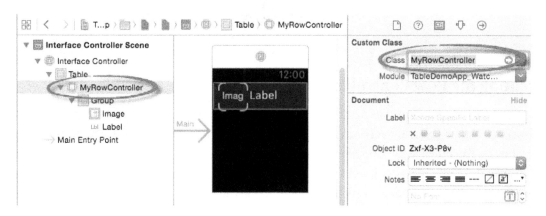

Figure 7-5

7.6 Establishing the Outlets

With the row controller class created, it is now time to establish the outlets for the image and label objects containing the row controller in the storyboard scene. Select the *Interface.storyboard* file so that it loads into

Interface Builder, select the image object and display the Assistant Editor panel using the button displaying interlocking rings in the Xcode toolbar:

Figure 7-6

Once the Assistant Editor has appeared, verify that it has loaded the *MyRowController.swift* file. In the event that it has not loaded the correct file, use the toolbar along the top of the editor panel to select the correct file. The small instance of the Assistant Editor icon in this toolbar can be used to switch to Manual mode allowing the file to be selected from a pull-right menu containing all the source files in the project. From this menu, select *Manual -> TableDemoApp -> TableDemoApp Watchkit Extension -> MyRowController.swift*.

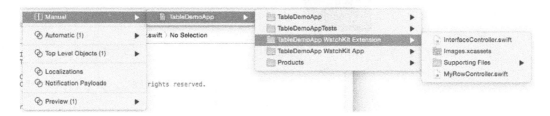

Figure 7-7

With the *MyRowController.swift* file displayed in the Assistant Editor panel, Ctrl-click on the image object in the storyboard scene and drag the resulting line to a location beneath the class declaration line in the Assistant Editor panel. Release the line and establish an outlet connection named *myImage*.

Repeat the above step to establish an outlet from the Label object named *myLabel*. Remaining within the Assistant Editor, edit the content of the file to import the WatchKit framework instead of UIKit. On completion of these steps, the *MyRowController.swift* file should read as follows:

```
import UIKit
import WatchKit

class MyRowController: NSObject {

    @IBOutlet weak var myImage: WKInterfaceImage!
    @IBOutlet weak var myLabel: WKInterfaceLabel!
}
```

With these steps completed, the next step is to create some data to be displayed and to add initialization code to the interface controller to display the rows at runtime.

7.7 **Connecting the Table Outlet**

In the course of initializing the table it will be necessary to access the table instance from within the interface controller class which will, in turn, require the establishment of an outlet. With the *Interface.storyboard* file selected and the Document Outline panel displayed, open the Assistant Editor panel and make sure that it is displaying the content of the *InterfaceController.swift* file. Ctrl-click on the *Table* entry in the Document Outline panel and drag the resulting line to a position immediately beneath the class declaration line in the Assistant Editor panel:

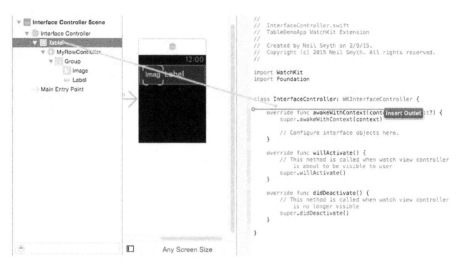

Figure 7-8

Release the line and establish an outlet named *myTable* in the resulting connection dialog.

7.8 **Creating the Data**

Clearly the rows within the table consist of an image and a label. The next step is to add some data to the project to serve as content for these two objects. This will take the form of two arrays declared within the interface controller class consisting of the names of the image files to be displayed on the Image object and strings to display on the Label object. Select the *InterfaceController.swift* file and edit it to add these two arrays as follows:

```
import WatchKit
import Foundation


class InterfaceController: WKInterfaceController {

    @IBOutlet weak var myTable: WKInterfaceTable!
```

```
    let stringData = ["Warm-up", "Cardio", "Weightlifting", "Core",
"Bike", "Cooldown"]

    let imageData = ["walking", "treadmill", "weights", "core",
"bikeriding", "cooldown"]
    .

    .

}
```

Next, a method needs to be added to the class to initialize the table with the content of the data arrays. Remaining within the *InterfaceController.swift* file, implement this method as follows:

```
func loadTable() {

    myTable.setNumberOfRows(stringData.count,
            withRowType: "MyRowController")

    for (index, labelText) in enumerate(stringData) {
        let row = myTable.rowControllerAtIndex(index)
            as! MyRowController
        row.myLabel.setText(labelText)
        row.myImage.setImage(UIImage(named: imageData[index]))
    }
}
```

The method identifies the number of elements in the string array and uses that value to set the number of rows within the table while specifying the row type as MyRowController. The code then iterates through each row in the table setting image and label properties using the two arrays as the data sources for the content to be displayed.

The *init* lifecycle method now needs to be overridden and implemented to call the new *loadTable* method when the scene loads within the WatchKit app. Add this method to the *InterfaceController.swift* file so that it reads as follows:

```
override init() {
    super.init()
    loadTable()
}
```

7.9 **Adding the Image Files to the Project**

The final task before testing the app is to add the image files referenced in the imageData array. These are contained within the *fitness_icons* folder of the sample code download which may be obtained from the following URL:

http://www.ebookfrenzy.com/print/watchkit/index.php

Within the code Project Navigator panel, select the *Images.xcassets* entry listed under the *TableDemoApp WatchKit App Extension* folder so that the asset catalog panel appears. Ctrl-click in the left hand panel of the asset catalog and select the *Import...* option from the resulting menu:

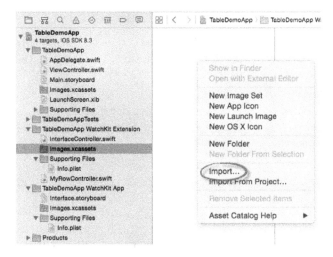

Figure 7-9

In the file import selection panel, navigate to and select the *fitness_icons* folder before clicking on the *Open* button. The images will be imported into the asset catalog as an image set named *fitness_icons* as shown in Figure 7-10:

Figure 7-10

7.10 **Testing the WatchKit App**

Select the current scheme in the toolbar and use the drop down menu (Figure 7-11) to select the *TableDemoApp WatchKit App -> iPhone 6* option:

Figure 7-11

With the correct build scheme and run target selected, click on the run button to launch the app on the simulator where it should appear as illustrated in Figure 7-12:

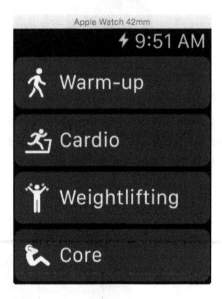

Figure 7-12

Assuming that the app runs as expected, note that it is possible to scroll through the rows but that selecting a row has no effect beyond some shadowing indicating that the row was selected. This functionality will be added in the chapter entitled *Implementing WatchKit Table Navigation*.

7.11 **Adding a Title Row to the Table**

The project will now be extended to demonstrate the steps involved in displaying multiple row controller types within a WatchKit app table. For the purposes of this project this will involve the addition of a title row to the top of the table.

The first step is to add another row controller to the table. Begin by selecting the *Interface.storyboard* file and displaying the Document Outline panel. Within the Document Outline panel, select the Table entry, display the Attributes Inspector and set the *Rows* property to 2 as outlined in Figure 7-13:

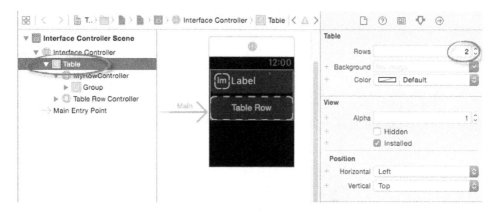

Figure 7-13

Drag a Label from the Object Library panel and drop it onto the new table row within the storyboard scene. With the new label selected, display the Attributes Inspector panel and set both the *Horizontal* and *Vertical* Position attributes to *Center*. On completion of these steps the scene should match that shown in Figure 7-14:

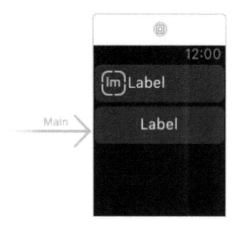

Figure 7-14

In the Document Outline panel, select the new *Table Row Controller* entry and enter *MyTitleRowController* into the Identifier field in the Attributes Inspector panel. Since this is a title row and is not intended to be selectable by the user, turn off the *Selectable* attribute.

As with the first row controller, this new controller will need a corresponding row controller class within the app extension. Locate and Ctrl-click on the *TableDemoApp WatchKit Extension* entry and select the *New File...* option from the menu. Repeat the steps performed earlier in this chapter to add a new Cocoa Touch Class named *MyTitleRowController* subclassed from NSObject. Edit the *MyTitleRowController.swift* file and modify the import directive so that the file imports the Watchkit framework instead of UIKit:

```
import UIKit
import WatchKit


class MyTitleRowController: NSObject {


}
```

7.12 Connecting the Outlet and Initializing the Second Table Row

Load the *Interface.storyboard* file into Interface Builder, display the Document Outline and Identity Inspector panels. In the Document Outline panel, select the MyTitleRowController entry and, from the Class menu in the Identity Inspector, select the newly created MyTitleRowController class.

Select the title Label object, display the Assistant Editor and make sure that it is displaying the content of the *MyTitleRowController.swift* file. Following the usual steps, establish an outlet for the Label object in the second row named *titleLabel*.

Finally, edit the *InterfaceController.swift* file and re-write the *loadTable* method so that it reads as follows:

```
func loadTable() {

    myTable.setRowTypes(["MyTitleRowController",
        "MyRowController",
        "MyRowController",
        "MyRowController",
        "MyRowController",
        "MyRowController",
        "MyRowController"])

    let titleRow = myTable.rowControllerAtIndex(0)
            as! MyTitleRowController

    titleRow.titleLabel.setText("Workout Plan")
```

```
for index in 0..<stringData.count {
    let row = myTable.rowControllerAtIndex(index+1)
                as! MyRowController
    row.myLabel.setText(stringData[index])
    row.myImage.setImage(UIImage(named: imageData[index]))
}
}
```

This time, the method is calling the *setRowTypes* method of the table and passing through an array containing the identifier of the title row and six instances of the MyRowController row type. This will ensure that the first row is the title row.

Next, the code obtains a reference to the title row at index position 0 in the table's internal array and sets a string value on the text property that reads "Workout Plan". Finally, the method iterates through the remaining rows configuring the properties of the Image and Label objects accordingly.

Compile and run the app once again, noting that the title row now appears at the top of the table:

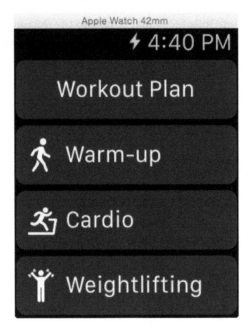

Figure 7-15

7.13 **Summary**

This chapter has worked through the creation of a project designed to demonstrate the steps involved in creating a table-based scene within a WatchKit app. Topics covered included the creation of a table scene, implementation of the supporting classes in the app extension and the process of supporting multiple row controller types within a single table.

8. Implementing WatchKit Table Navigation

The previous chapter introduced the concept of tables within WatchKit app scenes. An area of WatchKit tables that has been mentioned but not yet explored in detail involves the use of tables to implement navigation between storyboard scenes. This chapter will provide an overview of table based navigation (also referred to as hierarchical navigation) within WatchKit apps. Once the basics have been covered, the TableDemoApp project from the previous chapter will be extended to add navigation support.

8.1 Table Navigation in WatchKit Apps

Table based navigation, also referred to as hierarchical navigation, allows an app to transition from one scene to another scene when a row within a table is selected by the user. When a table row is selected, the *didSelectRow* method of the interface controller associated with the current scene is called and passed a reference to the table object in which the selection took place together with an integer value representing the index value of the selected row. It is then the responsibility of this method to perform the steps necessary to transition to the next scene.

8.2 Performing a Scene Transition

When implementing navigation-based behavior in a WatchKit app, each scene still has a corresponding interface controller. As the user navigates through scenes, the app framework maintains an internal navigation stack of the interface controllers. When a new scene is displayed it is *pushed* onto the navigation stack and becomes the currently active controller. The framework also places a left pointing chevron in the upper left hand corner (Figure 8-1) of the newly displayed scene which, when tapped, returns to the previous scene. When this happens, the current interface controller is *popped* off the stack and the interface controller beneath it moved to the top becoming the currently active and visible controller. In addition to the user tapping the chevron, a return to the previous scene may also be achieved programmatically via a call to the *popController* method of the current interface controller instance.

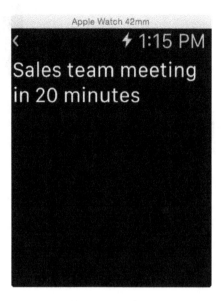

Figure 8-1

The interface controller for the first scene to be pushed onto the navigation stack is referred to as the *root interface controller*.

This stack based approach enables multiple levels of navigation to be implemented allowing the user to navigate back and forth through many scene levels. In this scenario it is also possible to trigger navigation back to the root interface controller, skipping all intermediate scenes in the navigation stack, via a call to the *popToRootController* method of the current interface controller instance.

The transition from one scene to another is initiated via a call to the *pushControllerWithName* method. This method takes as parameters the identifier name of the destination interface controller and an optional context object. The context object can be an object of any type and is intended to provide the destination interface controller with any data necessary to configure the new scene appropriate to the context of the selected row.

The *pushControllerWithName* method will initialize the destination interface controller and pass the context object through as a parameter to the controller's *awakeWithContext* lifecycle method.

8.3 Extending the TableDemoApp Project

In the remainder of this chapter, the TableDemoApp project will be extended so that when rows are selected within the table the app will transition to a second scene in which additional information about the selected item will be displayed. The first step in this tutorial is to add an additional scene and interface controller to the project to act as the detail scene.

8.4 Adding the Detail Scene to the Storyboard

Begin by launching Xcode and opening the TableDemoApp project created in the previous chapter. Once loaded, select the *Interface.storyboard* file so that it appears within the Interface Builder tool. The storyboard should currently consist of a single scene containing the table implementation. Add a second scene to the storyboard by locating the Interface Controller object in the Object Library panel and dragging and dropping it so that it is positioned to the right of the existing scene.

The detailed information about the selected workout step will be displayed on the second scene using a Label object so drag and drop a Label object from the Object Library onto the second scene. Once these steps have been performed the storyboard should resemble Figure 8-2:

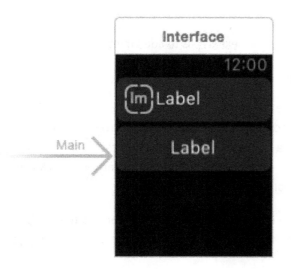

Figure 8-2

With the new scene added to the storyboard and selected so it is highlighted in blue, display the Attributes Inspector and enter "DetailInterfaceController" into the Identifier field.

By default, labels are configured to display a single line of text which will be clipped if the text exceeds the width of the watch display. To avoid this problem, configure the label to wrap the text over multiple lines by selecting the label in the second scene, displaying the Attributes Inspector and increasing the *Lines* attribute to 5.

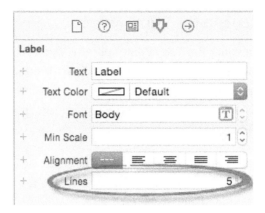

Figure 8-3

The design of the second scene is now complete. The next step is to add an interface controller to go with it.

8.5 Adding the Detail Interface Controller

Add the interface controller for the detail scene by locating the *TableDemoApp WatchKit Extension* entry in the Xcode Project Navigator panel, Ctrl-clicking on it and selecting *New File...* from the menu. In the template panel select the options to create an iOS Cocoa Touch Class source file and click *Next.* Name the new class *DetailInterfaceController* and configure it to be a subclass of WKInterfaceController. Click *Next,* make sure that the file is to be generated into the extension folder then click *Create.*

Load the *Interface.storyboard* file into Interface Builder. Select the second scene so that it highlights in blue, display the Identity Inspector panel and change the *Class* menu setting to the new *DetailInterfaceController* class as illustrated in Figure 8-4:

Figure 8-4

Select the Label object in the detail scene in the storyboard and display the Assistant Editor panel. Make sure that the Assistant Editor is displaying the *DetailInterfaceController.swift* file and then control click and drag from the Label object to a position just beneath the class declaration line in the Assistant Editor panel. Release the line and configure an outlet for the label named *detailLabel.* The outlet should now be declared within the class file as follows:

```
import WatchKit
import Foundation

class DetailInterfaceController: WKInterfaceController {

    @IBOutlet weak var detailLabel: WKInterfaceLabel!

    override func awakeWithContext(context: AnyObject?) {
        super.awakeWithContext(context)

        // Configure interface objects here.
    }
    .
    .
    .
}
```

8.6 Adding the Detail Data Array

When the user selects a row in the table the detail scene will appear on the display. The label within this scene is intended to provide a more detailed explanation of the exercise to be performed. The text displayed will depend on which row was selected by the user. In other words, when the user selects the "Warm-up" row, the detail scene will provide details on how the user should perform the warm-up routine. For the purposes of this example, the array containing the detailed descriptions will be placed in the interface controller of the first scene. The appropriate text will then be extracted from the array based on the row chosen by the user and passed through to the detail view controller as the context object.

Select the *InterfaceController.swift* file and modify it to add the detailData array as follows:

```
import WatchKit
import Foundation

class InterfaceController: WKInterfaceController {

    @IBOutlet weak var myTable: WKInterfaceTable!


    let stringData = ["Warm-up", "Cardio", "Weightlifting", "Core",
"Bike", "Cooldown"]

    let imageData = ["walking", "treadmill", "weights", "core",
"bikeriding", "cooldown"]
```

```
        let detailData = ["Walk at a moderate pace for 20 minutes keeping
heart rate below 110.",
            "Run for 30 minutes keeping heart rate between 130 and 140.",
            "Perform 3 sets of 10 repetitions increasing weight by 5lb on each
set.",
            "Perform 2 sets of 20 crunches.",
            "Ride bike at moderate pace for 20 minutes.",
            "Walk for 10 minutes then stretch for 5 minutes."]

    override init() {
        super.init()
        loadTable()
    }
    .
    .
    .
}
```

8.7 Implementing the didSelectRow Method

As previously discussed, the selection of a row within a table (assuming that the row has been configured as being selectable) results in a call to the *didSelectRow* method within the corresponding interface controller instance. This method now needs to be added to the *InterfaceController.swift* file as follows:

```
override func table(table: WKInterfaceTable, didSelectRowAtIndex rowIndex:
Int) {
    pushControllerWithName("DetailInterfaceController",
        context: detailData[rowIndex-1])
}
```

The code within this method simply calls the *pushControllerWithName* method passing through as a parameter the Identifier of the interface controller to be displayed (in this case our DetailInterfaceController scene). The code also extracts the string from the detailData array based on the number of the row selected by the user. The first element in the array is at index position zero while the first selectable row in the table is row 1 due to the presence of the title row. Consequently, the rowIndex value is decremented by one to compensate.

Run the application and test that selecting a row transitions to the detail scene. The next step is to add some code to display the detail text on the label of the detail scene.

8.8 Modifying the awakeWithContext Method

The *awakeWithContext* method is one of the lifecycle methods called on an interface controller during the app initialization process. The parameter passed to the method when it is called is the context object referenced in the *pushControllerWithName* method call. Code now needs to be added to the *awakeWithContext* method within the DetailInterfaceController class file to display the context string via the *detailText* outlet. Select the *DetailInterfaceController.swift* file, locate the *awakeWithContext* method and modify it so it reads as follows:

```
override func awakeWithContext(context: AnyObject?) {
    super.awakeWithContext(context)
    detailLabel.setText(context as? String)
}
```

Compile and run the app once again and verify that selecting a row transitions to the detail scene and that the label displays the text that corresponds to the chosen row:

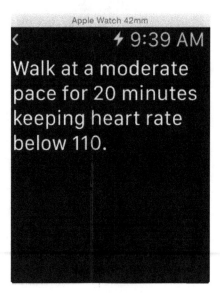

Figure 8-5

8.9 Adjusting the Interface Controller Insets

Although the text is displayed on the Label object in the detail scene, it appears a little too close to the outer edges of the display. The scene would probably be more visually appealing with a margin of some sort around the label content. This can be achieved by increasing the inset values on the interface controller. Modify these attributes by selecting the DetailInterfaceController object in the storyboard scene. This object can be selected by clicking on the black background of the scene, or via the Document Outline panel. Once selected, display the Attributes Inspector panel and change the *Insets* menu from *Default* to *Custom* to display the range of inset settings options. Set all four inset options to 5 as shown in Figure 8-6:

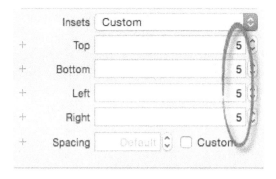

Figure 8-6

Re-run the app once again and verify that the label is now indented within the detail scene:

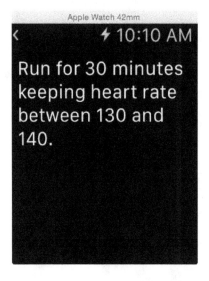

Figure 8-7

8.10 **Summary**

The WatchKit table provides an ideal starting point for providing a range of scene navigation options to the user. This chapter has extended the TableDemoApp project to implement navigation from the main scene to a detail scene. This example demonstrated the addition of new scenes to a storyboard and the passing of context data from one interface controller to another during a scene transition. The chapter also explored the use of insets to place a margin around the content of a scene.

9. WatchKit Page-based User Interfaces and Modal Interface Controllers

The WatchKit framework provides the infrastructure to create what Apple refers to as page-based interfaces within WatchKit Apps. A page-based interface consists of two or more WatchKit scenes through which the user is able to navigate by making left and right swiping motions on the Apple Watch screen.

Another form of transition between scenes involves the modal presentation of interface controller scenes within a WatchKit app. Since the modal interface controller is a useful mechanism for transitioning to an interface controller from a page-based scene, both topics will be covered in this chapter.

9.1 The Elements of a Page-based WatchKit Interface

A page-based WatchKit interface provides a way to navigate through a sequence of scenes by making left and right swiping motions on the display. Each scene within the navigation sequence is represented by a dot along the bottom edge of the display with the dot representing the currently displayed scene highlighted. Figure 9-1, for example, shows a page-based interface containing three scenes in which the third scene is currently displayed:

Figure 9-1

When implementing page-based navigation, each scene will typically be assigned its own unique interface controller. As will be demonstrated in the next chapter, however, it also is possible to make use of context data to configure multiple scenes to use the same interface controller class.

9.2 Associating Page Scenes

The scenes that are to be collected into a page-based navigation interface are connected together using *next page* segues within the WatchKit app storyboard file. Segues are transitions that have been configured between one scene and another within a storyboard and are typically implemented within the Interface Builder environment. Consider, for example, a storyboard containing two scenes. A segue between the two scenes can be created within Interface Builder by Ctrl-clicking on the first scene and dragging the resulting line to the second scene as shown in Figure 9-2.

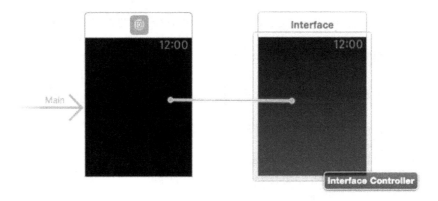

Figure 9-2

Upon releasing the line, a menu will appear providing a list of segue types available based on the context of the scene selections. Figure 9-3, for example, shows the segue menu providing the option to create a *next page* relationship segue between two scenes.

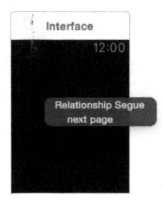

Figure 9-3

Once a segue has been established, it appears as a line and arrow between the two connected scenes (Figure 9-4). As with other items within a storyboard, a segue line can be selected and deleted. Certain types of segue may also be selected and given an identifier which, as will be shown later in the chapter, can be used to provide context during the transition from one scene to another.

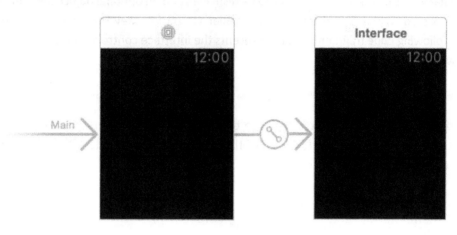

Figure 9-4

9.3 Managing Pages at Runtime

The interface controllers and ordering sequence for a paging interface may also be specified from within the application code via a call to the *reloadRootControllersWithNames* WKInterfaceController class method, passing through an array containing the identifiers of the interface controllers to be included in the page navigation together with a second array containing context data to be passed to each controller during scene transitions, for example:

```
WKInterfaceController.reloadRootControllersWithNames(
        ["controllerOne", "controllerTwo"],
            contexts: [contextObj1, contextObj2])
```

It is also possible to make an interface controller the currently displayed controller within the page sequence via a call to the *becomeCurrentPage* method within an initialization method of the interface controller to be displayed.

9.4 Modal Presentation of Interface Controllers

Interface controller scenes can be displayed modally using either storyboard segues, or programmatically from within a WatchKit app extension. Modal interface controllers are typically used to display information to the user and result in the scene associated with the controller appearing to the user together with an option located in the top left hand corner to dismiss the scene and return to the previous controller.

9.5 **Modal Presentation in Code**

Modal interface controllers can be displayed individually, or as a paging group. A single interface controller can be presented in code via a call to the *presentControllerWithName* method, passing through as parameters the identifier name of the interface controller to be displayed and an optional object containing context data which will be passed to the modal interface controller via the *awakeWithContext* lifecycle method. For example, the following code fragment modally presents the interface controller with the identifier matching "controllerTwo":

```
presentControllerWithName("controllerTwo", context: contextObj)
```

A set of interface controllers organized using page-based navigation may be presented modally from within code using the *presentControllerWithNames* method passing through arrays containing the controller identifiers and corresponding context objects:

```
presentControllerWithNames(["controllerOne", "controllerTwo"],
        contexts: [contextObj1, contextObj2])
```

By default, the dismissal option displayed in the modal scene will be labelled "Cancel". This can be changed by setting the title property of the interface controller to the desired text.

9.6 **Modal Presentation using Storyboard Segues**

An alternative to writing code to present an interface controller modally involves the use of storyboard segues. All that is required to implement a modal segue is to Ctrl-click on the user interface object within the scene that is to trigger the modal transition and then drag the line to the scene that is to be presented. If a modal segue can be established, the destination scene will highlight as shown in Figure 9-5. If the scene does not highlight, a segue cannot be established. It is not possible, for example, to establish a segue from a Label object because labels, unlike Button objects, do not trigger an event when tapped by the user.

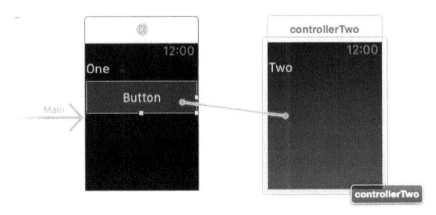

Figure 9-5

Upon release of the line, the segue menu will appear from which the *modal* option should be selected:

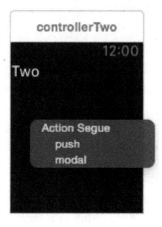

Figure 9-6

To modally present a collection of interface controllers grouped together using page-based navigation, simply connect the scenes together within the storyboard using *next page* segues as previously described.

9.7 Passing Context Data During a Modal Segue

The segue connection illustrated in Figure 9-5 above will cause the second interface controller to be presented modally when the button in the first interface controller is tapped by the user. If that is the only functionality that is required then no further steps are necessary when working with modal segues. If, on the other hand, context data needs to be passed during the segue transition then an additional step is needed.

When working with segues, the context data to be passed to the destination interface controllers can be specified by overriding either the *contextForSegueWithIdentifier* or *contextsForSegueWithIdentifier* method within the interface controller from which the segue is originating. The *contextForSegueWithIdentifier* method can be used to pass context data when presenting a single modal interface controller while the *contextsForSegueWithIdentifier* method is used when passing multiple context objects during the transition to a page-based set of interface controllers. In each case, the method will be called by the WatchKit framework during the scene transition and must return either a single context object, or in the case of the *contextsForSegueWithIdentifier* method, an array of context objects. The following code listing shows an example implementation of the method configured to return a string as the context object:

```
override func contextForSegueWithIdentifier(segueIdentifier: String)
        -> AnyObject? {
    return("MyContextString")
}
```

The context objects returned by these methods are passed to the corresponding destination interface controllers via the *awakeWithContext* lifecycle method.

9.8 **Summary**

Page-based navigation within WatchKit apps allows a sequence of interface controller scenes to be navigated by the user through left and right swiping motions performed on the display of the Apple Watch device. The interface controllers that comprise a page-based collection are grouped together within a storyboard file through the implementation of *next page* segues between each controller. Page-based interface controller groups may also be managed at runtime using the *reloadRootControllersWithNames* and *becomeCurrentPage* methods.

Interface controllers may be presented modally either by setting up a modal segue within a storyboard file, or from within code via method calls. The destination of a modal transition can take the form of either a single interface controller or a group of page-based controllers. Each modal controller displays an option for the user to return to the originating interface controller. Mechanisms are also provided for passing context data to the modal interface controller from the originating controller.

10. A WatchKit Page-based Interface Tutorial

This chapter will work through the creation of an example that makes use of both page-based navigation and modal interface controller presentation within a WatchKit app.

The project created in this chapter will involve a variation on the fitness app created in the chapter entitled *A WatchKit Table Tutorial*. In this case, the user interface will consist of a sequence of scenes within a page-based interface, each containing a fitness exercise image and a button. When selected by the user, the button will cause a modal interface controller to appear containing a Timer object which will show the user how much time is left to perform the corresponding workout step. When the countdown reaches zero, the app extension will play an alert sound to notify the user that the time has expired.

10.1 Creating the Page Example Project

Start Xcode and create a new iOS project. On the template screen choose the *Application* option located under *iOS* in the left hand panel and select *Single View Application*. Click *Next,* set the product name to *PageDemoApp,* enter your organization identifier and make sure that the *Devices* menu is set to *Universal*. Before clicking *Next*, change the *Language* menu to Swift. On the final screen, choose a location in which to store the project files and click on *Create* to proceed to the main Xcode project window.

10.2 Adding the WatchKit App Target

For the purposes of this example we will, once again, assume that the iOS app has already been implemented. The next step, therefore, is to add the WatchKit app target to the project. Within Xcode, select the *File -> New -> Target…* menu option. In the target template dialog, select the *Apple Watch* option listed beneath the *iOS* heading. In the main panel, select the *WatchKit App* icon and click on *Next*. On the subsequent screen turn off the *Include Glance Scene* and *Include Notification Scene* options before clicking on the *Finish* button.

As soon as the extension target has been created, a new panel will appear requesting permission to activate the new scheme for the extension target. Activate this scheme now by clicking on the *Activate* button in the request panel.

10.3 **Adding the Image Files to the Project**

Before designing the interface controller scene, some image files need to be added to the project. These are contained within the *fitness_icons_large* folder of the sample code download which may be obtained from the following URL:

http://www.ebookfrenzy.com/print/watchkit/index.php

Within the Project Navigator panel, select the *Images.xcassets* entry listed under the *PageDemoApp WatchKit App* folder so that the asset catalog panel appears. Ctrl-click in the left hand panel of the asset catalog and select the *Import...* option from the resulting menu.

In the file import selection panel, navigate to and select the *fitness_icons_large* folder before clicking on the *Open* button. The images will be imported into the asset catalog as an image set named *fitness_icons_large*.

10.4 **Designing the First Interface Controller Scene**

The user interface for the app is going to consist of three scenes, each containing an Image object and a Button. Select the *Interface.storyboard* file located under *PageDemoApp WatchKit App* in the Project Navigator panel, locate the main scene in the Interface Builder tool and add an Image and a Button object to the scene so that it appears as shown in Figure 10-1:

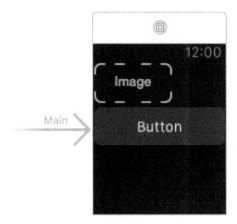

Figure 10-1

Select the Image object in the scene, display the Attributes Inspector and select the *walking* image from the *Image* menu. With the image object still selected and remaining in the Attributes Inspector, change the *Mode* setting to *Aspect Fit* and the *Horizontal* position attribute to *Center*.

Double click on the Button object and change the text so it reads "Start". Keep the Button object selected and change the *Vertical* position property in the Attributes Inspector to *Bottom*. On completion of these settings the layout should match that shown in Figure 10-2:

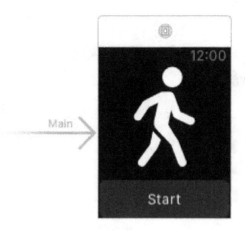

Figure 10-2

10.5 Adding More Interface Controllers

This phase of the project requires that an additional two interface controllers be added to the storyboard file. Locate the Interface Controller item in the Object Library panel and drag and drop two instances onto the storyboard canvas so that the objects are positioned to the right of the main controller (Figure 10-3):

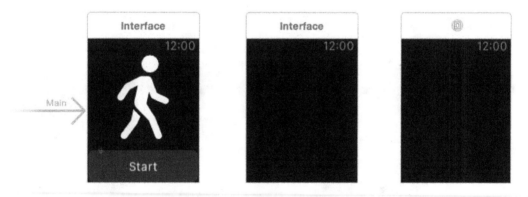

Figure 10-3

Since the user interface design for the remaining two scenes will be similar to that of the first, a quicker option than manually designing the scenes is to cut and paste the objects from the first scene. Hold down the Shift key and click on the Image and Button objects in the main scene. Press Cmd-C to copy the objects, select the second interface controller scene and use Cmd-V to paste the objects into the scene. Select the third scene and perform the paste operation once again.

Select the Image object in the second scene, display the Attributes Inspector and change the image value to the *treadmill* image. Repeat this step to change the image in the third scene to *weights*. On completion of these steps, the three interface controller scenes should appear as shown in Figure 10-4:

Figure 10-4

10.6 Establishing the Segues

For the three interface controllers to work within a page-based navigation interface, the controllers must be connected using *next page* segues. To achieve this, Ctrl-click on the title bar of the first scene (the title bar is the area which currently shows a time of 12:00). Drag the resulting line to the second interface controller until it highlights (Figure 10-5) and release the line. In the segue relationship menu select the *next page* option.

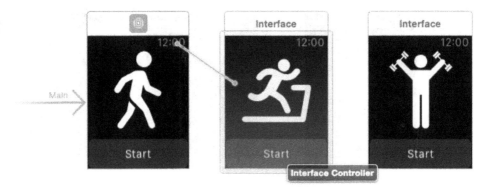

Figure 10-5

Repeat the above steps to establish a segue between the second and third interface controllers so that the storyboard matches that of Figure 10-6:

Figure 10-6

Run the app and test that the three scenes can now be navigated by making swiping motions on the display:

Figure 10-7

10.7 Assigning Interface Controllers

The scene now consists of three scenes but at the moment only the first scene has an Interface Controller associated with it. One approach to take at this point might be to add two new interface controller classes to the project, one for each of the two remaining scenes in the page-based navigation set. Since all three scenes essentially perform the same task, however, a more efficient approach is to use the same interface controller class for all three. The first scene is already assigned to the InterfaceController class, so select the second scene so that it is highlighted in blue, display the Identity Inspector panel and change the *Class* menu setting to *InterfaceController* (Figure 10-8). Repeat these steps with the third interface controller selected.

Figure 10-8

In each case, make sure that the *Module* menu is set to *PageDemoApp_WatchKit_Extension*.

10.8 Adding the Timer Interface Controller

When the Start button is tapped on any of the paged controller scenes an additional scene will be modally displayed to the user. This scene will contain a single object in the form of a WKInterfaceTimer instance. Start by dragging and dropping an Interface Controller object from the Object Library panel so that it is positioned beneath the three existing scenes in the storyboard:

Figure 10-9

Drag and drop a Timer object from the Object Library onto the newly added scene. With the Timer object selected, display the Attributes Inspector panel and set the *Horizontal* and *Vertical* position attributes to *Center*.

Click on the "T" button within the Font text field, select *System* from the popup panel, *Bold* from the *Style* menu and set the *Size* setting to 28 as shown in Figure 10-10:

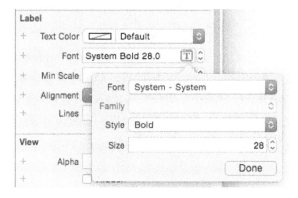

Figure 10-10

On completion of these steps the scene should match that illustrated in Figure 10-11:

Figure 10-11

By default, the Timer object displays hours, minutes and seconds as numbers (referred to as *positional* format). A range of other configuration alternatives is available within the Attributes Inspector for changing both what is displayed on the timer and how it is displayed. It is, for example, possible to also display month, week, day and year values. It is also possible to change the way in which this information is displayed, including fully spelling out the time and date in words instead of numbers. Although this example will use the default setting, it is worth reviewing the options in the Attributes Inspector panel for future reference.

Locate and select the *PageDemoApp WatchKit Extension* entry in the Xcode Project Navigator panel, Ctrl-click on it and select the *New File...* menu option. Create a new iOS Cocoa Touch Class named *TimerInterfaceController* subclassed from *WKInterfaceController* and proceed with the steps to generate the class source file into the *PageDemoApp WatchKit Extension* project folder.

Return to the *Interface.storyboard* file, select the timer scene so that it is highlighted in blue and, using the Identity Inspector panel, change the *Class* menu to *TimerInterfaceController*. Switch to the Attributes Inspector panel and enter *TimerInterfaceController* into the *Identifier* field.

Select the Timer object in the timer scene, display the Assistant Editor panel and verify that it is displaying the source code for the *TimerInterfaceController.swift* file. Ctrl-click on the Timer object and drag the resulting line to a position immediately after the class declaration line in the Assistant Editor panel. Release the line and establish an outlet named *workoutTimer*. On completion of these steps the start of the *TimerInterfaceController.swift* file should read as follows:

```
import WatchKit
import Foundation

class TimerInterfaceController: WKInterfaceController {

    @IBOutlet weak var workoutTimer: WKInterfaceTimer!

    override func awakeWithContext(context: AnyObject?) {
        super.awakeWithContext(context)

        // Configure interface objects here.
    }
    .
    .
    .
}
```

With the timer interface controller added and configured, the next step is to implement the modal segues so that the interface controller is presented when the Start buttons are tapped.

10.9 Adding the Modal Segues

When the buttons on the three paged scenes are tapped by the user, the timer scene will need to be displayed modally. Establish the first segue by Ctrl-clicking on the Button object in the first scene and dragging to the timer scene. Release the line and select the *modal* option from the Action Segue menu. Repeat these steps for the Button objects on the remaining two scenes so that the storyboard resembles Figure 10-12:

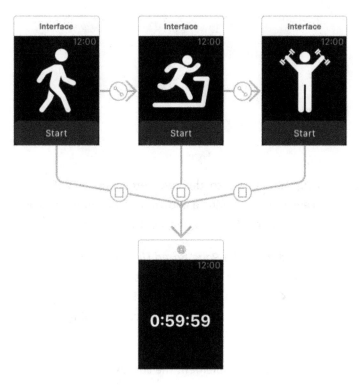

Figure 10-12

Compile and run the app and verify that tapping the button on each of the scenes causes the scene for the timer interface controller to appear. Note that a Cancel option is provided on the timer scene to return to the original scene.

10.10 Configuring the Context Data

When the timer interface controller is presented it will need to be initialized with a countdown time. The amount of time will vary depending on the scene from which the timer was launched. This means that we will need to find a way to identify which of the three modal segues triggered the appearance of the timer interface controller and, based on that information, pass the appropriate time duration through as context data.

The first step in this process is to establish a way to distinguish one segue from another by assigning identifiers. Begin by selecting the segue line from the left most scene to the timer scene and displaying the Attributes Inspector panel. Within the panel, enter *walkSegue* into the *Identifier* field as shown in Figure 10-13:

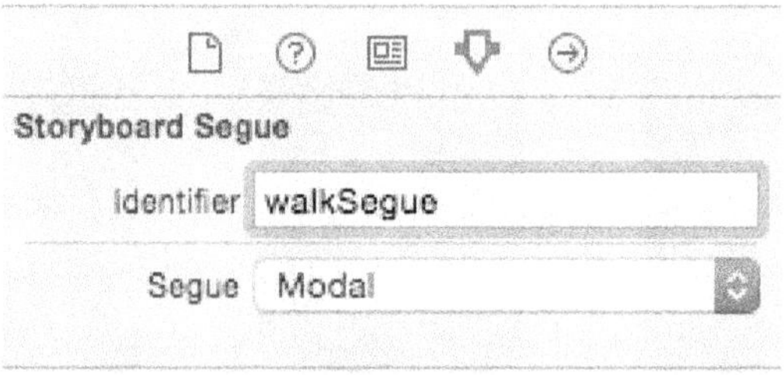

Figure 10-13

Follow the same steps to assign identifiers to the two remaining modal segues named *runSegue* and *weightsSegue* respectively. To avoid encountering a known problem with Xcode whereby the identifiers are not saved, be sure to save the storyboard after entering identifier (Cmd-S).

As explained in the chapter entitled *WatchKit Page Based User Interfaces and Modal Interface Controllers*, context data can be passed during a modal segue transition by implementing the *contextForSegueWithIdentifier* method within the originating interface controller. Passed as a parameter to this method is the identifier of the segue that triggered the call, allowing us to configure the context data according to the segue.

Select the *InterfaceController.swift* file and implement the *contextForSegueWithIdentifier* method so that it reads as follows:

```
override func contextForSegueWithIdentifier(segueIdentifier: String) ->
AnyObject? {

    var contextValue: NSTimeInterval?

    switch (segueIdentifier) {
        case "walkSegue":
            contextValue = 10
        case "runSegue":
            contextValue = 20
        case "weightsSegue":
            contextValue = 30
        default:
            break
    }
    return(contextValue)
}
```

The code in the above method declares a variable in which to store the countdown time before using a switch construct to identify the current segue and select a time value which is then returned. The duration value will then be passed by the WatchKit framework to the destination interface controller via the *awakeWithContext* method of that class. For testing purposes, the duration values are set to seconds rather than minutes.

10.11 Configuring the Timer

When the timer interface controller is now displayed it will be passed a time duration value via the *awakeWithContext* lifecycle method. This time duration will subsequently need to be assigned to the Timer object in the scene and the countdown started. The WatchKit Timer object is initialized by passing through an NSDate object configured to the current time, a time in the future or a time in the past. Passing through the current time and date will cause the timer to begin counting upwards from 0:00. Passing through a date and time in the future will cause the timer to begin counting down towards that time and date. Specifying a date and time in the past, on the other hand, will start the timer at that date and time and begin counting upwards from that point.

Select the *TimerInterfaceController.swift* file, locate the *awakeWithContext* method and modify it so that it reads as follows:

```
override func awakeWithContext(context: AnyObject?) {
    super.awakeWithContext(context)

    if let duration: AnyObject = context {
        let date = NSDate(timeIntervalSinceNow:
                            duration as! NSTimeInterval)
        workoutTimer.setDate(date)
        workoutTimer.start()
    }
}
```

The code verifies that a time value was passed through as the context object and uses that value to create an NSDate object configured to a time point in the future. The configured NSDate object is then used to initialize the Timer object using the previously configured outlet before the countdown is started.

Run the application and note that the timer is now initialized and begins counting down when the timer scene is presented. The time duration should also differ depending on which scene triggers the segue as defined in the earlier switch statement:

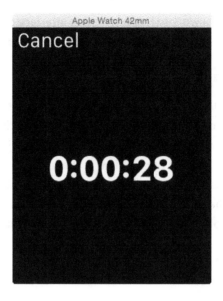

Figure 10-14

10.12 Playing the Alert Sound

The final feature to be added to the project is to set up an alert sound to play to notify the user that the timer has reached zero. The problem that arises in implementing this behavior is that the WatchKit Timer object does not trigger an action when it reaches zero. The solution is to initialize an NSTimer instance to run for the same amount of time as the WatchKit Timer object and configured to call a selector method when the time has elapsed. The code to set up the NSTimer object needs to be added to the *awakeWithContext* method as follows:

```
override func awakeWithContext(context: AnyObject?) {
    super.awakeWithContext(context)

    if let duration: AnyObject = context {

        var timer = NSTimer.scheduledTimerWithTimeInterval(
            duration as! NSTimeInterval,
            target: self,
            selector: Selector("playAlert"),
            userInfo: nil,
            repeats: false)

        let date = NSDate(timeIntervalSinceNow:
                    duration as NSTimeInterval)
        workoutTimer.setDate(date)
        workoutTimer.start()
```

```
        }
}
```

The NSTimer object is configured to call a selector method named *playAlert* when the designated time has elapsed. The code in this method will require that the AVFoundation framework be imported and that an AVAudioPlayer variable be declared within the *TimerInterfaceController.swift* file as follows:

```
import WatchKit
import Foundation
import AVFoundation

class TimerInterfaceController: WKInterfaceController {

    @IBOutlet weak var workoutTimer: WKInterfaceTimer!

    var audioPlayer: AVAudioPlayer?
.
.
.
```

With these changes made, the next step is to add the *playAlert* method to the class:

```
func playAlert() {

    let url = NSURL.fileURLWithPath(
        NSBundle.mainBundle().pathForResource("alert_sound",
            ofType: "mp3")!)

    var error: NSError?

    audioPlayer = AVAudioPlayer(contentsOfURL: url, error: &error)

    if let err = error {
        println("audioPlayer error \(err.localizedDescription)")
    } else {
        audioPlayer?.prepareToPlay()
        audioPlayer?.play()
    }
}
```

The code creates a URL that references an audio file named *alert_sound.mp3*, initializes an AVAudioPlayer instance with the URL and assigns it to the *audioPlayer* variable declared at the top of the class file. Assuming no errors are detected, the audio player is instructed to begin playing the sound.

All that remains before testing the app again is to add the audio file to the project. The audio file is located in the *audio_files* folder of the sample code download.

Once located, drag and drop the *alert_sound.mp3* file onto the *Supporting Files* folder located under *PageDemoApp WatchKit Extension* in the Xcode Project Navigator panel.

With the audio file added to the project, compile and run the app on a Simulator or physical Apple Watch device and test that the alert sound plays when the countdown reaches zero in the timer interface controller scene.

10.13 **Summary**

This chapter has worked through the design and implementation of an example WatchKit app containing a page-based scene navigation interface. The example also highlighted the steps involved in implementing modal interface controller presentation and the passing of context during segue transitions. The chapter also introduced the WatchKit Timer object and explored the use of an NSTimer instance in parallel with a Timer object to receive notification of the timer reaching zero.

11. Handling User Input in a WatchKit App

Unlike the iPhone, the Apple Watch display is too small to accommodate a virtual keyboard to allow the user to input text into an app. This does not, however, mean that it is not possible to accept user input. In fact, the WatchKit framework provides a mechanism for user input in the form of selections from a list of phrases, voice dictation and emoji image selection.

This chapter will provide an overview of how to accept user input from within a WatchKit app before providing a brief tutorial.

11.1 Getting User Input

The WatchKit framework supports three types of user input in the form of phrase selection, voice dictation and emoji image selection. All three forms of input are available via a single modal scene, an example of which is illustrated in Figure 11-1:

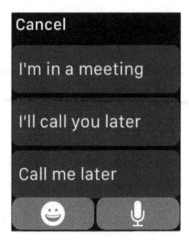

Figure 11-1

This screen is referred to as the *text input controller* and can be configured with a list of phrases to be displayed, to enable or disable support for emoji selection, or to go directly to dictation input.

11.2 **Displaying the Text Input Controller**

The text input controller screen is displayed via a call to the *presentTextInputControllerWithSuggestions* method of the currently active interface controller instance. The method accepts as parameters an array of phrase suggestion strings and an input mode value indicating what forms of input are to be accepted. The method also requires a completion handler block to be called when the input session is completed. This completion block is passed an array containing the results of the input.

The following code, for example, invokes the text input controller with emoji support and a range of phrase suggestions. The completion handler block simply outputs the input string from the reply array to the console:

```
let phrases = ["I'm in a meeting", "I'll call you later", "Call me later"]

presentTextInputControllerWithSuggestions(phrases,
                    allowedInputMode: .AllowEmoji,
                    completion: { (result) -> Void in

    if let choice = result[0] as? String {
            println(choice)
    }
})
```

The above code used the *.AllowEmoji* option (or more precisely the *WKTextInputMode.AllowEmoji* option) to include static emoji images as selection options. The three input mode options supported by WatchKit are as follows:

- **WKTextInputMode.Plain** – Allows the user to generate input from the phrase selection list and dictation only. The emoji button is absent from the text input controller screen in this mode.
- **WKTextInputMode.AllowEmoji** - Allows the user to generate input using the phrase list, dictation and non-animated emoji images.
- **WKTextInputMode.AllowAnimatedEmoji** - Allows the user to generate input using the phrase list, dictation and both animated and non-animated emoji images.

The text input controller screen will automatically dismiss when the user has made an input selection or tapped the Cancel button. The controller may also be dismissed from within the code of the interface controller via a call to the *dismissTextInputController* method. When the text input controller is dismissed in this way, the code within the completion handler block is not executed.

When testing text input, it is important to note that emoji and dictation modes are not available from within the simulator environment.

11.3 Detecting if Input is a String or NSData Object

If the input is in the form of text or a non-animated emoji, the input will be returned in the form of a Unicode string contained within a String object. If the user selects an animated emoji, however, the image will be returned in the form of an NSData object. The following code can be used to identify whether the returned result is a String or NSData object:

```
if result[0] is String {
    // Result is a String object
    // Handle as a text string
}

if result[0] is NSData {
    // Result is an NSData object
    // Handle as an image
}
```

11.4 Direct Dictation Input

In many situations, input will be needed only through the use of dictation. To move directly to dictation based input, call the *presentTextInputControllerWithSuggestions* method without any suggested phrases and with the input mode set to .*Plain*. For example:

```
presentTextInputControllerWithSuggestions(nil,
        allowedInputMode: .Plain,
        completion: { (result) -> Void in


    }
})
```

11.5 Creating the User Input Example Project

Start Xcode and create a new iOS project. On the template screen choose the *Application* option located under *iOS* in the left hand panel and select *Single View Application*. Click *Next,* set the product name to *TextInputApp,* enter your organization identifier and make sure that the *Devices* menu is set to *Universal*. Before clicking *Next*, change the *Language* menu to Swift. On the final screen, choose a location in which to store the project files and click on *Create* to proceed to the main Xcode project window.

11.6 Adding the WatchKit App Target

The next step is to add the WatchKit app target to the project. Within Xcode, select the *File -> New -> Target...* menu option. In the target template dialog, select the *Apple Watch* option listed beneath the *iOS* heading. In the main panel, select the *WatchKit App* icon and click on *Next*. On the subsequent screen turn off the *Include Glance Scene* and *Include Notification Scene* options before clicking on the *Finish* button.

As soon as the extension target has been created, a new panel will appear requesting permission to activate the new scheme for the extension target. Activate this scheme now by clicking on the *Activate* button in the request panel.

11.7 **Designing the WatchKit App Main Scene**

Locate and select the *Interface.storyboard* file so that it loads into Interface Builder. Drag and drop a Button object from the Object Library panel, double-click on it and change the text so that it reads "Get Input".

Add a Label object to the scene and set both the *Horizontal* and *Vertical* position properties in the Attributes Inspector panel to *Center* so that the scene layout matches that of Figure 11-2. Also, increase the *Lines* property to 4 so that multiple lines of text input can be displayed if necessary:

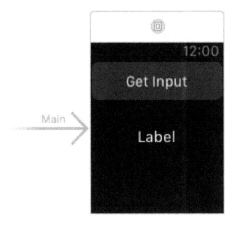

Figure 11-2

Display the Assistant Editor, Ctrl-click on the Label object in the storyboard scene and drag the resulting line to a position immediately beneath the class declaration line in the Assistant Editor panel. On releasing the line, establish an outlet named *labelObject* in the connection panel.

Repeat these steps on the Button object, this time establishing an action connection to a method named *getUserInput.*

11.8 **Getting the User Input**

The code to get input from the user now needs to be implemented within the *getUserInput* action method. For the purposes of this example, input will be accepted in the form of dictation, non-animated emoji and via phrase list selection. Once obtained, the user input will be displayed on the Label object within the main scene. Locate and select the *InterfaceController.swift* file for the WatchKit app extension in the Project Navigator panel and modify the *getUserInput* method so that it reads as follows:

```
@IBAction func getUserInput() {
    let phrases = ["I'm in a meeting", "I'll call you later", "Call me
later"]

    presentTextInputControllerWithSuggestions(phrases,
            allowedInputMode: .AllowEmoji,
            completion: { (result) -> Void in

        if let choice = result[0] as? String {
            self.labelObject.setText(choice)
        }
    })
}
```

11.9 Testing the Application

Compile and run the WatchKit app on a physical Apple Watch device, tap on the *Get Input* button and use dictation to enter some text. On tapping the Done button the dictated text will appear on the Label object in the main scene of the app. Repeat these steps to test the phrase selection and emoji forms of input.

11.10 Summary

WatchKit provides support for user input via phrase selection, dictation and emoji images. Input is initiated using the *presentTextInputControllerWithSuggestions* method of the currently active interface controller instance. This chapter has covered the basics of user input in WatchKit and worked through the creation of an example WatchKit app project.

12. WatchKit App and Parent iOS App Communication

Up until this point, most of the areas covered in this book have related primarily to the interaction between the WatchKit app and the WatchKit extension. There is, of course, a third element that needs to be taken into consideration in the form of the parent iOS app with which the WatchKit app is bundled. As has been demonstrated in the preceding chapters, much can be achieved within the WatchKit app extension. There are, however, certain tasks that can only be performed in the iOS application. In recognition of this fact, the WatchKit framework provides a mechanism for the WatchKit extension to launch the parent iOS app, send a request to the app and receive data in response once that request has been fulfilled.

This chapter will describe the way in which a WatchKit app extension can communicate directly with the parent iOS app. The next chapter (*A WatchKit openParentApplication Example Project*) will work through a tutorial that makes practical use of this technique.

12.1 Parent iOS App Communication

A WatchKit app implementation consists of the WatchKit app, the WatchKit app extension and the parent or containing iOS 8 app. When the user launches the WatchKit app on the Apple Watch device, the corresponding extension is launched on the iPhone device with which the watch is paired. In most cases, the WatchKit app extension contains all of the code that implements the logic and behavior of WatchKit app and this is often all that is needed to create a fully functional WatchKit app.

One characteristic of the WatchKit app extension that can make this configuration unsuitable for some requirements, however, is the fact that the extension is suspended when the user stops interacting with the corresponding WatchKit app on the watch device. In many instances this is not a problem unless the WatchKit app requires some task to continue running even when the user is no longer interacting with the app. Consider, for example, a WatchKit app designed to control the playback of music tracks on the iPhone device. If the audio playback is initiated from within the WatchKit app extension, the playback will stop when the WatchKit framework detects that the user is no longer using the WatchKit app on the watch. The app, on the other hand, requires the music to continue playing until the user requests that it stop by tapping a button on the WatchKit app. In such a scenario, the WatchKit extension clearly does not meet the needs of the app.

The solution to this dilemma is to hand off to the parent iOS app any tasks that need to continue to execute after the extension has been suspended. This can be achieved by making a call to the WatchKit framework *openParentApplication* class method from within the app extension.

12.2 **The openParentApplication Method**

When called, the *openParentApplication* method either wakes up or, if it is not already running, launches the parent iOS app such that it is executing in the background. In addition to launching the parent app, the method allows data to be passed to the parent app and to specify a block of code to be called and passed return data when the iOS app responds to the request.

The syntax for the *openParentApplication* method can be summarized as follows:

```
WKInterfaceController.openParentApplication(requestDictionary,
        reply: { (replyDictionary, error) -> Void in
            // Code to be executed when parent app replies
        })
}
```

The first point to note is that the *openParentApplication* method is a class method. As such it is called on the WKInterfaceController class rather than on an instance of the class. The first parameter to the method (named *requestDictionary* in the above example) is a Dictionary object containing any data that needs to be passed to the parent iOS app in order for the app to perform the necessary tasks.

The second parameter to the method is a closure expression containing the code that will be called and executed by the parent iOS app in order to reply to the *openParentApplication* call. When the closure expression is called it can be passed a Dictionary object (represented by *replyDictionary* in the above example) containing any data that needs to be returned to the extension together with an NSError object (or a nil value if no error occurred) used to report any problems encountered whilst the request was being fulfilled by the parent app.

The following code, for example, creates a dictionary containing a key-value pair and calls the *openParentApplication* method using a closure expression which outputs the value of the reply dictionary object based on a key of "replyString":

```
let requestValues = ["myValue" : "startPlay"]

WKInterfaceController.openParentApplication(requestValues,
        reply: { (replyValues, error) -> Void in
    println(replyValues["replyString"])
})
```

12.3 The handleWatchKitExtensionRequest Method

When the *openParentApplication* method is called, the *handleWatchKitExtensionRequest* method is called on the app delegate of the parent iOS app. This method is passed the Dictionary object declared in the *openParentApplication* method call and a reference to the reply closure expression.

The *handleWatchKitExtensionRequest* method will typically extract data from the dictionary, perform any necessary tasks, create a new dictionary populated with the reply data and then pass that through as a parameter when calling the reply closure expression. The following code shows an example implementation of the *handleWatchKitExtensionRequest* method:

```
func application(application: UIApplication,
handleWatchKitExtensionRequest userInfo: [NSObject : AnyObject]?, reply:
(([NSObject : AnyObject]!) -> Void)!) {

    var replyValues = Dictionary<String, AnyObject>()
    replyValues["replyString"] = "Playback started"
    reply(replyValues)
}
```

12.4 Understanding iOS Background Modes

Although the parent iOS app is not automatically suspended when the user is no longer interacting with the matching WatchKit app, there are still situations where the iOS app running in the background may be suspended or terminated by the iOS operating system. There are a number of ways to mitigate this risk depending on whether the tasks being performed by the iOS app on behalf of the WatchKit app are short or long-term in nature.

12.4.1 Using the beginBackgroundTaskWithName Method

If the iOS app needs to perform a task which is short-term, and where suspension prior to replying to the WatchKit app would be detrimental to the user experience, the use of the UIApplication *beginBackgroundTaskWithName* and *endBackgroundTask* methods is recommended.

The *beginBackgroundTaskWithName* method indicates to the operating system that the app needs extra time to complete a task. The *endBackgroundTask* method is called to notify the operating system that the task is complete and that the application can be suspended. A background task request of this type does not provide an app with an indefinite amount of time to complete a task. When the operating system decides that sufficient time has been used, it will call the handler method declared when the *beginBackgroundTaskWithName* method was called to notify the app that the time has expired. The amount of time remaining can be checked at any time via the *backgroundTimeRemaining* property of the

UIApplication instance. The following code, for example, might be placed within the *handleWatchKitExtensionRequest* method to request time to complete the designated task:

```
    .
    .
    .

let bgIdentifier = application.beginBackgroundTaskWithName("MyTask",
        expirationHandler: { () -> Void in
    // Code here will be called when time expires.
    // Perform any necessary clean up tasks here.
    // Report failure to complete task to app extension if
    // necessary.
})

// Place code here to perform task on behalf of WatchKit app

reply(replyValues) // Reply to WatchKit App Extension

application.endBackgroundTask(bgIdentifier) // Notify OS of completion
    .
    .
```

12.4.2 Using Background Modes

For long-term background execution of an iOS app, Apple recognizes nine categories in which application suspension would be detrimental to the user experience, these being audio, location updates, voice over IP (VOIP), Newsstand updates, external and Bluetooth accessory communication, background fetch and remote notifications.

The background execution modes supported by an application are configured in the application's *Info.plist* file using the *UIBackgroundModes* key. The value for the key is actually an array allowing an application to register for more than one background execution mode. The easiest way to enable the background modes required by an application is to select the application target at the top of the project navigator panel, select the *Capabilities* tab and switch the *Background Modes* option from *Off* to *On*. Once background modes are enabled, individual modes may be activated using the checkboxes provided as shown in Figure 12-1:

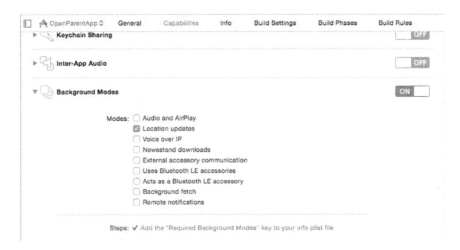

Figure 12-1

With the necessary modes enabled, the app will not be suspended as long as it continues to perform tasks associated with the selected background mode. For example, as long as an iOS app configured for audio background mode continues to play music using the standard iOS frameworks it will not be suspended by the operating system.

12.5 **Summary**

Each WatchKit app has associated with it a WatchKit app extension which runs on the iPhone device while the user is using the app on the Apple Watch. When the user stops interacting with the app, the corresponding app extension is suspended by the operating system. This means that tasks that need to continue running after the extension is suspended need to be performed by the parent iOS app. This can be achieved using the *openParentApp* method. This method causes the parent iOS app to be woken up or launched in the background. The *handleWatchKitExtensionRequest* of the app delegate is called and passed a dictionary object containing data passed from the app extension. Once the iOS app has completed any required tasks it is able to reply to the app extension, passing through another dictionary object containing response data.

When using the iOS app to perform background tasks for a WatchKit app it is also important to be aware the iOS app may also be subject to suspension and termination. The risks of this can be reduced by making use of the various background task methods of the UIApplication instance, or the use of one or more the supported iOS app background modes.

13. A WatchKit openParentApplication Example Project

The previous chapter explored the use of the openParentApplication method to enable a WatchKit app to communicate with the containing iOS application with which it is bundled. The tutorial outlined in this chapter will make use of this technique to play audio on the iPhone device under the control of a WatchKit app.

13.1 About the Project

The project created in this chapter will consist of two parts. The first is an iOS application that allows the user to playback music and to adjust the volume level from an iPhone device. The second part of the project involves the creation of a WatchKit app which also allows the user the same level of music playback control from the paired Apple Watch device. The communication back and forth between the WatchKit and iOS apps will be implemented entirely using the *openParentApplication* method.

13.2 Creating the Project

Start Xcode and create a new iOS project. On the template screen choose the *Application* option located under *iOS* in the left hand panel and select *Single View Application*. Click *Next,* set the product name to *OpenParentApp,* enter your organization identifier and make sure that the *Devices* menu is set to *Universal*. Before clicking *Next*, change the *Language* menu to Swift. On the final screen, choose a location in which to store the project files and click on *Create* to proceed to the main Xcode project window.

13.3 Enabling Audio Background Mode

When the user begins audio playback it should not stop until the user taps the stop button, or the end of the track is reached. To ensure that the iOS app is not suspended by the operating system the Audio background mode needs to be enabled. Within Xcode, select the *OpenParentApp* target at the top of the project navigator panel, select the Capabilities tab and switch the Background Modes option from *Off* to *On*. Once background modes are enabled, enable the checkbox next to Audio and Airplay as outlined in Figure 13-1:

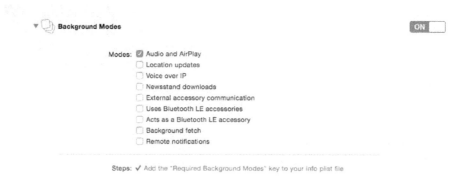

Figure 13-1

With this mode enabled, the background iOS app will not be suspended as long as it continues to play audio.

13.4 Designing the iOS App User Interface

The user interface for the iOS app will consist of a Play button, a Stop button and a slider with which to control the volume level. Locate and select the *Main.storyboard* file in the Xcode Project Navigator panel and drag and drop two Buttons and one Slider view onto the scene canvas so that they are centered horizontally within the scene. Double click on each button, changing the text to "Play" and "Stop" respectively, and stretch the slider so that it is slightly wider than the default width. On completion of these steps the layout should resemble that of Figure 13-2:

Figure 13-2

Using the *Resolve Auto Layout Issues* menu (indicated in Figure 13-3) select the *Reset to Suggested Constraints* option to configure appropriate layout behavior for the three views in the scene:

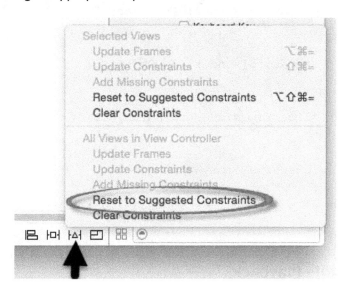

Figure 13-3

13.5 Establishing Outlets and Actions

With the *Main.storyboard* file still loaded into Interface Builder, display the Assistant Editor panel and verify that it is displaying the content of the *ViewController.swift* file. Ctrl-click on the Slider object in the storyboard scene and drag the resulting line to a position immediately beneath the class declaration line in the Assistant Editor panel. On releasing the line, establish an outlet named *volumeControl* in the connection panel.

Repeat these steps on both of the Button views, this time establishing action connections to methods named *playAudio* and *stopAudio* respectively.

Finally, establish an action connection for the Slider view to a method named *sliderMoved* based on the *Value Changed* event. On completion of these steps the *ViewController.swift* file should read as follows:

```
import UIKit

class ViewController: UIViewController {

    @IBOutlet weak var volumeControl: UISlider!

    override func viewDidLoad() {
        super.viewDidLoad()
        // Do any additional setup after loading the view, typically from
a nib.
```

```
    }

    @IBAction func playAudio(sender: AnyObject) {
    }

    @IBAction func stopAudio(sender: AnyObject) {
    }

    @IBAction func sliderMoved(sender: AnyObject) {
    }

    override func didReceiveMemoryWarning() {
        super.didReceiveMemoryWarning()
        // Dispose of any resources that can be recreated.
    }
}
```

13.6 Initializing Audio Playback

Before sounds can be played within the iOS app a number of steps need to be taken. First, an audio file needs to be added to the project. The music to be played in this tutorial is contained in a file named *vivaldi.mp3* located in the *audio_files* folder of the sample code download available from the following URL:

http://www.ebookfrenzy.com/print/watchkit/index.php

Locate the file in a Finder window and drag and drop it onto the *Supporting Files* entry of the *OpenParentApp* folder in the Project Navigator panel as shown in Figure 13-4, clicking on the *Finish* button in the options panel:

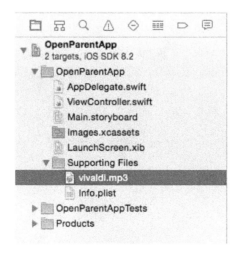

Figure 13-4

With the audio file added to the project, code now needs to be added to the *viewDidLoad* method of the *ViewController.swift* file to initialize an AVAudioPlayer instance so that playback is ready to start when the user taps the Play button. Select the *ViewController.swift* file and modify it to import the AVFoundation framework, declare AVAudioSession and AVAudioPlayer instance variables and to initialize the player:

```
import UIKit
import AVFoundation
import MediaPlayer

class ViewController: UIViewController {

    var audioSession: AVAudioSession = AVAudioSession.sharedInstance()
    var audioPlayer: AVAudioPlayer?

    @IBOutlet weak var volumeControl: UISlider!

    override func viewDidLoad() {
        super.viewDidLoad()

        var error: NSError?

        let success = audioSession.setCategory(
            AVAudioSessionCategoryPlayback, error: &error)

        if success {
            let url = NSURL.fileURLWithPath(
                NSBundle.mainBundle().pathForResource("vivaldi",
                    ofType: "mp3")!)

            audioPlayer = AVAudioPlayer(contentsOfURL: url,
                    error: &error)

            if let err = error {
                println("audioPlayer error \(err.localizedDescription)")
            } else {
                audioPlayer?.prepareToPlay()
                audioPlayer?.volume = 0.1
            }
        }
    }
    .
    .
    .
}
```

The code configures the audio session to allow audio playback to be initiated from the background even when the device is locked and the ring switch on the side of the device is set to silent mode. The audio player instance is then configured with the mp3 file containing the audio to be played and an initial volume level set.

13.7 Implementing the Audio Control Methods

With the audio player configured and initialized, the next step is to add some methods to control the playback of the music. Remaining within the *ViewController.swift* file, implement these three methods as follows:

```
func stopPlay() {
    audioPlayer?.stop()
}

func startPlay() {
    audioPlayer?.play()
}

func adjustVolume(level: Float)
{
    audioPlayer?.volume = level
}
```

Each of these methods will need to be called by the corresponding action methods as follows:

```
@IBAction func playAudio(sender: AnyObject) {
    startPlay()
}

@IBAction func stopAudio(sender: AnyObject) {
    stopPlay()
}

@IBAction func sliderMoved(sender: AnyObject) {
    adjustVolume(volumeControl.value)
}
```

Compile and run the iOS app and test that the user interface controls allow playback to be started and stopped via the two buttons and that the slider provides control over the volume level.

With the iOS app now functioning, it is time to focus on creating the matching WatchKit app.

13.8 Adding the WatchKit App Target

Within Xcode, select the *File -> New -> Target...* menu option. In the target template dialog, select the *Apple Watch* option listed beneath the *iOS* heading. In the main panel, select the *WatchKit App* icon and click on *Next*. On the subsequent screen, turn off the *Include Glance Scene* and *Include Notification Scene* options before clicking on the *Finish* button.

As soon as the extension target has been created, a new panel will appear requesting permission to activate the new scheme for the extension target. Activate this scheme now by clicking on the *Activate* button in the request panel.

13.9 Designing the WatchKit App Scene

Select the *Interface.storyboard* file located under *OpenParentApp WatchKit App* so that the storyboard loads into Interface Builder. Drag and drop a Label, two Buttons and a Slider from the Object Library onto the scene canvas so that the layout matches that shown in Figure 13-5:

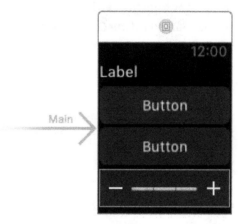

Figure 13-5

Select the Label object, display the Attributes Inspector panel and set the *Alignment* property to center the displayed text. Within the *Position* section of the panel, change the *Horizontal* menu to *Center*.

Double click on the uppermost of the two buttons and change the text to "Play". Repeat this step for the second button, this time changing the text so that it reads "Stop".

Select the Slider object and, in the Attributes Inspector panel, change both the *Maximum* and *Steps* properties to 10.

On completion of the above steps, the scene layout should resemble Figure 13-6:

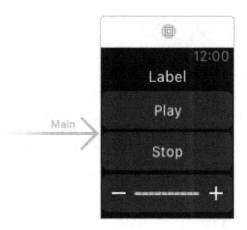

Figure 13-6

Display the Assistant Editor and verify that it is showing the contents of the *InterfaceController.swift* file. Using the Assistant Editor, establish an outlet connection from the Label object in the user interface named *statusLabel.* Next, create action connections from the two buttons named *startPlay* and *stopPlay* respectively and an action connection from the slider named *volumeChange*. With these connections established, the top section of the *InterfaceController.swift* file should read as follows:

```
import WatchKit
import Foundation

class InterfaceController: WKInterfaceController {

    @IBOutlet weak var statusLabel: WKInterfaceLabel!

    override func awakeWithContext(context: AnyObject?) {
        super.awakeWithContext(context)

        // Configure interface objects here.
    }

    @IBAction func startPlay() {
    }

    @IBAction func stopPlay() {
    }

    @IBAction func volumeChange(value: Float) {
    }
```

```
            .
            .
}
```

13.10 **Opening the Parent Application**

Now that the WatchKit app user interface is wired up to methods in the interface controller class, the next step is to implement the calls to the *openParentApplication* method in those action methods.

Each *openParentApplication* method call will include a dictionary consisting of a key named "command" and a value of either "play", "stop" or "volume". In the case of the volume command, an additional key-value pair will be provided within the dictionary with the value set to the current value of the slider. The *openParentApplication* method calls will also declare and pass through a *reply closure*. This is essentially a block of code that will be called and passed data by the parent application once the request has been handled.

Within the *InterfaceController.swift* file, implement this code within the action methods so that they read as follows:

```
@IBAction func startPlay() {
    let parentValues = [
        "command" : "start"
    ]

    WKInterfaceController.openParentApplication(parentValues,
            reply: { (replyValues, error) -> Void in
        self.statusLabel.setText(replyValues["status"] as? String)
    })
}

@IBAction func stopPlay() {
    let parentValues = [
        "command" : "stop"
    ]

    WKInterfaceController.openParentApplication(parentValues,
            reply: { (replyValues, error) -> Void in
        self.statusLabel.setText(replyValues["status"] as? String)
    })
}

@IBAction func volumeChange(value: Float) {
    let parentValues = [
        "command" : "volume",
        "level" : value/10
```

```
    ]

    WKInterfaceController.openParentApplication(parentValues
                                    as [NSObject : AnyObject],
            reply: { (replyValues, error) -> Void in
        self.statusLabel.setText(replyValues["status"] as? String)
    })
}
```

Note that the slider will contain a value between 0 and 10. Since the AVAudioPlayer class has a range of 0.0 to 1.0 for the volume level, the slider value is divided by 10 before being passed to the parent application.

In the above code, the reply closure code in each method call reads as follows:

```
(replyValues, error) -> Void in
        self.statusLabel.setText(replyValues["status"] as? String)
```

The closure expects as parameters a dictionary and an error object. In the case of this example, the closure code simply extracts the string value for the "status" key from the reply dictionary and displays it on the status Label object in the main WatchKit app scene.

13.11 Handling the WatchKit Extension Request

When the *openParentApplication* method is called, the parent iOS application will be notified via a call to the *handleWatchKitExtensionRequest* method within the application delegate class. The next step in this tutorial is to implement this method.

Locate and select the *AppDelegate.swift* file in the Project Navigator panel so that it loads into the editor. Once loaded, add an implementation of the *handleWatchKitExtensionRequest* method as follows:

```
func application(application: UIApplication,
handleWatchKitExtensionRequest userInfo: [NSObject : AnyObject]?, reply:
(([NSObject : AnyObject]!) -> Void)!) {

    var replyValues = Dictionary<String, AnyObject>()

    var viewController = self.window!.rootViewController
                                    as! ViewController

    switch userInfo!["command"] as! String {
        case "start" :
            viewController.startPlay()
            replyValues["status"] = "Playing"
```

```
        case "stop" :
                viewController.stopPlay()
                replyValues["status"] = "Stopped"
        case "volume" :
                var level = userInfo!["level"] as! Float
                viewController.adjustVolume(level)
                replyValues["status"] = "Vol = \(level)"
        default:
                break
    }
    reply(replyValues)
}
```

The code begins by creating and initializing a Dictionary instance in which to store the data to be returned to the WatchKit Extension. Next, a reference to the root view controller instance of the iOS app is obtained so that the playback methods in that class can be called later in the method.

One of the arguments passed through to the *handleWatchKitExtensionRequest* method is a dictionary named *userInfo*. This is the dictionary that was passed through when the *openParentApplication* method was called from the WatchKit app extension (in other words the *parentValues* dictionary declared in the extension action methods). The method uses a switch statement to identify which command has been passed through within this dictionary. Based on the command detected, the corresponding method within the view controller is called. For example, if the "command" key in the *userInfo* dictionary has the string value "play" then the *startPlay* method of the view controller is called to begin audio playback. The value for the "status" key in the *replyValues* dictionary is then configured with the text to be displayed via the status label in the WatchKit app scene.

Also passed through as an argument to the *handleWatchKitExtensionRequest* method is a reference to the *reply closure* declared as part of the *openParentApplication* method call. The last task performed by the *handleWatchKitExtensionRequest* method is to call this closure, passing through the *replyValues* dictionary. As previously described, the reply closure code will then display the status text to the user via the previously declared *statusLabel* outlet.

13.12 Testing the Application

In the Xcode toolbar, make sure that the run target menu is set to *OpenParentApp WatchKit App* before clicking on the run button. Once the WatchKit app appears, click on the Play button in the scene. The status label should update to display "Playing" and the music should begin to play within the iOS app. Test that the slider changes the volume and that the Stop button stops the playback. In each case, the response from the parent iOS app should be displayed by the status label.

13.13 **Summary**

This chapter has created an example project intended to demonstrate the use of the *openParentApplication* method to launch and communicate with the iOS parent application of a WatchKit app. The example has shown how to call the *openParentApplication* method and implement the *handleWatchKitExtensionRequest* method within the app delegate of the parent iOS app.

14. Sharing Data Between a WatchKit App and the Containing iOS App

It has already been established in previous chapters that the elements that make up a WatchKit app are bundled into the same package as the containing (or parent) iOS app and that the WatchKit app extension executes on the same device as the iOS app. Regardless of these facts, however, the WatchKit app extension and the containing iOS app each run within separate processes. This process separation (sometimes referred to as "sandboxing") means that the extension and parent iOS app do not, by default, have access to each other's data and file storage. This chapter will explore the use of app groups to enable a WatchKit extension and iOS app to share access to files and data.

14.1 Sandboxes, Containers and User Defaults

Although both the containing iOS app and the corresponding extension for a WatchKit app both execute on the same physical iPhone device they are said to run in separate sandbox environments. Sandboxes are a security mechanism that enforce sets of rules in terms of what an app can and cannot do when running on an iOS device. Sandboxing, for example, prevents one app on a device from interfering with, or accessing files and data belonging to another app installed on the same device.

Included within the sandbox of each app is a *container*. This is essentially a file system area containing directories into which the app can store and access files. These can be any type of file including images, videos, plain text files or even SQLite or Core Data databases. The sandbox rules dictate that an app in one sandbox cannot access the files in the container of a second app and these same rules apply equally to the relationship between a WatchKit extension and the containing iOS app.

In addition to files, each app can have associated with it a set of user defaults. User defaults are used to store preferences selected by the user for the way in which an app appears and functions. Consider, for example, an iOS app that provides the user with the ability to configure a range of preferences such as the preferred currency in which to display monetary values or the font to be used when displaying text. The ideal location to store such settings is in the user's defaults database. As with file access, each app or extension has its own set of defaults data and sandboxing prevents one process from accessing the user defaults data of another sandboxed process.

14.2 **Sharing Data Using App Groups**

The sharing of files and data between a WatchKit extension and the parent iOS app can be achieved through the use of shared app groups. When the iOS app and WatchKit extension are enrolled in the same app group they are given access to a shared container and shared user defaults data. This allows files to be shared between the parent app and the extension, along with any user defaults configured using the NSUserDefaults class. The diagram in Figure 14-1 illustrates this concept:

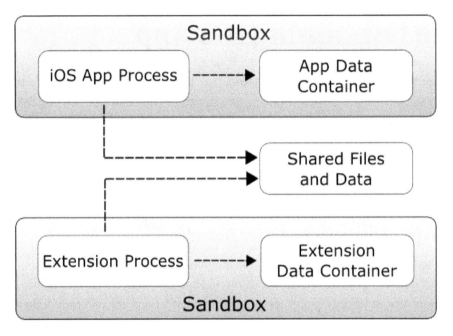

Figure 14-1

14.3 **Adding an App or Extension to an App Group**

App Group settings are contained in entitlement files using the *com.apple.security.application-groups* key. Both the WatchKit app Extension and the parent iOS app must include this entitlement. The value assigned to the *com.apple.security.application-groups* key indicates the app group to which membership is required. This value is typically set to the package name of the iOS app prefixed with "group." and must match in both the parent app and extension entitlement files.

While it is possible to manually create the necessary entitlement files, by far the easiest way to configure app group membership is to do so through the Xcode Capabilities panel. To configure app group support for the iOS app, select the target located at the top of the Project Navigator panel and click on the *Capabilities* tab in the main panel. Within the capabilities panel, locate the *App Groups* section and switch it to the *On* position:

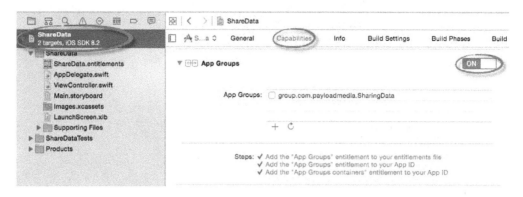

Figure 14-2

When app groups have been enabled in the Capabilities screen, any existing app groups associated with your Apple developer account will be listed. To make the current app a member of any of those groups simply enable the checkbox next to the group name:

Figure 14-3

To add a new app group to your account, simply click on the + button and enter the new app group name. Add the current app to the newly added app group by enabling the checkbox next to the group name. The app group will subsequently appear as an option in all other project targets within the Xcode Capabilities panel.

With the iOS app added to the app group, the WatchKit app extension must also be added as a member of the same group in order to gain access to the shared container. By default, the Capabilities panel displays the settings for the iOS app target. To access the capability settings for the WatchKit Extension, use the menu located in the top left-hand corner of the Capabilities panel as indicated in Figure 14-4:

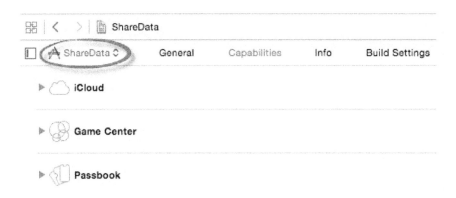

Figure 14-4

When clicked, this menu will present a list of targets contained within the current project as shown in Figure 14-5, one of which will be the WatchKit extension. Select this option and repeat the steps followed for the iOS app to enable and configure app group support, making sure to select the same group name as that chosen for the iOS app.

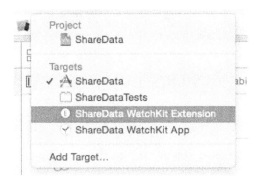

Figure 14-5

A review of the files in the Project Navigator panel will reveal that entitlement files have been added for each of the two targets, the contents of which will read as follows (allowing for differences in the app group name):

```
<?xml version="1.0" encoding="UTF-8"?>
<!DOCTYPE plist PUBLIC "-//Apple//DTD PLIST 1.0//EN"
"http://www.apple.com/DTDs/PropertyList-1.0.dtd">
<plist version="1.0">
<dict>
        <key>com.apple.security.application-groups</key>
        <array>
                <string>group.com.ebookfrenzy.SharingData</string>
        </array>
</dict>
```

```
</plist>
```

With both the parent iOS app and the WatchKit extension added to the same app group, code can now be written to access the shared data container.

14.4 App Group File Sharing

The first step in terms of sharing files via an app group is to identify the URL of the shared container. This can be achieved by obtaining a reference to the app's default NSFileManager instance and making a call to the *containerURLForSecurityApplicationGroupIdentifier* method of that object, passing through as an argument the name of the app group. For example:

```
let fileManager = NSFileManager.defaultManager()

let url =
    fileManager.containerURLForSecurityApplicationGroupIdentifier(
                        "group.com.ebookfrenzy.SharingData")
```

Once the URL has been obtained, it can be used to share data in terms of files and SQLite or Core Data based databases. When writing data to flat files in a container shared by an extension and a containing app, Apple advices against using the standard file coordination techniques and recommends using atomic write operations to avoid deadlocks occurring. An atomic write operation writes new data to a temporary file and then renames it to replace the original file. The following code, for example, obtains a reference to the shared container, appends a file name (datafile.dat) to the URL, checks that the file exists and then atomically writes a string to it:

```
let fileManager = NSFileManager.defaultManager()

let url =
    fileManager.containerURLForSecurityApplicationGroupIdentifier(
                "group.com.ebookfrenzy.SharingData")

let dirPath = url?.path
let filePath = dirPath?.stringByAppendingPathComponent("datafile.dat")

if fileManager.fileExistsAtPath(filePath!) {
    let databuffer = ("hello world"
            as NSString).dataUsingEncoding(NSUTF8StringEncoding)
    databuffer?.writeToFile(filePath!, atomically: true)
}
```

14.5 **App Group User Default Sharing**

iOS allows applications to access and store user settings via the NSUserDefaults class. These settings are stored in the user's defaults database by the app and can be accessed via a variety of methods provided by the NSUserDefaults class.

As with file storage, the rules imposed by sandbox security prevent the default settings for one app from being accessed by another app or app extension. In terms of WatchKit app development, therefore, app group sharing must be used if the extension and parent app need to share user default settings. In addition to sharing user default settings, this technique also provides a useful and efficient way to share small amounts of data that are not necessarily related to user default preferences between the iOS app and the WatchKit extension.

When sharing user defaults, the shared database is identified by a *suite name* which is the name assigned to the app group when it was created. The following code, for example, obtains a reference to a shared user defaults suite before storing into it a string value in the form of a key-value pair:

```
let myDefaults = NSUserDefaults(suiteName:
                    "group.com.ebookfrenzy.SharingData")

myDefaults?.setObject("sterling", forKey: "currency")
```

Once a default has been set, it can then be accessed from within the WatchKit app extension (as long as it is a member of the same app group) as follows:

```
let myDefaults = NSUserDefaults(suiteName:
                "group.com.ebookfrenzy.SharingData")

let preference = myDefaults?.stringForKey("currency")
```

The data shared using this approach can take the form of NSString, NSData, NSArray, NSDictionary, NSNumber and NSDate objects, allowing for a wide range of data sharing options.

14.6 **Summary**

The WatchKit extension and containing iOS app are separate processes that execute within individual sandbox environments. The purpose of sandboxing is to prevent one process from accessing the files and data stored by another process. In order for files and data to be shared between the iOS app and the WatchKit extension, both must belong to the same app group. App groups allow processes to share files through a shared container and to gain access to shared data using the NSUserDefaults class.

15. WatchKit Extension and iOS App File and Data Sharing - A Tutorial

The objective of this chapter is to put the theory from the previous chapter into practice by creating a project that makes use of app groups to implement a simple example of sharing both file content and user default data between a WatchKit extension and the containing iOS app.

15.1 About the App Group Sharing Example

The project created in this chapter will consist of an iOS app in which the user can enter text and change the setting of a switch control. On selection of a "save" button, the text entered by the user will be saved to a file in a shared container and the current switch setting stored using shared user defaults.

The companion WatchKit app will present a Label and a Switch object configured to display the same text and switch setting as those entered by the user on the iOS app. Changes made to the Switch object in the WatchKit app will also be stored and used by the iOS app.

15.2 Creating the Sharing Project

Start Xcode and create a new iOS project. On the template screen choose the *Application* option located under *iOS* in the left hand panel and select *Single View Application*. Click *Next,* set the product name to *SharingData,* enter your organization identifier and make sure that the *Devices* menu is set to *Universal.* Before clicking *Next,* change the *Language* menu to Swift. On the final screen, choose a location in which to store the project files and click on *Create* to proceed to the main Xcode project window.

15.3 Designing the iOS App User Interface

Locate and select the *Main.storyboard* file in the Project Navigator panel and drag and drop a Text View, Switch and Button object onto the scene canvas. Configure and position the views so that the layout of the user interface matches that of Figure 15-1:

Figure 15-1

Having designed the layout, click on the white background of the scene so that no views are selected. Display the *Resolve Auto Layout Issues* menu and select the *Reset to Suggested Constraints* option listed under *All Views in View Controller* as shown in Figure 15-2:

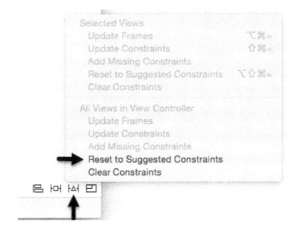

Figure 15-2

Finally, double click on the Text View object so that the Latin text highlights before tapping the keyboard delete key to remove the sample text.

15.4 **Connecting Actions and Outlets**

With the scene still displayed in Interface Builder, open the Assistant Editor and verify that it is displaying the content of the *ViewController.swift* file. Ctrl-click on the Text View object in the scene and drag the resulting line to a position beneath the class declaration line in the *ViewController.swift* file. Release the line and establish an outlet connection named *textView*.

Repeat the above steps to establish an outlet from the Switch object named *mySwitch*. Finally, Ctrl-click on the Button view, drag to a position beneath the *viewDidLoad* method and establish an action connection to a method named *saveData*. On completion of these steps, the *ViewController.swift* file should read as follows:

```
import UIKit

class ViewController: UIViewController, UIImagePickerControllerDelegate,
UINavigationControllerDelegate {

    @IBOutlet weak var mySwitch: UISwitch!
    @IBOutlet weak var textView: UITextView!

    override func viewDidLoad() {
        super.viewDidLoad()
    }

    @IBAction func saveData(sender: AnyObject) {
    }
    .
    .
    .
}
```

15.5 **Creating the App Group**

In order for the iOS app and WatchKit extension to be able to share files and data they must both be enrolled as members of the same app group. To do this, begin by selecting the *SharingData* target located at the top of the project navigator and clicking on the *Capabilities* tab in the main panel. Within the Capabilities panel, locate the *App Groups* section and move the switch to the *On* position. When prompted, select an Apple Developer account to be associated with the app group.

When app groups have been enabled in the Capabilities screen, any existing app groups associated with your Apple developer account will be listed.

To add a new app group to your account, simply click on the + button and enter the new app group name, for example:

```
group.com.example.SharingData
```

Add the current app to the newly added app group by enabling the checkbox next to the group name.

15.6 Performing Initialization Tasks

When the iOS app launches it will need to obtain a reference to the default file manager and then use that to get the URL of the shared container. Using this URL, the full path to the file that will be shared between the iOS app and the WatchKit extension will need to be constructed. These tasks can be performed in the *viewDidLoad* method as follows (noting that the app group identifier will need to be changed to match the one you created in the previous section):

```
class ViewController: UIViewController {

    @IBOutlet weak var mySwitch: UISwitch!
    @IBOutlet weak var textView: UITextView!

    var sharedFilePath: String?
    var sharedDefaults: NSUserDefaults?
    let fileManager = NSFileManager.defaultManager()

    override func viewDidLoad() {
        super.viewDidLoad()

        let sharedContainer = fileManager
            .containerURLForSecurityApplicationGroupIdentifier(
                "<YOUR APP GROUP IDENTIFIER HERE>")

        let dirPath = sharedContainer?.path
        sharedFilePath = dirPath?.stringByAppendingPathComponent(
                                   "sharedtext.doc")
    }
    .
    .
    .
}
```

Next, the *viewDidLoad* method needs to check if the *sharedtext.doc* file already exists in the shared container and, if so, read the content of the file into a data buffer before displaying it to the user via the Text View:

```
override func viewDidLoad() {
    super.viewDidLoad()
```

```
        let sharedContainer = fileManager
                .containerURLForSecurityApplicationGroupIdentifier(
                        "<YOUR APP GROUP IDENTIFIER HERE>")

        let dirPath = sharedContainer?.path
        sharedFilePath = dirPath?.stringByAppendingPathComponent(
                        "sharedtext.doc")

        if fileManager.fileExistsAtPath(sharedFilePath!) {
           let databuffer = fileManager.contentsAtPath(sharedFilePath!)
           textView.text = NSString(data: databuffer!,
                encoding: NSUTF8StringEncoding) as! String
        }
}
```

Finally, the method needs to check for the presence of a user default value for the "switch" key and, in the event that a default exists, set the state of the Switch view accordingly, once again making sure to use your own app group identifier:

```
override func viewDidLoad() {
    super.viewDidLoad()

    let sharedContainer = fileManager
                .containerURLForSecurityApplicationGroupIdentifier(
                        "<YOUR APP GROUP IDENTIFIER HERE>")

    let dirPath = sharedContainer?.path
    sharedFilePath = dirPath?.stringByAppendingPathComponent(
                        "sharedtext.doc")

    if fileManager.fileExistsAtPath(sharedFilePath!) {
        let databuffer = fileManager.contentsAtPath(sharedFilePath!)
        textView.text = NSString(data: databuffer!,
                encoding: NSUTF8StringEncoding)
    }

    sharedDefaults = NSUserDefaults(
        suiteName: "<YOUR APP GROUP IDENTIFIER HERE>")

    let switchSetting = sharedDefaults?.boolForKey("switch")

    if let setting = switchSetting {
        mySwitch.on = setting
```

```
        }
    }
```

15.7 **Saving the Data**

The next step in implementing the iOS app is to write the code for the *saveData* method. Locate this method in the *ViewController.swift* file and modify it to read as follows:

```
@IBAction func saveData(sender: AnyObject) {
    let databuffer = (textView.text
            as NSString).dataUsingEncoding(NSUTF8StringEncoding)

    if fileManager.fileExistsAtPath(sharedFilePath!) {
        databuffer?.writeToFile(sharedFilePath!, atomically: true)
    } else {
        fileManager.createFileAtPath(sharedFilePath!,
            contents: databuffer, attributes: nil)
    }
    sharedDefaults?.setBool(mySwitch.on, forKey: "switch")
}
```

The method begins by encoding the text entered into the Text View into an NSData object and writing that data to the shared file. Next, the switch setting is saved to the shared defaults storage as a Boolean value.

Compile and run the application. Once running, enter some text into the Text View and change the setting of the Switch view. Stop the app from the Xcode toolbar and then re-launch it. On restarting, both the text and switch mode should have been preserved.

With the iOS app functioning as expected the next step is to add and implement the WatchKit app.

15.8 **Adding the WatchKit App Target**

Within Xcode, select the *File -> New -> Target...* menu option. In the target template dialog, select the *Apple Watch* option listed beneath the *iOS* heading. In the main panel, select the *WatchKit App* icon and click on *Next*. On the subsequent screen, turn off the *Include Glance Scene* and *Include Notification Scene* options before clicking on the *Finish* button.

As soon as the extension target has been created, a new panel will appear requesting permission to activate the new scheme for the extension target. Activate this scheme now by clicking on the *Activate* button in the request panel.

15.9 **Adding the WatchKit App to the App Group**

With the iOS app added to the app group, the WatchKit extension must also be added as a member of the same group in order to gain access to the shared container. To access the capability settings for the WatchKit extension, use the menu located in the top left-hand corner of the Capabilities panel as indicated in Figure 15-3:

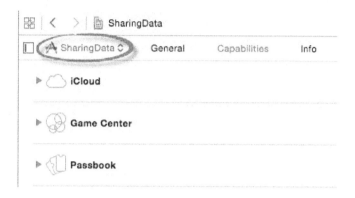

Figure 15-3

When clicked, this menu will present a list of targets contained within the current project, one of which will be the *SharingData WatchKit Extension*. Select this option and repeat the steps followed for the iOS app to enable membership in the same app group as that configured for the iOS app.

15.10 **Designing the WatchKit App Scene**

Select the *Interface.storyboard* file located under *SharingData WatchKit App* so that the storyboard loads into Interface Builder. Drag and drop a Label and a Switch from the Object Library onto the scene. Select the Label object and use the Attributes Inspector to change the *Horizontal* position property to *Center*. On completion of these steps, the scene layout should match that shown in Figure 15-4:

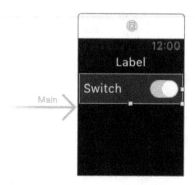

Figure 15-4

The final task is to allow the label to display more than a single line of text. With the Label object selected, increase the *Lines* property to 8.

15.11 Adding the WatchKit App Actions and Outlets

Display the Assistant Editor and verify that it is displaying the *InterfaceController.swift* file. Establish outlet connections from the Label and Switch objects named *watchLabel* and *watchSwitch* respectively. Also establish an action connection on the Switch object so that a method named *switchChanged* is called when the user changes the switch setting. On completion of these steps the *InterfaceController.swift* file should read as follows:

```
import WatchKit
import Foundation

class InterfaceController: WKInterfaceController {

    @IBOutlet weak var watchLabel: WKInterfaceLabel!
    @IBOutlet weak var watchSwitch: WKInterfaceSwitch!

    override func awakeWithContext(context: AnyObject?) {
        super.awakeWithContext(context)

        // Configure interface objects here.
    }

    @IBAction func switchChanged(value: Bool) {
    }
    .
    .
}
```

15.12 Performing the WatchKit App Initialization

The WatchKit extension will need to perform many of the same tasks as the iOS app in order to load the text from the shared file and identify the current switch setting. These tasks can best be performed in the *awakeWithContext* method. Locate this method in the *InterfaceController.swift* file and modify it to read the content of the *sharedtext.doc* file and display it on the Label object (noting that the app group identifier will once again need to be changed to match the one you created).

```
class InterfaceController: WKInterfaceController {

    @IBOutlet weak var watchLabel: WKInterfaceLabel!
    @IBOutlet weak var watchSwitch: WKInterfaceSwitch!
```

```
    var sharedDefaults: NSUserDefaults?

override func awakeWithContext(context: AnyObject?) {
    super.awakeWithContext(context)

    let fileManager = NSFileManager.defaultManager()

    let sharedContainer = fileManager
        .containerURLForSecurityApplicationGroupIdentifier(
            "<YOUR APP GROUP IDENTIFIER HERE>")

    let dirPath = sharedContainer?.path
    let sharedFilePath =
        dirPath?.stringByAppendingPathComponent("sharedtext.doc")

    if fileManager.fileExistsAtPath(sharedFilePath!) {
        let databuffer =
            fileManager.contentsAtPath(sharedFilePath!)
        watchLabel.setText(NSString(data: databuffer!,
            encoding: NSUTF8StringEncoding) as? String)
    }
}
.
.
}
```

Next, add the code to access the shared user defaults using the "switch" key to obtain the Boolean switch setting value:

```
class InterfaceController: WKInterfaceController {

    @IBOutlet weak var watchLabel: WKInterfaceLabel!
    @IBOutlet weak var watchSwitch: WKInterfaceSwitch!

    var sharedDefaults: NSUserDefaults?

    override func awakeWithContext(context: AnyObject?) {
        super.awakeWithContext(context)

        let fileManager = NSFileManager.defaultManager()

        let sharedContainer = fileManager
```

```
        .containerURLForSecurityApplicationGroupIdentifier(
            "<YOUR APP GROUP IDENTIFIER HERE>")

    let dirPath = sharedContainer?.path
    let sharedFilePath =
        dirPath?.stringByAppendingPathComponent("sharedtext.doc")

    if fileManager.fileExistsAtPath(sharedFilePath!) {
        let databuffer =
            fileManager.contentsAtPath(sharedFilePath!)

        watchLabel.setText(NSString(data: databuffer!,
            encoding: NSUTF8StringEncoding) as? String)
    }

    sharedDefaults = NSUserDefaults(suiteName:
        "<YOUR APP GROUP IDENTIFIER HERE>")

    if let setting = sharedDefaults?.boolForKey("switch") {
        watchSwitch.setOn(setting)
    }
  }
  .
  .
}
```

15.13 Implementing the switchChanged Method

The final task required to complete the project is to add the code to the *switchChanged* method so that changes to the switch are stored in the shared user defaults. Remaining in the *InterfaceController.swift* file, locate the stub method created by the Assistant Editor and modify it so that it reads as follows:

```
@IBAction func switchChanged(value: Bool) {
    sharedDefaults?.setBool(value, forKey: "switch")
}
```

When the user changes the switch setting this method is called and passed as a parameter a Boolean value indicating the new switch state. The code added to the method stores this new value into the shared defaults storage using the "switch" key.

15.14 **Testing the Project**

Use the run target menu in the Xcode toolbar to select the *SharingData* iOS app target together with a suitable device or emulator as shown in Figure 15-5:

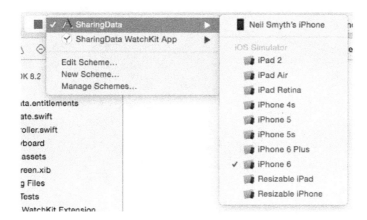

Figure 15-5

When the iOS app launches, enter new text into the Text View, change the switch setting and click the Save button. Change the run target menu to *SharingData WatchKit App* and click the run button to invoke the WatchKit app. When the app appears it should do so displaying the text entered into the iOS app and the current switch state.

Within the WatchKit app, change the switch setting, re-launch the iOS app and verify that the switch state change has been picked up by the switch view.

15.15 **Summary**

This chapter has put the theory of the previous chapter into practice through the creation of a project that utilizes app groups to share file and user defaults data between an iOS app and a WatchKit extension.

16. Configuring Preferences with the WatchKit Settings Bundle

The preceding chapters have explored the concept of sharing small amounts of data between a WatchKit app and the containing iOS app using the NSUserDefaults class and app group sharing. Clearly, this approach could also be used for sharing user preferences between the iOS app and the WatchKit app. The containing iOS app might, for example, provide a screen within which the user is able to configure the text color and font size used to display text within the corresponding WatchKit app. A more consistent approach to providing preference settings for a WatchKit app, however, is to make those settings available via the Apple Watch app on the iPhone using a WatchKit settings bundle.

This chapter will provide an overview of the WatchKit settings bundle while the next chapter, entitled *A WatchKit Settings Bundle Tutorial*, will work through the creation of a settings bundle example project.

16.1 An Overview of the WatchKit Settings Bundle

iOS running on the iPhone now includes the *Apple Watch* app (Figure 16-1). In addition to configuring the pairing of the iPhone with an Apple Watch device, the app also provides access to preference settings tailored for each installed WatchKit app.

Apple Watch

Figure 16-1

When a WatchKit app is selected from the list within the Apple Watch app, the preferences available for that app are listed. By default, the only preference listed is whether or not the WatchKit app is shown on the paired watch device as shown in Figure 16-2:

Figure 16-2

Additional preference settings can be made available from within the Apple Watch app through the use of a WatchKit Settings Bundle.

The WatchKit settings bundle defines which settings controls are to be displayed on the Apple Watch app preferences page and stores the results using the NSUserDefaults class. Access to the chosen preferences from within both the iOS and WatchKit apps is achieved through the use of a shared app group as outlined in the *Sharing Data Between a WatchKit App and the Containing iOS App* chapter of this book.

16.2 Adding a WatchKit Settings Bundle to a Project

To add a WatchKit settings bundle to an Xcode project, select the *File -> New -> File...* menu option and, from within the resulting panel, select the *Apple Watch* option in the left hand panel and the *WatchKit Settings Bundle* option in the main panel before clicking on the *Next* Button:

Figure 16-3

On the subsequent screen, make sure that the iOS app target is selected in the *Targets* section of the "Save As" panel as shown in Figure 16-4. The filename will be specified as *Settings-Watch* by default and should not be changed.

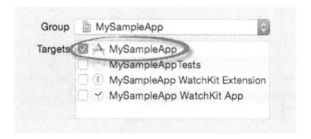

Figure 16-4

Once the settings bundle has been added to the project it will appear within the project navigator panel:

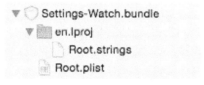

Figure 16-5

16.3 **WatchKit Bundle Settings Controls**

Preferences are set by the user within the preferences screens of the Apple Watch app using a variety of controls which are specified within the *Root.plist* property list file. The options available for inclusion within the panel are as follows:

- **Toggle Switch** – An On/Off switch mechanism allowing the user to select one of two values for a preference.
- **Slider** – Allows the user to make a preference selection within a range of values.
- **Text Field** – An editable text field into which information can be typed by the user.
- **Multi-value** – Provides a mechanism for the user to make a selection from multiple options. When selected, a second screen is displayed listing the options from which a selection can be made.
- **Title** – Displays read-only text to the user.
- **Group** – Used to group preferences together under a specified heading.
- **Child Pane** – Allows the user to navigate to additional pages of preference settings.

The controls are added to the *Root.plist* file and configured using the Xcode Property List Editor. When a control is added to the property list file it needs to be assigned an identifier key. This is the key that will be used to extract and set the current preference value from within the code of the iOS app and WatchKit extension.

Figure 16-6 shows an example *Root.plist* file loaded into the Xcode Property List Editor. In this case, the list consists of a single preference control item in the form of a toggle switch. The toggle is configured to display a title which reads "Use Large Font" and to be enabled by default. The item has also been assigned *font_preference* as the identifier.

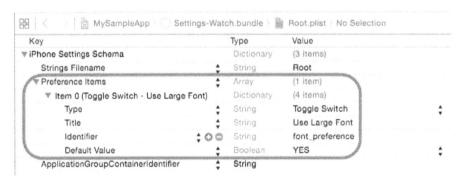

Figure 16-6

Figure 16-7 shows the above preference item as it appears within an Apple Watch app settings panel:

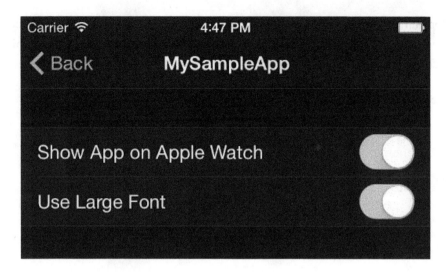

Figure 16-7

16.4 Accessing WatchKit Bundle Settings from Code

Obviously preference settings are of little use if the WatchKit app does not identify the current settings and act upon them. The WatchKit bundle settings reside within the containing iOS app but will need to be accessed from the WatchKit app extension. This sharing can be achieved by creating an app group and configuring both the containing iOS app and WatchKit extension to be group members as outlined in the chapter entitled *Sharing Data Between a WatchKit App and the Containing iOS App*.

Once an app group has been created as outlined, it needs to be added to the *Root.plist* file of the settings bundle using the *ApplicationGroupContainerIdentifier* key. Figure 16-8, for example, shows an app group identifier assigned to this key:

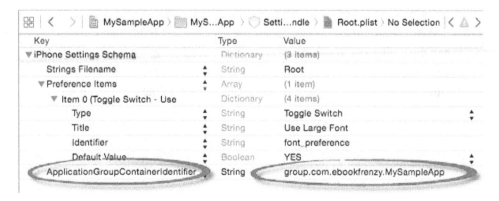

Figure 16-8

Assuming a Boolean preference with an identifier of *font_preference* and an app group identifier of *group.com.ebookfrenzy.MySampleApp*, the code to access the preference setting from within either the iOS app or the WatchKit extension would read as follows:

```
let defaults = NSUserDefaults(suiteName:
                    "group.com.ebookfrenzy.MySampleApp")

if let preference = defaults?.boolForKey("font_preference")
{
    if preference {
        // The preference setting is enabled
    } else {
        // The preference setting is disabled
    }
}
```

16.5 Registering Default Preference Values

Each item added to the *Root.plist* file through the Property List Editor has associated with it an optional *default value*. In Figure 16-8, for example, the toggle switch was configured to have a default Boolean value of YES (or true).

A common mistake made when working with user defaults is to assume that the defaults set in the properties list file are the values that will be stored in the settings bundle in the absence of the selection being made by the user. In reality, these settings only define the appearance of the control when it appears in the preferences screen for a WatchKit app. In fact, a preference value is only saved to the settings bundle when the user makes a change to that value using the control in the preference screen.

It is important, therefore, to write code to configure user default settings within the settings bundle so that a sensible default value is returned in the event that the user has yet to change the setting. This operation should be performed each time the app launches and is achieved using the *registerDefaults* method of the settings bundle NSUserDefaults object. This method takes as a parameter a dictionary object containing the keys for which defaults are to be set and the corresponding default values.

The ideal location to add the code to register default values is the *init* method of the interface controller of the main WatchKit app scene. The following code, for example, overrides the *init* method and registers default values for three keys previously declared in a settings bundle *Root.plist* file:

```
override init() {

    let defaults = NSUserDefaults(suiteName:
                "group.com.ebookfrenzy.MySampleApp")
```

```
let defaultSettings = ["display_preference" : true,
                       "fontsize_preference" : 19,
                       "color_preference" : "red"]

    defaults?.registerDefaults(defaultSettings)
}
```

Code such as that shown above ensures that default values will be returned when accessing the corresponding keys from within code. Since the *registerDefaults* method does not overwrite any settings already saved into the settings bundle as a result of user preference selections, it can be called safely each time the app is run.

16.6 **Configuring a Settings Icon**

When the Apple Watch app on the iPhone lists the WatchKit apps for which settings are available it will display both the app name and an app icon within this list. Until a *Companion Settings* icon is added to the image assets catalog of the WatchKit app, the default icon will be displayed.

The app icons for a WatchKit app are managed by selecting the *Image.xcassets* entry listed under the WatchKit app target folder within the Project Navigator panel. Once the catalog has loaded into Xcode, selecting the *AppIcon* image set will display the categories for which icons may be provided:

Figure 16-9

The icons for the Apple Watch app need to be placed in the *Apple Watch Companion Settings* category. Icon images should be provided for both the 2x and 3x image scales. Since 1x image size is specified as being 29x29 pixels (29pt), the 2x and 3x icons need to be 58x58 pixels and 87x87 pixels respectively. Once the icons have been created, simply drag and drop them onto the icon placeholders in the asset catalog.

16.7 **Summary**

With the introduction of iOS 8.2, the Apple Watch app is now installed by default on all iPhone devices. Among the features provided by this app is the ability to modify the preference settings for any WatchKit app installed on the watch device. By default the settings provide control only over whether or not a specific WatchKit app is visible on the paired Apple Watch. Through the use of the WatchKit settings bundle, however, the Apple Watch app can be used to provide the user with a central and consistent location through which to change any number of preference settings for a WatchKit app.

A range of different settings controls can be defined within the settings bundle property list file including text fields, sliders, switches and multiple value lists. Through the declaration of settings identifiers and app groups, the preferences stored within a WatchKit settings bundle can be accessed in code from both the containing iOS app and the WatchKit extension.

Chapter 17

17. A WatchKit Settings Bundle Tutorial

The objective of this chapter is to build upon the overview of the WatchKit settings bundle provided in the preceding chapter through the implementation of an example app. The chapter will cover the steps involved in adding a WatchKit settings bundle to an Xcode project, defining the preference controls and accessing and responding to those settings within the WatchKit app.

17.1 About the WatchKit Settings Bundle Example

The WatchKit app created within this chapter will consist of a scene containing a single Label interface object. The label will initially display text using the default font size and foreground color. A settings bundle will then be added to the project and configured to allow the user to control whether or not the label is visible and to adjust both the font size and foreground color. This will involve the use of toggle switch, group, slider and multi-value controls within the bundle settings properties list.

17.2 Creating the WatchKit Settings Bundle Project

Start Xcode and create a new iOS project. On the template screen choose the *Application* option located under *iOS* in the left hand panel and select *Single View Application.* Click *Next,* set the product name to *SettingsBundle,* enter your organization identifier and make sure that the *Devices* menu is set to *Universal.* Before clicking *Next*, change the *Language* menu to Swift. On the final screen, choose a location in which to store the project files and click on *Create* to proceed to the main Xcode project window.

17.3 Adding the WatchKit App Target

For the purposes of this example we will, once again, assume that the iOS app has already been implemented. The next step, therefore, is to add the WatchKit app target to the project. Within Xcode, select the *File -> New -> Target...* menu option. In the target template dialog, select the *Apple Watch* option listed beneath the *iOS* heading. In the main panel, select the *WatchKit App* icon and click on *Next.* On the subsequent screen turn off the *Include Glance Scene* and *Include Notification Scene* options before clicking on the *Finish* button.

As soon as the extension target has been created, a new panel will appear requesting permission to activate the new scheme for the extension target. Activate this scheme now by clicking on the *Activate* button in the request panel.

141

17.4 Designing the WatchKit App Scene

Within the Project Navigator panel, locate and select the *Interface.storyboard* file located under the *SettingsBundle WatchKit App* folder so that it loads into the Interface Builder environment. From the Object Library panel, drag and drop a Label interface object onto the scene canvas. Double-click on the new label and change the text so it reads "Hello Watch". With the label still selected in the scene, display the Attributes Inspector panel and set both the *Vertical* and *Horizontal* position properties to *Center*.

Figure 17-1

Display the Assistant Editor and verify that it is displaying the *InterfaceController.swift* source file. Ctrl-click on the Label object and drag to a line immediately beneath the class declaration line in the Assistant Editor panel. Release the line and establish an outlet connection named *titleLabel*.

17.5 Adding the WatchKit Settings Bundle

Add a WatchKit settings bundle to the project by Ctrl-clicking on the *SettingsBundle* folder entry in the Project Navigator panel and selecting the *New -> File...* menu option. In the resulting panel, select the *Apple Watch* category in the side bar followed by *WatchKit Settings Bundle* in the main panel as shown in Figure 17-2:

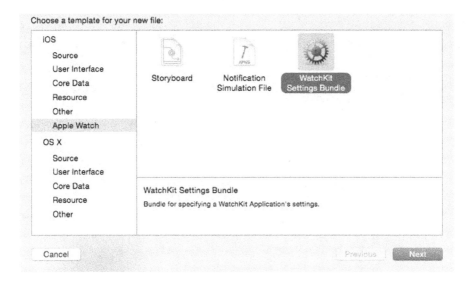

Figure 17-2

Click the *Next* button and on the following screen make sure that the *Group* menu is set to the *SettingsBundle* folder option and that *SettingsBundle* is enabled in the *Targets* section:

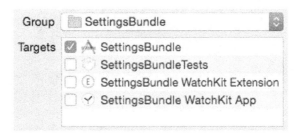

Figure 17-3

With the settings bundle configured, click on the *Create* button to add the settings bundle to the project. Within the Project Navigator panel, locate the settings bundle and select the *Root.plist* file so that it appears in the Property List Editor as illustrated in Figure 17-4:

Figure 17-4

If the list does not appear as shown above, Ctrl-click on the editor panel and select the *Property List Type ->* *iPhone Settings plist* option from the resulting menu to switch the editor into the correct mode.

By default, the property list file will contain a group, text field, toggle switch and slider. To view the current preference items, click on the right facing arrow to the left of the *Preference Items* heading to unfold the list of items:

Figure 17-5

For the purposes of this example we will start with an empty list of preference items. Select each of the items in turn, pressing the keyboard delete key to remove the item from the list.

17.6 **Adding a Switch Control to the Settings Bundle**

The first control to be added to the preferences list is a switch control. Select the *Preference Items* entry in the editor panel and click on the + button when it appears. In the resulting menu, select the *Toggle Switch* option as outlined in Figure 17-6:

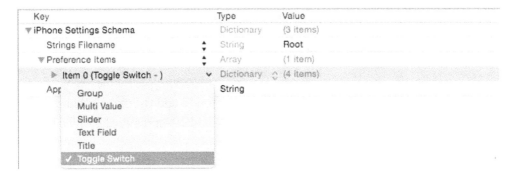

Figure 17-6

With the sub-items for the newly added preference item unfolded and visible within the property list editor, set the *Title* value to "Show Title", the *Identifier* to *show_label_preference* and the *Default Value* to *YES*:

Item 0 (Toggle Switch - Show		Dictionary	(4 items)
Type	⬍	String	Toggle Switch
Title	⬍	String	Show Title
Identifier	⬍	String	show_label_preference
Default Value	⬍	Boolean	YES

Figure 17-7

Select the *SettingsBundle* target from the Xcode toolbar and then run the iOS app to install the settings bundle on the device. Once the app is installed and running, stop the app and then navigate to and launch the Apple Watch app on the iPhone device or simulator. Within the Apple Watch app select the *My Watch* tab and scroll down to and select the *SettingsBundle* app from the list of installed WatchKit apps. The preferences screen should appear and include the new Toggle Switch control:

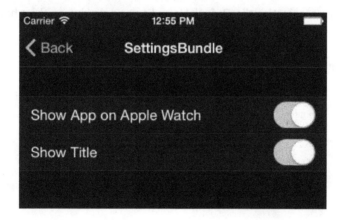

Figure 17-8

17.7 Adding a Slider Control to the Settings Bundle

The remaining controls will appear within a group section on the preferences screen. Begin by clicking on the down arrow to the left of the Item 0 entry so that the sub-items are folded and out of sight. Next, Ctrl-click on the *Item 0* entry and select the *Add Row* menu option. Select the *Group* item type from the menu and configure the title value to read "Font and Color":

▶ Item 0 (Toggle Switch - Show		Dictionary	(4 items)
▼ Item 1 (Group - Font and Color)		Dictionary	(2 items)
Type	⬍	String	Group
Title	⬍	String	Font and Color

Figure 17-9

Click on the down arrow on the Item 1 line to fold the sub-items and then Ctrl-click on the item, once again selecting the *Add Row* menu option but this time choosing *Slider* from the list of preference item types. Unfold the new item and set the *Identifier* field to *font_preference*, the *Minimum* value to 10, the *Maximum* value to 30 and the *Default Value* to 15.

17.8 Adding a Multi Value Control to the Settings Bundle

The multi-value control will provide the user with a choice of white, blue or green for the color of the text on the label in the WatchKit app. Add this item by folding the sub-items of Item 2, Ctrl-clicking on the item line and selecting the *Add Row* menu option. From the list of item types choose the *Multi Value* option. Edit the values for the new item so that the title reads "Foreground Color" and the identifier is set to *color_preference*.

The multi value control requires a list of titles to display to the user together with a set of corresponding values. Add the Titles entry by selecting the *Default Value* line and clicking on the + button. From the resulting menu, select the *Titles* entry:

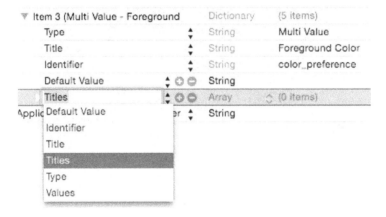

Figure 17-10

Unfold the new Titles entry (so that the arrow is pointing down) and click on the + button to add the first title to the list which will appear with a key of *Item 0*. Enter *White* into the value field for this item before clicking on the + button on the Item 0 line to add the next title. Enter *Green* as the value for this key. Repeat this step once more, this time setting the title text to *Blue*.

On completion of these steps the multi value section of the properties file should match Figure 17-11:

Figure 17-11

Each of the titles added to the multi-value control now needs to have a corresponding value. Select and fold the Titles section of the properties list so that the title sub-items are hidden. With the Titles line still selected, click on the + button and add a new item of type *Values*.

Select the *Values* line, unfold it and click on the + button to add a new value item to the array. The type of a value is set to String by default. This can be changed by clicking on the type field and selecting a different type from the resulting menu as shown in Figure 17-12:

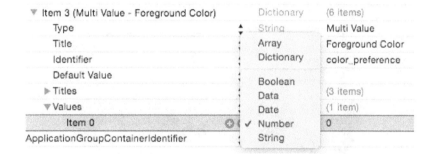

Figure 17-12

Using this technique, change the value type for the new value from *String* to *Number* and set the value to 0.

Repeat the above steps to add two more values, configured as numbers set to 1 and 2 respectively. Review the Titles and Values settings which should now resemble those configured in Figure 17-13:

▼ Titles	▲ ◯ ⊖	Array	(3 items)
Item 0		String	White
Item 1		String	Green
Item 2		String	Blue
▼ Values	▲ ▼	Array	(3 items)
Item 0		Number	0
Item 1		Number	1
Item 2		Number	2

Figure 17-13

The last task in this phase of the tutorial is to configure the default value setting for the multi-value control. Within the multi-value section of the list (listed as Item 3) locate the *Default Value* key, change the value type to *Number* and set the value to 0.

Compile and run the iOS app target and then use the Apple Watch app to test that the preference items are configured correctly. If the Apple Watch app launches directly into the SettingsBundle preferences page it may be necessary to use the Back button to return to the list of WatchKit apps and then reselect the SettingsBundle app in order to see the new configuration. The first screen should match Figure 17-14:

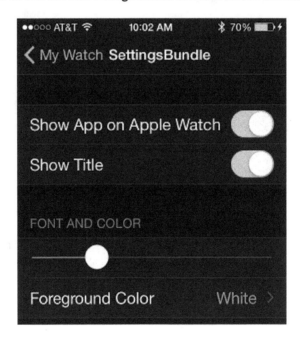

Figure 17-14

Selecting the Foreground Color control should display a second screen (Figure 17-15) listing the full range of color choices available for selection by the user:

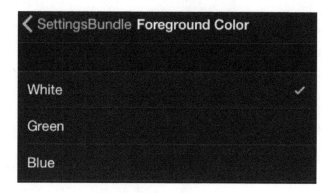

Figure 17-15

17.9 Setting Up the App Group

The WatchKit settings bundle is packaged with the containing iOS app. This means that an app group is required if the WatchKit extension is to be able to access the preferences contained within the settings bundle.

Begin by selecting the *SettingsBundle* target located at the top of the Project Navigator panel and clicking on the *Capabilities* tab in the main panel. Within the capabilities panel, locate the *App Groups* section and switch the setting to the *On* position.

To add a new app group to your account, simply click on the + button and enter a suitable app group name, with a format similar to the following:

```
group.com.example.SettingsBundle
```

Add the current app to the newly added app group by enabling the checkbox next to the group name.

With the iOS app added to the app group, the WatchKit extension must also be added as a member of the same group in order to gain access to the shared container. To access the capability settings for the WatchKit extension, use the menu located in the top left-hand corner of the capabilities panel as indicated in Figure 17-16:

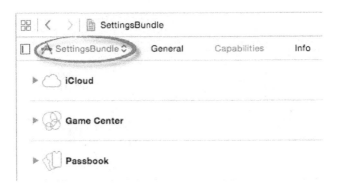

Figure 17-16

When clicked, this menu will present a list of targets contained within the current project as shown in Figure 17-16, one of which will be the *SettingsBundle WatchKit Extension*. Select this option and repeat the steps followed for the iOS app to enable membership in the same app group as that configured for the iOS app.

17.10 **Adding the App Group to the Settings Bundle**

The final step in configuring the app group is to add the group container identifier to the settings bundle. This is achieved by selecting the *Root.plist* file from the settings bundle folder in the Project Navigator and entering the app group identifier into the value field of the *ApplicationGroupContainerIdentifier* key line:

Figure 17-17

17.11 **Accessing Preference Settings from the WatchKit Extension**

The intention in this example is for the preferences saved in the settings bundle to be applied to the user interface of the WatchKit app each time that the app launches on the Apple Watch device. This will require the addition of some code to the *awakeWithContext* method in the WatchKit extension *InterfaceController.swift* file. With this file loaded into the editing panel, locate and modify this method so that it reads as follows making sure to use the app group identifier you configured earlier in the chapter:

```
override func awakeWithContext(context: AnyObject?) {
    super.awakeWithContext(context)

    let defaults = NSUserDefaults(suiteName:
            "<YOUR APP GROUP ID HERE>")
```

```
        if let preference = defaults?.boolForKey("show_label_preference")
        {
            titleLabel.setHidden(!preference)
        }
    }
}
```

This code gets the user default settings for the app group and extracts the Boolean value assigned to the *show_label_preference* key. This value is then inverted (since a *true* value from the settings bundle means the title should not be hidden) and used to control whether or not the title label is visible in the scene.

The next preference to be handled is the font size setting. Remaining within *awakeWithContext*, further modify the method so that it reads as follows:

```
override func awakeWithContext(context: AnyObject?) {
    super.awakeWithContext(context)

    let defaults = NSUserDefaults(suiteName:
            "<YOUR APP GROUP ID HERE>")


    if let preference = defaults?.boolForKey("show_label_preference")
    {
        titleLabel.setHidden(!preference)
    }

    let sliderVal = defaults?.floatForKey("font_preference")

    let fontSize = CGFloat(sliderVal!)

    var attrs = [NSFontAttributeName :
            UIFont.systemFontOfSize(fontSize)]

    var attributedString = NSAttributedString(string: "Hello Watch",
            attributes: attrs)

    titleLabel.setAttributedText(attributedString)
}
```

The font code begins by getting the current value of the slider in the settings bundle and converting it to a CGFloat value. It then creates a dictionary object consisting of a key represented by NSFontAttributesName and a UIFont object using the system font with the size set to the value defined by the slider.

If anything other than plain text with a pre-configured font is to be displayed on a WatchKit Label interface object it is necessary to use an NSAttributedString instance to do so. The NSAttributedString class allows text and a variety of attributes such as font settings to be combined within a single object.

In the method code, an NSAttributedString object is created and initialized with the text to be displayed and the attributes dictionary containing the font setting. Finally, the attributed string object is set on the title label.

The last addition to the method is to add a switch statement based on the multi value preference selection to set the foreground color of the label text:

```
override func awakeWithContext(context: AnyObject?) {
    super.awakeWithContext(context)

    let defaults = NSUserDefaults(suiteName:
            "<YOUR APP GROUP ID HERE>")


    if let preference = defaults?.boolForKey("show_label_preference")
    {
        titleLabel.setHidden(!preference)
    }

    let sliderVal = defaults?.floatForKey("font_preference")

    let fontSize = CGFloat(sliderVal!)

    var attrs = [NSFontAttributeName :
            UIFont.systemFontOfSize(fontSize)]

    var attributedString = NSAttributedString(string: "Hello Watch",
            attributes: attrs)

    titleLabel.setAttributedText(attributedString)

    if let color = defaults?.integerForKey("color_preference") {
        switch color {
        case 0:
            titleLabel.setTextColor(UIColor.whiteColor())
        case 1:
            titleLabel.setTextColor(UIColor.greenColor())
        case 2:
            titleLabel.setTextColor(UIColor.blueColor())
```

```
    default:
        break
    }
  }
}
```

When the multi-value control was created it was configured to store integer values between 0 and 2 to indicate the color chosen by the user. The code added above uses a switch statement to set the text color on the label according to the integer retrieved from the bundle.

17.12 Registering the Default Preference Settings

As outlined in the previous chapter, the defaults value configured within the settings bundle properties file define only how the controls will appear when the preferences screen for the WatchKit app is displayed to the user. A preference value is not saved to the settings bundle until the user changes that setting in the preference screen. Default values must, therefore, be registered in the code when the main WatchKit app interface controller initializes. Edit the *InterfaceController.swift* file and implement the *init* method to register the default values for the preference settings:

```
override init() {

    let defaults = NSUserDefaults(suiteName:
            "<YOUR APP GROUP ID HERE>")

    let defaultSettings = ["show_label_preference" : true,
                           "font_preference" : 15,
                           "color_preference" : 0]

    defaults?.registerDefaults(defaultSettings)
}
```

17.13 Adding the Companion Settings Icons

The last task before testing the project is to add the app icons that will appear within the Apple Watch app. The icons for this purpose are contained within the *app_icons* folder of the sample code download, available from the following URL:

http://www.ebookfrenzy.com/print/watchkit/index.php

To add the icons, begin by selecting the *Image.xcassets* entry listed under the *SettingsBundle WatchKit App* folder in the Project Navigator panel and selecting the *AppIcon* image set. Open a Finder window and locate the *app_icons* folder in the code samples. Once located, drag and drop the *AppleWatchIcon@2x.png* icon file onto the 2x placeholder for the *Companion Settings* icons. Repeat this step to place the

AppleWatchIcon@3x.png file into the 3x placeholder so that the icon settings appear as shown in Figure 17-18:

2x   3x

Apple Watch
Companion Settings
29pt

Figure 17-18

Finally, drag and drop the *HomeIcon@2x.png* file onto the Apple Watch Home Screen (All) location.

17.14 Testing the Settings Bundle Project

Compile and run the iOS app so that the latest version of the settings bundle is installed. Change the run target in the Xcode toolbar to the *Settings Bundle WatchKit Extension* target, run the app on the watch device and note that the text appears with a white foreground.

Return to the iPhone, launch the Apple Watch app and navigate to the preferences screen. Note that SettingsBundle app icon appears in the list of WatchKit apps:

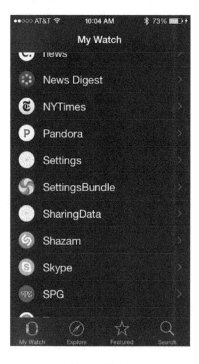

Figure 17-19

Select the app to display the preferences screen, change the font size and color settings and then stop and restart the WatchKit app from the Xcode toolbar. This time the label should display the text using the new color and font size preferences. Repeat these steps once again, this time turning off the switch control to hide the label.

17.15 **Summary**

The tutorial in this chapter has produced a project designed to demonstrate the use of a WatchKit settings bundle to provide the user with the ability to configure the preferences for a WatchKit app using the iPhone Apple Watch app.

18. An Overview of WatchKit Glances

A WatchKit glance is an optional additional scene intended to provide a quick and lightweight view of the key information provided by a WatchKit app. A WatchKit app can have only one glance scene, which is non-interactive and non-scrollable. Tapping the screen while a glance is displayed opens the corresponding WatchKit app.

This chapter will provide an overview of WatchKit glances. The next chapter, entitled *A WatchKit Glance Tutorial*, will provide a practical implementation of a glance scene for an existing WatchKit app.

18.1 WatchKit Glances

A WatchKit glance is an optional scene that can be added to a WatchKit app. Glances are accessed on the Apple Watch device by performing an upward swipe starting at the bottom of the device display. Glances are displayed in a page-based navigation format allowing the user to swipe left and right to navigate through the glance scenes for the various apps installed on the watch.

WatchKit scenes are intended to show only a subset of the information provided by the WatchKit app and containing iOS app and cannot contain interactive controls such as buttons, sliders or switches. Since glance scenes are non-scrollable it is also essential that the information displayed by the glance fit onto a single screen.

The only user interaction supported in a glance scene is a tap to launch the corresponding WatchKit app. When a WatchKit app is launched via its glance scene, context information can be passed from the glance to the WatchKit app.

A glance should be designed to display the minimum amount of information necessary to inform the user and do so as quickly as possible.

18.2 The Architecture of a WatchKit Glance

A WatchKit glance consists of a scene and a corresponding interface controller derived from the WKInterfaceController class, essentially mirroring the architecture of a standard WatchKit scene. The glance scene is contained within the same storyboard file as all the other scenes within a WatchKit app and the glance interface controller resides within the WatchKit extension.

The lifecycle of the glance interface controller is the same as that of any other interface controller as described in the chapter entitled *An Overview of WatchKit App Architecture*.

A key difference between a glance interface controller and the interface controller for a standard scene is that the operating system will call the initialization lifecycle methods earlier for a glance controller, allowing for a greater amount of time to elapse between the *init* and *awakeWithContext* initialization lifecycle method calls and the call to the *willActivate* lifecycle method immediately before the scene is shown to the user. It is recommended, therefore, that the *willActivate* method be used within glance interface controllers to perform a final check that the information being displayed to the user is still up to date before the scene appears to the user.

18.3 Adding a Glance During WatchKit App Creation

A glance may be included when the WatchKit app target is first created within an Xcode project, or added later to an existing WatchKit app extension. To include a glance when first creating a WatchKit app target, simply enable the *Include Glance Scene* checkbox in the new target options panel as highlighted in Figure 18-1:

Figure 18-1

With this option selected, Xcode will add a glance scene to the *Interface.storyboard* file in addition to the standard main scene:

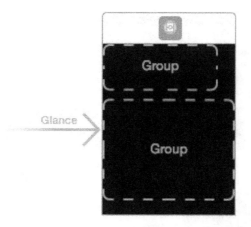

Figure 18-2

In addition to the scene, Xcode will also add a corresponding interface controller source file to the WatchKit extension named *GlanceController.swift* and associate it with the glance storyboard scene.

The last element automatically added to the project by Xcode is a new build scheme configured to compile and run the glance scene. This build scheme appears as an option within the Xcode run target menu as shown in Figure 18-3 and is named *Glance - <app name> WatchKit App*.

Figure 18-3

18.4 Adding a Glance to an Existing WatchKit App

The inclusion of a glance scene to an existing WatchKit app is a multi-step process that begins with the addition of a Glance Interface Controller scene to the WatchKit app storyboard file. To add the scene, select the *Interface.storyboard* file so that it loads into the Interface Builder tool and drag and drop a *Glance Interface Controller* object from the Object Library panel onto the storyboard canvas (Figure 18-4):

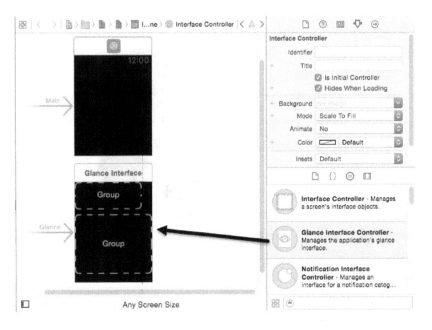

Figure 18-4

Next, add an interface controller to accompany the glance scene by Ctrl-clicking on the WatchKit Extension entry in the Project Navigator panel, selecting the *New File...* menu option and creating a new Cocoa Touch Class source file subclassed from the WKInterfaceController class.

Return to the *Interface.storyboard* file and select the Glance Interface Controller scene so that it highlights in blue. Display the Identity Inspector panel and select the newly added interface controller class from the *Class* drop-down menu.

The final step is to add a build scheme for the glance scene. The easiest way to achieve this is to duplicate the existing WatchKit App scheme and modify it for the glance scene. Begin this process by selecting the WatchKit App scheme in the run target menu as shown in Figure 18-5:

Figure 18-5

Display the run target menu again, this time selecting the *Edit Scheme...* menu option. Within the scheme editing panel, click on the *Duplicate Scheme* button located in the lower left hand corner and, in the name field located in the upper left hand corner, replace the "Copy of" text with a "Glance – " prefix:

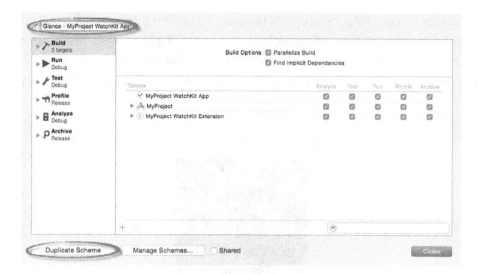

Figure 18-6

With the new scheme created and appropriately named, select the *Run* option on the left hand panel and change the *Watch Interface* option menu in the main panel from *Main* to *Glance* as shown in Figure 18-7:

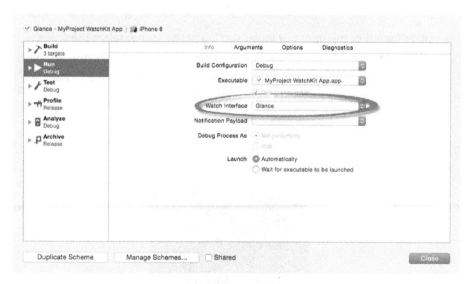

Figure 18-7

With these steps complete the glance is now added and fully integrated into the WatchKit app.

18.5 WatchKit Glance Scene Layout Templates

The layout for a WatchKit glance must be based on one of a number of templates provided within the Xcode environment. Glance scenes are divided into upper and lower sections. Xcode currently provides 12 template options for the upper section of the scene and 24 template options for the lower section. The templates vary in the amount of customization that can be performed in terms of adding other visual elements. The most flexible is the default template shown in Figure 18-8. This consists of a Group object in each of the upper and lower sections, allowing additional interface objects to be added to meet the requirements of the glance layout:

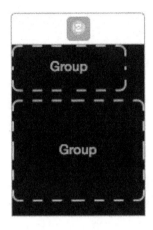

Figure 18-8

To change the template for either the upper or lower section of the scene, select the scene in the storyboard and display the Attributes Inspector in the utilities panel. This will display the current template selections for both sections. Clicking on a section in the panel will display a menu of available alternatives. Figure 18-9, for example, shows the template options for the upper section of the glance scene:

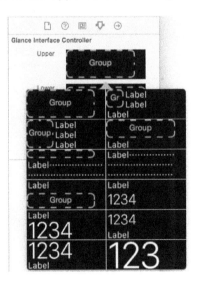

Figure 18-9

18.6 **Passing Context Data to the WatchKit App**

When the user taps a glance scene on the watch display the WatchKit app associated with that glance is launched. In some situations it might be useful to pass some context data from the glance interface controller to the initial interface controller of the WatchKit app. Based on this data the appearance of the WatchKit app can then be changed. A WatchKit app consisting of a number of different scenes might, for example, display a particular scene when launched in this way based on the context data passed through from the glance.

The context data to be passed to the WatchKit app when the user taps on the glance scene is configured by making a call to the *updateUserActivity* method within the glance interface controller. This method takes as parameters a string uniquely identifying the activity, a dictionary object containing the context data and a web page URL. When working with WatchKit glances, only the type string and dictionary parameter are used. The following code, for example, calls the *updateUserActivity* method passing through a dictionary object:

```
updateUserActivity("com.ebookFrenzy.MyProjectApp",
        userInfo: myDictionary, webpageURL: nil)
```

When the WatchKit app launches, the *handleUserActivity* method, if implemented in the initial interface controller class, will be called and passed the userInfo dictionary object. For example:

```
override func handleUserActivity(userInfo: [NSObject : AnyObject]?) {
        // Extract data from dictionary and handle context
}
```

When called, the *handleUserActivity* method can extract the context data from the dictionary and decide how to tailor the launch of the app in response.

18.7 **Summary**

A WatchKit glance is an optional scene that can be added to a WatchKit app. Glances are accessed when the user performs an upward swipe starting at the bottom of the watch display. All of the glances available on the device are displayed using a page-based navigation interface through which the user moves using left and right swiping motions.

The purpose of a glance is to provide quick access to a subset of the information provided by the corresponding WatchKit app. Glance scenes are non-scrollable and do not respond to user interaction with the exception that a tap will launch the corresponding WatchKit app. When the WatchKit app is launched from the glance scene, context data may be passed to the initial interface controller of the WatchKit app.

A glance scene may be created either at the point that a WatchKit app target is added to a project, or added manually to an existing WatchKit app extension. A number of template options are provided within Xcode as the basis for the layout of glance scenes.

An Overview of WatchKit Glances

Glances are intended to launch and display information quickly. To achieve this, the operating system will "pre-initialize" the glance interface controller by making early calls to the two initialization lifecycle methods. Any last minute updates to the data to be displayed should, therefore, be performed immediately before the scene appears within the *willActivate* method. Tasks that take a long time to complete should be avoided when performing this final update.

19. A WatchKit Glance Tutorial

The tutorial outlined in this chapter will add a glance scene to the TableDemoApp created in the chapter entitled *A WatchKit Table Tutorial* and will make use of the various glance capabilities outlined in the previous chapter, including the addition of a glance to an existing Xcode project and the passing of context data from the glance to the main interface controller of the WatchKit app.

19.1 About the Glance Scene

The TableDemoApp project consists of a table containing a list of workout exercises for a fitness app. When a table row is selected by the user the app navigates to a second scene containing more detailed information about the chosen exercise. In this chapter, a glance scene will be added to this project, the purpose of which is to allow the user to display a summary of the exercise last selected in the WatchKit app. Through the use of context data, tapping the display from within the glance scene will launch the WatchKit app and automatically navigate to the corresponding detail scene.

If you have already completed the TableDemoApp project as outlined in the *A WatchKit Table Tutorial* and *Implementing WatchKit Table Navigation* chapters of this book, open the project in Xcode now. Alternatively, the completed project may be downloaded along with the other sample projects at the following URL:

http://www.ebookfrenzy.com/print/watchkit/index.php

19.2 Adding the Glance to the Project

To add the glance scene to the WatchKit app storyboard, select the *Interface.storyboard* file so that it loads into the Interface Builder tool and drag and drop a *Glance Interface Controller* object from the Object Library panel onto the storyboard canvas (Figure 19-1):

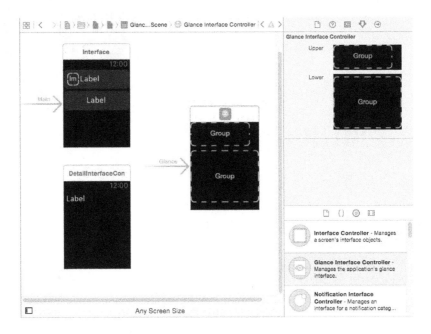

Figure 19-1

Next, add an interface controller to accompany the glance scene by Ctrl-clicking on the *TableDemoApp WatchKit Extension* entry in the Project Navigator panel, selecting the *New File...* menu option and creating a new Cocoa Touch Class named *GlanceController* and subclassed from the WKInterfaceController class.

Return to the *Interface.storyboard* file and select the Glance Interface Controller scene so that it highlights in blue. Display the Identity Inspector panel and select the newly added interface controller class from the *Class* drop-down menu.

The final step is to add a build scheme for the glance scene by duplicating and modifying the existing WatchKit App scheme. Begin by selecting the WatchKit App scheme in the run target menu as shown in Figure 19-2:

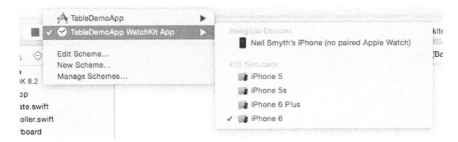

Figure 19-2

Display the run target menu again, this time selecting the *Edit Scheme...* menu option. Within the scheme editing panel, click on the *Duplicate Scheme* button located in the lower left hand corner and, in the name field located in the upper left hand corner, replace the "Copy of" text with a "Glance – " prefix.

With the new scheme created and appropriately named, select the *Run* option on the left hand panel and change the *Watch Interface* option menu in the main panel from *Main* to *Glance* as shown in Figure 19-3:

Figure 19-3

Close the panel to commit the changes, at which point the glance is now integrated into the TableDemoApp WatchKit app extension.

19.3 Designing the Glance Scene Layout

The glance scene will use the default template layout consisting of the two Group interface objects. With the *Interface.storyboard* file displayed within Interface Builder, drag a Label object into each of the group containers within the glance scene as shown in Figure 19-4:

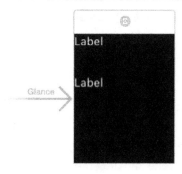

Figure 19-4

Select the Label object in the upper group container, display the Attributes Inspector panel and change the *Vertical* property listed under Position to *Center*.

Select the Label object located in the lower group and change both the *Horizontal* and *Vertical* properties in the Position section of the panel to *Center*. With the Label object still selected, click on the 'T' icon in the Font property field, change the *Font* menu to *System* and change the *Style* menu to *Bold*. Before clicking on the Done button, increase the *Size* value to 35:

Figure 19-5

On completion of these steps, the layout of the glance scene should match that outlined in Figure 19-6:

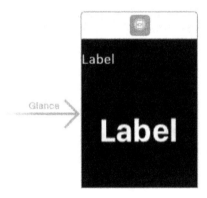

Figure 19-6

19.4 Establishing Outlet Connections

The interface controller for the glance scene will need access to the two labels to change the text that is displayed to the user. Keeping the *Interface.storyboard* file loaded in the Interface Builder tool, display the Assistant Editor panel and make sure that it is displaying the content of the *GlanceController.swift* file. Ctrl-click on the upper label in the glance scene and drag the resulting line to a position immediately beneath the class declaration line in the Assistant Editor panel. Release the line and create an outlet connection named *titleLabel.* Repeat this step to connect the lower label to an outlet named *mainLabel.* At this point the beginning of the *GlanceController.swift* file should read as follows:

```
import WatchKit
import Foundation

class GlanceController: WKInterfaceController {

    @IBOutlet weak var titleLabel: WKInterfaceLabel!
    @IBOutlet weak var mainLabel: WKInterfaceLabel!

    override func awakeWithContext(context: AnyObject?) {
        super.awakeWithContext(context)

        // Configure interface objects here.
    }
    .
    .
}
```

19.5 Adding Data to the Glance Interface Controller

Now that the user interface of the glance scene is designed and the Label objects are connected to outlets in the interface controller, some data needs to be added to represent the information to be presented when the glance is displayed by the user. The information contained within the glance will consist of the currently selected exercise and a reminder of the duration or number of repetitions to be performed.

Select the *GlanceController.swift* file and add two data arrays to the class so that it reads as follows:

```
import WatchKit
import Foundation

class GlanceController: WKInterfaceController {

    @IBOutlet weak var titleLabel: WKInterfaceLabel!
    @IBOutlet weak var mainLabel: WKInterfaceLabel!

    let titleData = ["Warm-up", "Cardio", "Weightlifting", "Core", "Bike",
"Cooldown"]
    let durationData = ["20 mins", "30 mins", "3 x 10", "2 x 20", "20
mins", "20 mins"]

    override func awakeWithContext(context: AnyObject?) {
```

```
        super.awakeWithContext(context)

        // Configure interface objects here.
    }
    .
    .
    .
}
```

19.6 Creating an App Group

When the glance is invoked by the user it will need to know which row within the corresponding WatchKit app was last selected by the user. The WatchKit app interface controller, therefore, needs to store this information in a location where it can also be accessed by the glance interface controller. Since this is a small amount of data, the ideal location is within app group user defaults as described in the chapter entitled *Sharing Data Between a WatchKit App and the Containing iOS App*.

Select the *TableDemoApp* target located at the top of the Project Navigator panel and click on the *Capabilities* tab in the main panel. By default, the Capabilities panel displays the settings for the iOS app target. To access the capability settings for the WatchKit Extension, use the menu located in the top left-hand corner of the capabilities panel as indicated in Figure 19-7:

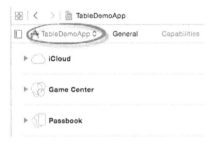

Figure 19-7

When clicked, this menu will present a list of targets contained within the current project, one of which will be the *TableDemoApp WatchKit Extension*. Select this option and scroll down the capabilities list until the App Groups section comes into view. Switch App Group support On and select a suitable Apple developer account with which to associate the group when prompted to do so.

Click on the + button within the App Group section of the capabilities panel and add a new app group based on the application name and your organization identifier, for example:

```
group.com.example.TableDemoApp
```

Once the new app group has been added, enable the checkbox next to it to ensure that the extension becomes part of the group as shown in the figure below:

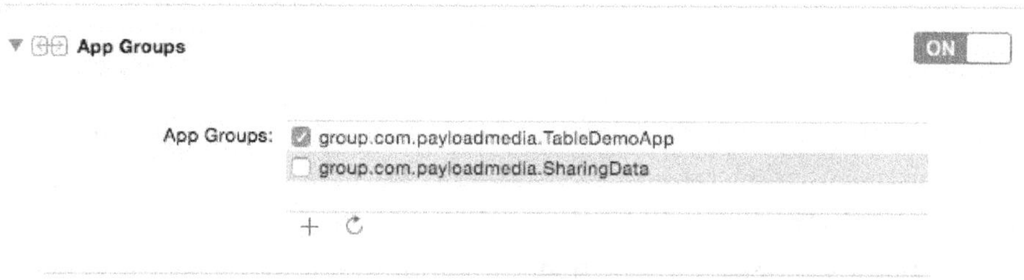

▼ ⊞ **App Groups**   ON

App Groups: ☑ group.com.payloadmedia.TableDemoApp
              ☐ group.com.payloadmedia.SharingData

              + ↻

Figure 19-8

19.7 **Storing and Retrieving the Currently Selected Table Row**

When the user selects a row within the WatchKit app, the index of that row needs to be saved into the app group user defaults. The selection of a table row results in a call to the *didSelectRowAtIndex* method of the main WatchKit app interface controller which now needs to be updated to save the current index value. Within the Project Navigator panel, select the *InterfaceController.swift* file, locate the *didSelectRowAtIndex* method and modify it as follows (noting that the app group identifier will need to be changed to match the one you created):

```
override func table(table: WKInterfaceTable, didSelectRowAtIndex rowIndex:
Int) {
    pushControllerWithName("DetailInterfaceController", context:
detailData[rowIndex-1])

    let sharedDefaults = NSUserDefaults(suiteName:
            "<YOUR APP GROUP IDENTIFIER HERE>")
    sharedDefaults?.setInteger(rowIndex, forKey: "index")
}
```

Within the glance interface controller, this stored index value needs to be retrieved and used to display the correct information within the glance scene. Edit the *GlanceController.swift* file and modify the *willActivate* method to update the labels in the scene with the current information:

```
override func willActivate() {
    super.willActivate()
    let sharedDefaults = NSUserDefaults(suiteName:
            "<YOUR APP GROUP IDENTIFIER HERE>")

    let index = sharedDefaults?.integerForKey("index")

    if let arrayIndex = index {
        titleLabel.setText(titleData[arrayIndex - 1])
        mainLabel.setText(durationData[arrayIndex - 1])
```

```
        }
    }
```

Test that the changes to the project work by running the WatchKit app within the Simulator environment and selecting the Warm-up row from the table so that the detail page appears. Next, within the Xcode toolbar change the run target to the *Glance – TableDemoApp WatchKit App* option and click on the run button. The glance scene should appear and display information relating to the selected Warm-up exercise as illustrated in Figure 19-9:

Figure 19-9

Tapping the glance scene will launch the WatchKit app. Note, however, that the app starts at the table scene and does not automatically navigate to the detail scene for the Warm-up exercise. To address this some code needs to be added to the project to pass context data from the glance to the WatchKit app.

19.8 Passing Context Data to the WatchKit App

As outlined in *An Overview of WatchKit Glances*, a glance interface controller specifies the context data to be passed to the WatchKit app via a call to the *updateUserActivity* method. The ideal location in which to place this method call is within the *willActivate* method of the glance interface controller.

Edit the *GlanceController.swift* file and modify this method as follows:

```
override func willActivate() {
    super.willActivate()
    let sharedDefaults = NSUserDefaults(suiteName:
            "<YOUR APP GROUP IDENTIFIER HERE>")

    let index = sharedDefaults?.integerForKey("index")
```

```
        if let arrayIndex = index {
            titleLabel.setText(titleData[arrayIndex - 1])
            mainLabel.setText(durationData[arrayIndex - 1])

            updateUserActivity("com.example.TableDemoApp",
                    userInfo: ["controller" : arrayIndex], webpageURL: nil)
        }
    }
```

The added code calls the *updateUserActivity* method, passing through a dictionary object consisting of a key ("controller") and the current array index value.

When the WatchKit app is launched by a tap on the glance scene, the *handleUserActivity* method of the main interface controller will be called and passed the dictionary object specified when the *updateUserActivity* method was called. This method now needs to be implemented in the *InterfaceController.swift* file as follows:

```
override func handleUserActivity(userInfo: [NSObject : AnyObject]?) {

    let controllerIndex = userInfo!["controller"] as! Int

    pushControllerWithName("DetailInterfaceController",
            context: detailData[controllerIndex-1])
}
```

This method extracts the value associated with the "controller" key within the userInfo dictionary and uses it to display the DetailInterfaceController with the appropriate detail content.

Run the WatchKit app once again on the Simulator, this time selecting a different row from the table. Run the glance and tap the screen to launch the WatchKit app. This time, the WatchKit app should launch and display the previously selected detail scene.

Having verified that the code works within the Simulator, install and run the app on a physical Apple Watch device. Once the table appears, select a row and then press the digital crown twice to exit the app and display the time. Perform an upward swiping motion on the screen to display the glances and navigate to the table demo glance scene where the title and time should match the row selected in the main WatchKit app. Tapping the glance scene should launch the WatchKit app and automatically navigate to the corresponding detail scene.

19.9 **Summary**

Glances provide a quick way for users to view key information contained within a WatchKit app. This chapter has added a glance scene to the TableDemoApp project, using app group user defaults and context data to pass data back and forth between the glance and the WatchKit app.

20. A WatchKit Context Menu Tutorial

The Apple Watch display includes touch based technology known as *Force Touch*. A Force Touch event is triggered when the user presses on the screen with slightly more pressure than would be needed to register a tap gesture. When a Force Touch gesture is detected while a WatchKit app is running a context menu will appear if one has been configured.

This chapter will provide an overview of context menus before working through a tutorial involving the use of context menus in a sample WatchKit app.

20.1 An Overview of WatchKit Context Menus

As previously outlined, a context menu appears when the user presses down on the watch display while an app is running. Each storyboard scene within a WatchKit app can have associated with it one context menu.

Each context menu can contain up to four menu items (also referred to as *actions*), each of which is represented by a menu icon. Figure 20-1, for example, shows a context menu containing four menu items:

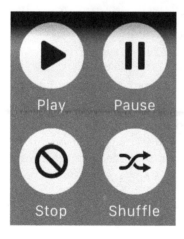

Figure 20-1

In practical terms, a context menu is actually an instance of the WKInterfaceMenu class while the menu items are represented by instances of the WKInterfaceMenuItem class. Menu items may be added to a context menu within the Interface Builder environment, or added dynamically at runtime from within the code of an interface controller instance. Menu items added dynamically may also be removed at runtime though the same is not true of those added using Interface Builder.

Each menu item needs to be connected to an action method within the interface controller class and will be called when the user taps that item. A tap performed outside any of the menu items dismisses the context menu and returns the user to the app scene.

20.2 Designing Menu Item Images

The icons displayed on menu items may be custom designed or selected from a list of pre-designed icons available from within Xcode. In terms of designing your own menu images some strict rules must be followed.

Each menu item image must be in PNG format and appears as a semi-opaque white circle. Opaque areas of the graphic in the center of the circle always appear in black, with transparent areas allowing the background scene to show through.

For the 38mm Apple Watch the canvas size of the menu image must be 70x70 pixels and for the 42mm device 80x80 pixels.

The background of the image must be fully transparent and must not contain the white circle (this is added automatically by WatchKit). When using a painting or graphic design tool, colors are defined by mixing red, green and blue (RGB) to make other colors. The level of transparency of an RGB-based color is defined by a fourth control referred to as the "Alpha channel" (which combines with RGB to create RGBA). This means that when designing a WatchKit menu image the RGBA alpha channel must be set to zero for the image background so that it is fully transparent. The visible area of the image, on the other hand, is defined by any graphic content that is not entirely transparent.

A sufficient margin must exist between the visible graphic and the outer edge of the white circle. Apple recommends that the non-transparent graphic content of the image not exceed 46x46 pixels and 54x54 pixels for the 38mm and 42mm Apple Watch models respectively. This, however, is only a guideline and it appears that the pre-designed images provided with Xcode use a more generous margin.

Figure 20-2 shows a graphical depiction of a menu image consisting of an opaque circle with a semi-transparent center designed for the 42mm Apple Watch:

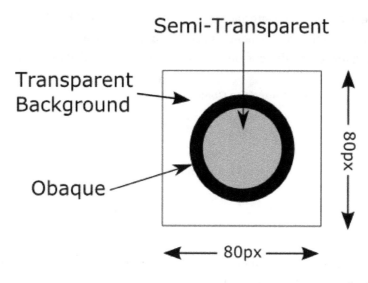

Figure 20-2

20.3 Creating a Context Menu in Interface Builder

To add a context menu to a scene in an Interface Builder storyboard simply locate the Menu object in the Object Library panel and drag and drop it onto the scene canvas as outlined in Figure 20-3 below:

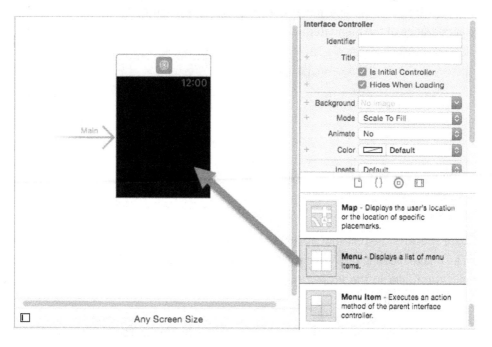

Figure 20-3

Once the menu has been added to the interface controller scene it will not be visible within the scene layout. The only evidence of the presence of the menu can be found in the Document Outline panel (Figure 20-4). As shown in the figure, the menu includes one default menu item when added to a scene:

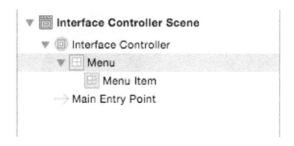

Figure 20-4

Additional menu items are added to the menu by dragging Menu Item objects from the Object Library onto the Menu entry in the Document Outline panel.

Action method connections are established by displaying the Assistant Editor panel, Ctrl-clicking and dragging from a menu item to an appropriate position in the interface controller source file and following the usual steps to establish an action connection.

Select a menu item from the outline panel and display the Attributes Inspector panel (Figure 20-5) to configure the appearance of the menu item.

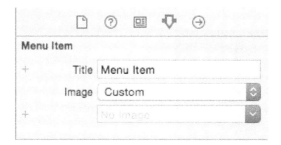

Figure 20-5

The title attribute specifies the text that appears beneath the menu item image circle. If the image menu is set to *Custom*, an image meeting the Apple style guidelines will need to be added to the image assets catalog of the WatchKit App folder in the Project Navigator panel and then selected from the drop down menu located beneath the Image menu.

To select a pre-defined image, simply click on the *Image* menu and make a selection:

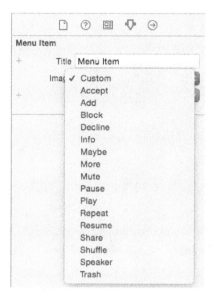

Figure 20-6

20.4 **Adding and Removing Menu Items in Code**

If a context menu has been added to a WatchKit storyboard scene, additional menu items may be added dynamically within the code of the interface controller using the following interface controller methods:

- **addMenuItemWithImage** – Takes as parameters a UIImage object containing the image to be displayed, the title string to display beneath the image and a reference to the method to be called when the item is selected.

- **addMenuItemWithImageNamed** – This method is used when the image to be displayed is already included in the WatchKit app resources. The method takes as parameters the name of the image file stored on the Apple Watch device, the title string to be displayed beneath the image and a reference to the method to be called when the item is selected.

- **addMenuItemWithIcon** – Allows one of the pre-designed template icons to be specified for the menu item image. In addition to the icon reference, this method also requires the title string to be displayed beneath the image and a reference to the method to be called when the item is selected.

When calling the *addMenuItemWithIcon* method, the icon options are defined within the *WKMenuItemIcon* enumeration and may be referenced as follows:

```
WKMenuItemIcon.Accept
WKMenuItemIcon.Add
WKMenuItemIcon.Block
WKMenuItemIcon.Decline
WKMenuItemIcon.Info
```

```
WKMenuItemIcon.Maybe
WKMenuItemIcon.More
WKMenuItemIcon.Mute
WKMenuItemIcon.Pause
WKMenuItemIcon.Play
WKMenuItemIcon.Repeat
WKMenuItemIcon.Resume
WKMenuItemIcon.Share
WKMenuItemIcon.Shuffle
WKMenuItemIcon.Speaker
WKMenuItemIcon.Trash
```

The following code, for example, adds a menu item to a context menu using the "Pause" template icon configured to call an action method named *pauseSelected*:

```
addMenuItemWithItemIcon(WKMenuItemIcon.Pause, title: "Pause",
                        action: "pauseSelected")
```

All of the menu items added from within the interface controller code may be removed via a call to the *clearAllMenuItems* method of the interface controller object. Any menu items added to the storyboard scene using Interface Builder are unaffected by this method call.

20.5 Creating the Context Menu Example Project

Start Xcode and create a new iOS project. On the template screen choose the *Application* option located under *iOS* in the left hand panel and select *Single View Application.* Click *Next,* set the product name to *ContextMenu,* enter your organization identifier and make sure that the *Devices* menu is set to *Universal.* Before clicking *Next*, change the *Language* menu to Swift. On the final screen, choose a location in which to store the project files and click on *Create* to proceed to the main Xcode project window.

20.6 Adding the WatchKit App Target

Within Xcode, select the *File -> New -> Target...* menu option. In the target template dialog, select the *Apple Watch* option listed beneath the *iOS* heading. In the main panel, select the *WatchKit App* icon and click on *Next.* On the subsequent screen turn off the *Include Glance Scene* and *Include Notification Scene* options before clicking on the *Finish* button.

As soon as the extension target has been created, a new panel will appear requesting permission to activate the new scheme for the extension target. Activate this scheme now by clicking on the *Activate* button in the request panel.

20.7 **Designing the WatchKit App User Interface**

When the project is complete, the WatchKit app will include a user interface comprising four menu items. When a menu item is selected, the text displayed on a Label object in the main scene will change to reflect the selected option. Select the *Interface.storyboard* file in the Project Navigator panel and drag and drop a Label interface object from the Object Library onto the main storyboard scene. With the newly added Label object selected, display the Attributes Inspector panel and change the *Horizontal* and *Vertical* position properties to *Center* at which point the scene should match Figure 20-7:

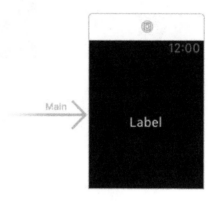

Figure 20-7

Display the Assistant Editor and verify that it is displaying the content of the *InterfaceController.Swift* file. Ctrl-click on the Label object in the scene and drag the resulting line to a position immediately beneath the class declaration line in the Assistant Editor panel. Release the line and establish an outlet connection named *statusLabel*.

20.8 **Designing the Context Menu**

Remaining within the *Interface.storyboard* file, drag a Menu object from the Object Library and drop it onto the main scene as previously illustrated in Figure 20-3. Display the Document Outline panel using the button in the bottom left hand corner of the Interface Builder panel (indicated in Figure 20-8) and select the first Menu Item located beneath the Menu entry:

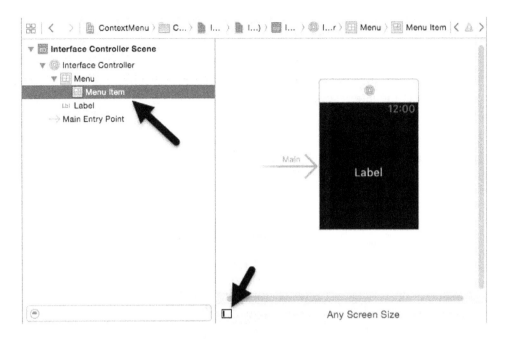

Figure 20-8

Display the Attributes Inspector and change the *Image* menu setting to *Play* and enter Play into the Title field.

Drag and drop three more Menu Item objects from the Object Library onto the *Menu* entry in the Document Outline panel, changing the *Image* property in the Attributes Inspector for each one to *Pause*, *Block* and *Shuffle* respectively. While configuring images, change the Title field for each Menu Item to Pause, Stop and Shuffle.

20.9 **Establishing the Action Connections**

Display the Assistant Editor, Ctrl-click on the uppermost Menu Item entry in the Document Outline panel and drag the line to a position beneath the *willActivate* method in the editor panel. Release the line and establish an action connection to a method named *playSelected*.

Repeat these steps for the remaining three Menu Items, connecting them to action methods named *pauseSelected*, *stopSelected* and *shuffleSelected*.

Next, edit the *InterfaceController.swift* file and implement the code in the four action method stubs to read as follows:

```
@IBAction func playSelected() {
    statusLabel.setText("Play")
}
```

```
@IBAction func pauseSelected() {
    statusLabel.setText("Pause")
}

@IBAction func stopSelected() {
    statusLabel.setText("Stop")
}

@IBAction func shuffleSelected() {
    statusLabel.setText("Shuffle")
}
```

20.10 Testing the Context Menu App

Compile and run the WatchKit app and when the app is running, press firmly on the device screen to invoke the context menu (if using the Simulator, move the mouse pointer over the watch simulator display and click and hold until the context menu appears). The context menu should appear as illustrated in Figure 20-9:

Figure 20-9

Selecting a menu item from the menu should dismiss the context menu and change the text on the Label object in the main scene to match the menu item selection.

20.11 Summary

The Force Touch technology built into the display of the Apple Watch is able to differentiate between a tap and a more forceful pressing motion on the device screen. When a force touch is detected by the device when an app is running the context menu associated with the current scene will be displayed. Each scene within a WatchKit app can have a single context menu, each of which can present up to four menu items available for selection by the user. Each menu item consists of an image and a title.

21. Working with Images in WatchKit

There are a number of factors that need to be taken into consideration when working with images within a WatchKit app such as whether the image can be included within the WatchKit app bundle or needs to be transferred from the iPhone to the Apple Watch device at runtime. Unlike iPhone based apps, the size of the images used within a WatchKit app is also of key importance, particularly when working with large image files.

The goal of this chapter is to explore the various options for managing and displaying images in a WatchKit app including topics such as image caching, named images, animation, image compression, asset catalogs and image templates.

21.1 Displaying Images in WatchKit Apps

WatchKit provides two ways in which images can be displayed within a WatchKit app. The first involves the use of the WKInterfaceImage interface object class. When added to the scene of a WatchKit app storyboard, this object can be used to display images to the user. Another option involves setting an image as a background on the WKInterfaceGroup, WKInterfaceButton and WKInterfaceController classes. In both scenarios, the image can be specified within the storyboard file or set dynamically from within the code of the interface controller at runtime.

Wherever possible, images should be in PNG or JPEG format and sized to match the display size of the interface object on which they are to be displayed. Whilst WatchKit is able to handle other image formats, Apple warns that app performance is likely to be impacted adversely when those images are rendered.

Images can be generated and stored within the WatchKit extension or included on the Apple Watch device as part of the WatchKit app bundle.

21.2 Images Originating in the WatchKit Extension

Whenever a UIImage object is created within the extension of a WatchKit app, that image is local to the iPhone device. The image contained within a UIImage object in a WatchKit extension can be displayed using the *setImage*, *setImageData*, *setBackgroundImage* and *setBackgroundImageData* methods of the interface object on which the image is to be displayed. The following code, for example, displays an image stored within a WatchKit extension onto a WKInterfaceImage object via an outlet connection named *myImage*:

```
let theImage = UIImage(named: "spaceship")
myImage.setImage(theImage)
```

At the point that the UIImage object is assigned to an interface object within the scene of a WatchKit app the image must be transmitted wirelessly to the Apple Watch device before it will be visible to the user. Depending on the size of the image this transfer can take a considerable amount of time.

To avoid such delays it is important to reduce the storage size of any image objects prior to displaying them within a WatchKit app. In fact, given the storage limitations of the Apple Watch device, this approach should be taken for all images.

An alternative to transferring image files from the iPhone to the watch device is to include image files as part of the WatchKit app bundle so that they are already installed on the watch device at the point that they need to be displayed to the user. Such images are referred to as *named images*.

21.3 Understanding Named Images

As previously outlined, whenever a UIImage object is created within the extension of a WatchKit app, that image is local to the iPhone device and must be transferred to the watch device before it can be displayed to the user.

Images that are bundled with the WatchKit app are referred to as *named images* and are displayed using the *setImageNamed* and *setBackgroundImageNamed* methods of the interface objects on which the image is to be displayed. The following code, for example, displays a named image as the background for a WKInterfaceGroup object instance:

```
myGroup.setBackgroundImageNamed("spaceship")
```

21.4 Adding Images to a WatchKit App

Images can be stored as part of the WatchKit app bundle or WatchKit extension by placing them in the target's *Images.xcassets* asset catalog. Figure 21-1, for example, highlights the image assets catalogs for WatchKit app and WatchKit extension targets within the Xcode project navigator panel:

Figure 21-1

When files are stored into the image asset catalog the file names should end with "@2x", for example *myimage@2x.png*. This indicates to the asset catalog that the images are suitable for display on the retina screen of the Apple Watch device family. For the purposes of an example, assume that we have a file named *spaceship@2x.png* and need to add this as a named image to the WatchKit app bundle image asset catalog. The first step would be to select the *Image.xcassets* catalog entry in the WatchKit app target as shown in Figure 21-2:

Figure 21-2

Making this selection will load the catalog into the main Xcode panel:

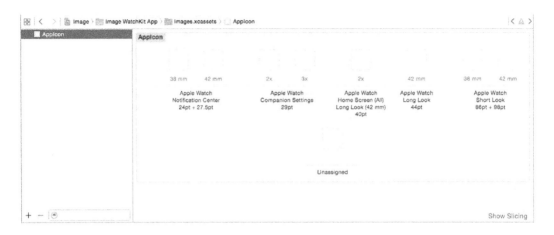

Figure 21-3

The left hand panel lists the *image sets* that are currently contained within the catalog. An image set collects together images in different sizes and resolutions. By default, the image asset catalog for a WatchKit app target contains a single image set named *AppIcon*. As the name suggests, this image set contains the icon used to represent the WatchKit app in a variety of locations such as the home screen and notification center.

To create a new image set for an image, simply locate the image in a Finder window and drag and drop it onto the image set panel as illustrated in Figure 21-4:

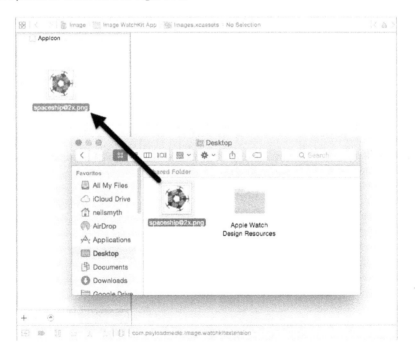

Figure 21-4

Multiple images may be imported by Ctrl-clicking within the image set panel, selecting the *Import...* menu option and navigating to the file system location containing the image files. If a folder is selected for import, all of the images in that folder will be imported into a single image set with a name reflecting that of the selected folder.

Once the image has been added, a new image set will be listed containing the 2x image. If this were an image set for an iOS app it would also be recommended to add 1x (for non-retina screens) and 3x (for iPhone 6 Plus and iPad devices) images to the image set. Since the Apple Watch has retina-only displays of similar sizes only the 2x image is required:

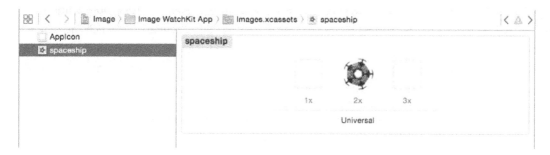

Figure 21-5

When referencing an image stored in an asset catalog, the "@2x" is dropped from the filename. With the image file named *spaceship@2x.png* contained in an image asset catalog for a WatchKit app target, the code to display this image on a WKInterfaceImage object would read as follows:

```
myImage.setImageNamed("spaceship")
```

21.5 Caching Extension-based Images on the Watch Device

As previously discussed, images either reside on the Apple Watch device or originate within the WatchKit extension and reside on the paired iPhone device. Images that reside on the iPhone device must be transferred to the watch device before they can be displayed to the user. This problem can be alleviated to a certain extent by bundling images as named images as part of the WatchKit app bundle. Situations may arise, however, where the images to be displayed are not known until app runtime such as when the image is selected or created dynamically within the WatchKit extension based on user activity. In this case, there is no option but to transfer the images to the device as the app is running. The impact of the transfer of images can be reduced by caching them on the watch prior to the point at which the images are needed.

Images can be cached onto the paired Apple Watch using the *addCachedImage* and *addCachedImageWithData* methods of the WKInterfaceDevice object. Each WatchKit app has 5MB of cache space available so caching should be used sparingly. When the cache for an app is exhausted, images must be removed using the *removeCachedImageWithName* or *removeAllCachedImages* methods of the WKInterfaceDevice object.

Once an image has been cached it is considered to be a *named image* and may be displayed using the standard named image methods. Once an image has been cached it will remain on the device until it is explicitly removed.

21.6 Compressing Large Images

Whilst caching is a useful way to store on the watch device frequently used images that originate in the WatchKit extension this still does not address the issue that it can take a considerable amount of time to transfer a large image from the iPhone to the Apple Watch. Consider a scenario in which the extension for a WatchKit app needs to display a photo that the user has taken using the iPhone camera. Transferring such an image could take over two minutes to transfer wirelessly from the iPhone to the watch. This is clearly an unacceptable amount of time to keep the user waiting.

In reality the image that is taken by the iPhone camera is orders of magnitude larger than is necessary to fit on the display of an Apple Watch. In fact, an image from the iPhone camera roll is measured in thousands of pixels while the display of even the largest Apple Watch model has a resolution of only 312 x 390 pixels. Clearly there is significant opportunity for reducing the size of any large images before they are transferred to the Apple Watch for display.

There are a number of options for reducing the size of any images both in terms of dimensions and storage space before the transfer to the watch takes place. The following code, for example, is useful for reducing the size of an image by a specified scale factor:

```
if let largeImage = UIImage(named: "myLargeImage") {

    let imageSize = largeImage.size
    let scale: CGFloat = 0.15 // Scale factor

    let reducedSize = CGSizeMake(imageSize.width * scale,
            imageSize.height * scale);

    UIGraphicsBeginImageContext(reducedSize)

    largeImage.drawInRect(CGRectMake(0, 0, reducedSize.width,
            reducedSize.height))

    let compressedImage = UIGraphicsGetImageFromCurrentImageContext()

    UIGraphicsEndImageContext()
```

```
myImage.setImage(compressedImage) // Display the image
}
```

In tests on an original PNG image file of 2448 x 3264 pixels with a size of 23MB the transfer time was reduced from approximately 3 minutes down to just 6 seconds after the image was compressed using the above code.

21.7 **Specifying the WKInterfaceImage Object Dimensions in Code**

When a WKInterfaceImage interface object is added to a storyboard scene using Interface Builder the dimensions of the object can be specified from within the Attributes Inspector panel (Figure 21-6). Options are available to allow the object to resize to accommodate the assigned image content, to size relative to the container in which the interface object is located, or to specify fixed height and width dimensions:

Figure 21-6

It is also possible to specify fixed height and width properties for a WKInterfaceImage object from within the code of the corresponding interface controller class. This involves establishing an outlet connection to the image object and making calls to the *setHeight* and *setWidth* methods of that instance, for example:

```
myImage.setHeight(100)
myImage.setWidth(170)
```

21.8 **Displaying Animated Images**

The WKInterfaceImage interface object is able to display animated images. This animation takes the form of a sequence of images with each image representing a single frame of the animation. To create an animation sequence, the image files should be added to the project (preferably bundled with the WatchKit app as named images) using a file naming convention of *name<sequence number>.png* (for example animation0.png, animation1.png, animation2.png and so on).

The way in which the sequence of animation images is converted into a single animation image and displayed to the user depends on whether the images are bundled with the WatchKit app as named images (the recommended approach for better performance), or reside on the iPhone as part of the extension.

If the animation images are bundled as named images within the WatchKit app, the animated image can be created and displayed using the *setImageNamed* method of the WKInterfaceImage instance, passing through the image file name prefix. Assuming a set of animation images named animation<*image number*>.png bundled with the WatchKit app, the animation would be displayed on a WKInterfaceImage instance with a single line of code as follows:

```
myImage.setImageNamed("animation")
```

When executed, the above method call collects together all of the appropriately named animation sequence images and uses them to create a single animated UIImage object which is then displayed on the corresponding WKInterfaceImage object.

In the case of extension-based animation images, an animated UIImage object must first be created using the *animatedImageNamed* method of the UIImage class which is then assigned to the WKInterfaceImage object via the object's *setImage* method. For example:

```
let animatedImage = UIImage.animatedImageNamed("animation",
            duration: 20)

myImage.setImage(animatedImage)
```

Once the animated image has been displayed, the *startAnimating* method of the WKInterfaceImage object can be used to begin the animation:

```
myImage.startAnimating()
```

The animation may be customized in terms of duration, repetition and the range of images used within the animation sequence using the *startAnimatingWithImagesInRange* method. The following code customizes an animation to use images from positions 1 through 4 of the image sequence with a 6 second duration and 2 repetitions:

```
myImage.startAnimatingWithImagesInRange(NSRange(location: 1,
                    length: 4), duration: 6, repeatCount: 2)
```

An animation sequence may be stopped at any time via a call to the *stopAnimating* method:

```
myImage.stopAnimating()
```

The implementation of animation within a WatchKit app will be covered in greater detail in the next chapter entitled *A WatchKit Animated Image Tutorial*.

21.9 Template Images and Tinting

Images contained within an image asset catalog may be designated as *template images*. When an image is configured as a template image all color information in the image is ignored and the graphic displayed is defined by the stencil that is created by the transparent areas of the image in relation to the non-transparent areas. In Figure 21-7, for example, the rocket image is drawn against a transparent background:

Figure 21-7

When configured as a template image, the colored, non-transparent area of the image is filled with a solid color (light blue by default) creating the stencil image shown in Figure 21-8:

Figure 21-8

To specify that an image is to be rendered as a template, select the image in the asset catalog, display the Attributes Inspector panel and change the *Render As* menu to *Template Image*:

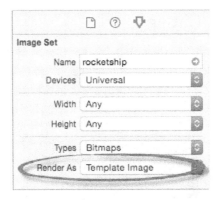

Figure 21-9

The default blue color used for the solid area of the image can be defined within Interface Builder by selecting the interface object on which the image is to be displayed and changing the *Tint* color setting. A tint color may also be assigned from within the interface controller code using the *setTintColor* method of the interface object, for example:

```
myImage.setTintColor(UIColor.redColor())
```

21.10 Summary

Images can be displayed within a WatchKit app scene either using an instance of the WKInterfaceImage class, or as a background image for WKInterfaceButton and WKInterfaceGroup classes. When images originate within the WatchKit extension they will be transferred wirelessly to the watch device before they are displayed to the user causing a time delay for larger images. This can be avoided by reducing image sizes or by including images as part of the WatchKit app bundle. Images included in the WatchKit app bundle are pre-installed in the Apple Watch device along with the app and are referred to as *named images*. As an alternative to named images, extension based images may be cached on the device so that they remain there for future app invocations.

In addition to static images, WatchKit also provides support for animated images, an example of which will be demonstrated in the next chapter.

22. A WatchKit Animated Image Tutorial

The previous chapter touched briefly on the subject of animated images within the context of a WatchKit app. This chapter will expand on this knowledge through the implementation of an example application that creates and displays an animated image within a WatchKit app scene.

22.1 Creating the Animation Example Project

Start Xcode and create a new iOS project. On the template screen choose the *Application* option located under *iOS* in the left hand panel and select *Single View Application.* Click *Next,* set the product name to *AnimationApp,* enter your organization identifier and make sure that the *Devices* menu is set to *Universal.* Before clicking *Next*, change the *Language* menu to Swift. On the final screen, choose a location in which to store the project files and click on *Create* to proceed to the main Xcode project window.

22.2 Adding the WatchKit App Target

Within Xcode, select the *File -> New -> Target…* menu option. In the target template dialog, select the *Apple Watch* option listed beneath the *iOS* heading. In the main panel, select the *WatchKit App* icon and click on *Next.* On the subsequent screen turn off the *Include Glance Scene* and *Include Notification Scene* options before clicking on the *Finish* button.

As soon as the extension target has been created, a new panel will appear requesting permission to activate the new scheme for the extension target. Activate this scheme now by clicking on the *Activate* button in the request panel.

22.3 Designing the Main Scene Layout

The only interface object required within the main WatchKit app scene is an Image object. Within the Xcode project navigator panel, locate and select the *Interface.storyboard* file so that it loads into the Interface Builder environment. Once loaded, locate the Image object in the Object Library panel and drag and drop it onto the main storyboard scene. With the newly added image object selected, display the Attributes Inspector and change both the *Horizontal* and *Vertical* position properties to *Center* so that the scene layout matches Figure 22-1:

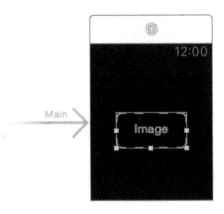

Figure 22-1

Display the Assistant Editor panel and establish an outlet connection from the Image object in the scene named *imageObject*.

22.4 Adding the Animation Sequence Images

The animation sequence in this example consists of 40 PNG image files, which combine to make up an animation of the planet Earth rotating. These files can be found in the *animation_images* folder of the sample code archive, available for download from the following link:

http://www.ebookfrenzy.com/print/watchkit/index.php

Locate and select the *Images.xcassets* entry listed under the *AnimationApp WatchKit App* folder within the Xcode Project Navigator panel. Ctrl-click in the left hand panel of the asset catalog and select the *Import...* option from the resulting menu. Within the file selection dialog, navigate to and select the *animation_images* folder and click on *Open*.

Once the images have been imported into the asset catalog a new image set will be created named *animation_images* containing all of the animation sequence images:

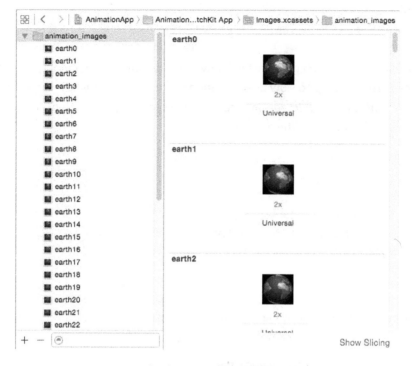

Figure 22-2

With the images added to the asset catalog, all that remains is to add some code in the interface controller class to create and initiate the animation.

22.5 Creating and Starting the Animated Image

Locate and edit the *InterfaceController.swift* file and modify the *awakeWithContext* method to create and display the animation image:

```
override func awakeWithContext(context: AnyObject?) {
    super.awakeWithContext(context)

    imageObject.setImageNamed("earth")
}
```

Compile and run the WatchKit app and note that image 0 appears but that the image object does not animate through the remaining frames. Modify the code further to start the animation sequence:

```
override func awakeWithContext(context: AnyObject?) {
    super.awakeWithContext(context)

    imageObject.setImageNamed("animation")
```

```
        imageObject.startAnimating()
    }
```

When the app is re-launched the image object will now cycle rapidly and repeatedly through the animation frames showing the Earth rotating. To slow the animation down, the *startAnimating* method can be replaced with a call to the *startAnimatingWithImagesInRange* method specifying a duration, repeat count and a range that encompasses all of the images in the animation:

```
override func awakeWithContext(context: AnyObject?) {
    super.awakeWithContext(context)

    imageObject.setImageNamed("animation")
    imageObject.startAnimatingWithImagesInRange(NSRange(location: 0,
        length: 40), duration: 7, repeatCount: 2)
}
```

When the app is now run, the animation frames will be run more slowly so that the entire sequence takes 7 seconds to complete. The animation should also now stop after 2 repetitions. To configure the animation loop to repeat indefinitely simply change the *repeatCount* value to 0.

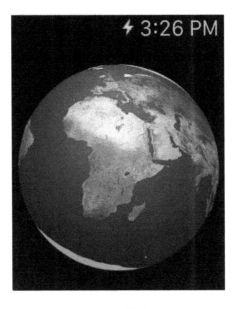

Figure 22-3

22.6 **Summary**

This chapter created a sample project that demonstrates the implementation of animated images within a WatchKit app. The tutorial covered the steps required to add animation sequence images to a WatchKit app target in Xcode and outlined the code required within the interface controller to convert those images to an animated image and display that animation to the user. The chapter also explored the different ways in which the animation may be customized in terms of duration, repetition and frame range.

23. Working with Fonts and Attributed Strings in WatchKit

Fonts are an important part of making a WatchKit app visually appealing and accessible to the user. WatchKit provides three options when making choices about the fonts to use within the scene of an app. These options consist of text style fonts, system fonts and custom fonts. The subject of custom fonts will be covered in detail in the next chapter entitled *A WatchKit App Custom Font Tutorial*. This chapter, however, will introduce the concepts of text styles and system fonts and outline how these can be used both from within Interface Builder and, through the use of attributed strings, via the code of an interface controller class.

23.1 Dynamic Text and Text Style Fonts

Apple Watch users are able to specify a preferred text size which WatchKit apps are expected to adopt when displaying text (also referred to as the *preferred content size*). The current text size can be configured via the Apple Watch app on the paired iPhone device. To access this setting, launch the Apple Watch app, select the *My Watch* tab followed by the *Brightness & Text Size* option. As shown in Figure 23-1, options are provided on this screen to adjust the font size and use bold text.

Almost without exception, the built-in WatchKit apps adopt the font size setting selected by the user when displaying text. Apple also recommends that third-party apps conform to the user's text size selection wherever possible. WatchKit specifies a variety of different preferred text styles for this purpose including headings, sub-headings, body, captions and footnotes. The text style used by an interface object in a scene can be configured either using Interface Builder or in code.

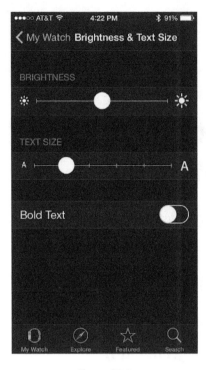

Figure 23-1

To configure the text style of an interface object in Interface Builder, select the interface object to which the style is to be applied, display the Attributes Inspector and click on the "T" button in the Font setting field. From the drop-down menu click on the Font menu button and select an item from the options listed under the *Text Styles* heading:

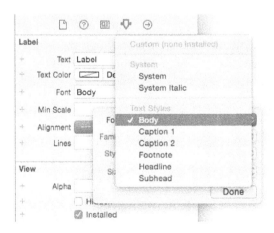

Figure 23-2

When the app is run, the text on the interface object on which the font setting was made will be displayed using the font for the selected text style and sized according to the user's preferred content size category setting.

Behind the scenes, the text style selections are translated to fonts from Apple's San Francisco Font Family. The Headline text style, for example, is displayed using the San Francisco Text font.

23.2 Using Text Style Fonts in Code

A text style font may be retrieved and used from within the code of an interface controller class using the *preferredFontForTextStyle* method of the UIFont class, passing through one of the following pre-configured text style values:

- UIFontTextStyleHeadline
- UIFontTextStyleSubheadline
- UIFontTextStyleBody
- UIFontTextStyleFootnote
- UIFontTextStyleCaption1
- UIFontTextStyleCaption2

The following code, for example, retrieves a Headline text style font object:

```
let headlineFont =
        UIFont.preferredFontForTextStyle(UIFontTextStyleHeadline)
```

When executed, the above code will request the preferred headline style font from the system. The method call will return a UIFont object configured with the headline font sized to match the user's current preferred content size category setting.

Having obtained the preferred font, the next step is to use the font to render the text displayed on a Label or Button interface object. As will be outlined in the next section, this involves the use of *attributed strings*.

23.3 Understanding Attributed Strings

To display text within a WatchKit app using a particular font it is necessary to use an attributed string. Attributed strings are represented using the NSAttributedString and NSMutableAttributedString classes and allow text to be combined with attributes such as fonts and colors.

Having obtained a font object as outlined in the previous section, the next task is to create a Dictionary object with a key set to *NSFontAttributeName* and the font object as the value. This dictionary is then used to specify the attributes for an NSAttributedString instance. The following code, for example, obtains a font object for the headline text style and uses it to create an attributed string that reads "Apple Watch":

```
let headlineFont =
        UIFont.preferredFontForTextStyle(UIFontTextStyleHeadline)

let fontAttribute = [NSFontAttributeName : headlineFont]

let attributedString = NSAttributedString(string: "Apple Watch",
            attributes: fontAttribute)
```

Once an attributed string has been created, it can be applied to Button and Label interface objects using the *setAttributedTitle* and *setAttributedText* methods respectively. The following code, for example, displays the *attributedString* text from the above example on a Label object:

```
myLabel.setAttributedText(attributedString)
```

When executed, text which reads "Apple Watch" will be rendered on the label referenced by the *myLabel* outlet using the headline font style sized according to the user's preferred content size setting as shown in Figure 23-3:

Figure 23-3

The above example uses an attributed string to set one attribute for the entire text string. In practice, attributed strings can contain multiple attributes covering different ranges of characters within the string. Multiple attributes within an attributed string require the use of the NSMutableAttributedString class. Once an instance of this class has been created and initialized with a string, the *addAttribute* method may be called to add attributes for ranges of characters in the string. For the purposes of the example project, this approach will be used to change the colors used to render the words "Apple" and "Watch" in the label in Figure 23-3. The code to achieve this reads as follows:

```
let headlineFont =
        UIFont.preferredFontForTextStyle(UIFontTextStyleHeadline)

let fontAttribute = [NSFontAttributeName : headlineFont]

let attributedText = NSMutableAttributedString(
                        string: "Apple Watch",
                        attributes: fontAttribute)

let firstRange = NSRange(location: 0, length: 5)
let secondRange = NSRange(location: 6, length: 5)

attributedText.addAttribute(
                    NSForegroundColorAttributeName,
                    value: UIColor.greenColor(),
                    range: firstRange)

attributedText.addAttribute(
                    NSForegroundColorAttributeName,
                    value: UIColor.redColor(),
                    range: secondRange)

myLabel.setAttributedText(attributedText)
```

The above code creates a mutable attributed string using the headline text style font. Two range objects are then created and initialized to encompass the first and second words of the "Apple Watch" text. These ranges are then used when adding color attributes to the string.

When the example is now run, the words displayed on the label will be rendered in green and red.

23.4 Using System Fonts

The system fonts use the same Apple San Francisco font family as the text style font options outlined earlier in this chapter. Unlike text styles, however, system fonts allow attributes such as point size and style (italic, bold etc) to be selected. System font sizes, however, are not subject to the prevailing preferred content size category setting and should be used only when the required results cannot be achieved using text style fonts.

As with text style fonts, system fonts may be selected at design-time within Interface Builder, or specified dynamically in the code of an interface controller.

To select a system font in Interface Builder, select the interface object to which the font is to be applied, display the Attributes Inspector and click on the "T" button in the Font setting field. From the drop-down menu, click on the Font menu button and select either the *System* or *System Italic* option from the options listed under the *System* heading as shown in Figure 23-4:

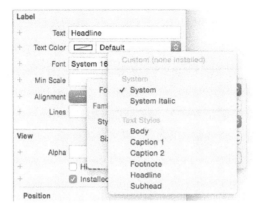

Figure 23-4

Once a system font setting has been selected, a variety of options are available to configure the size and appearance of the font when used to render text. In Figure 23-5, for example, the range of style selections is displayed in the Attribute Inspector font menu:

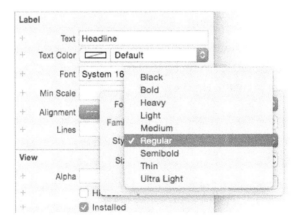

Figure 23-5

As with text style fonts, system font objects can be obtained by making calls to methods of the UIFont class, specifying as a parameter the required point size of the font. Among the system font methods supported by the UIFont class are methods to obtain regular, bold and italic font objects of a specified point size:

```
// Returns a regular 12 pt system font
let regularFont = UIFont.systemFontOfSize(12)
```

```
// Returns an italic 14 pt system font
let italicFont = UIFont.italicSystemFontOfSize(14)

// Returns a bold 16 pt system font
let boldFont = UIFont.boldSystemFontOfSize(16)
```

As with text style fonts, a system font object can be used when rendering text within a WatchKit app scene through the use of attributed strings.

23.5 Summary

WatchKit provides support for text style, system and custom fonts. Text style fonts are referenced by style (body, headline, sub-heading etc) and are tailored automatically by the UIFont class to match the user's preferred content size category setting.

System fonts, on the other hand, use the same font family as text style fonts but allow the selection of style and point size attributes. System fonts are not subject to the user's preferred content size setting and, as such, should be used only when the desired results cannot be achieved using text styles.

When using fonts in WatchKit app code, it is necessary to use attributed strings to incorporate the font in the text string being displayed. The use of mutable attributed strings allows multiple attributes such as fonts and colors to be included in a single string.

24. A WatchKit App Custom Font Tutorial

WatchKit provides a set of built-in "system" fonts available for use when displaying text within a WatchKit app. In addition to these system fonts it is also possible to install and use custom fonts within a WatchKit app user interface. This chapter will present the steps involved in installing and using a custom font within a WatchKit app project.

24.1 Using Custom Fonts in WatchKit

The system fonts supported by WatchKit can be selected at design time from the Font menu (Figure 24-1) which can be found in the Attributes Inspector when an interface object containing text is selected in the storyboard scene.

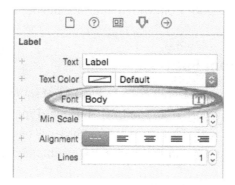

Figure 24-1

When custom fonts are bundled with the project they can be applied to interface objects by clicking on the "T" icon in the Font field and, in the resulting panel, clicking on the current Font setting and selecting the *Custom* option (Figure 24-2) from the resulting menu. If the *Custom* option is not selectable then custom fonts have yet to be added to the project:

Figure 24-2

Custom fonts may also be applied to text at runtime from within the interface controller class of a scene through the use of *attributed strings*. Custom fonts cannot, however, be used within Notification and Glance scenes.

The remainder of this chapter will work through a tutorial that demonstrates how custom fonts can be added to a WatchKit app project and used both from within Interface Builder and within the code of an interface controller class.

24.2 Downloading a Custom Font

Fonts are supplied in *font files* and can be obtained from a variety of sources at a range of prices including for free. WatchKit and iOS currently support TrueType (.ttf) and OpenType (.otf) formats. For the purposes of this example the Sofia font bundled with the sample code archive will be used as the custom font. If you have not already downloaded the sample code for the book it can be obtained from the following URL:

http://www.ebookfrenzy.com/print/watchkit/index.php

Once the package has been downloaded and unpacked, navigate in a Finder window to the *custom_font* folder which contains the *Sofia-Regular.otf* file as outlined in Figure 24-3:

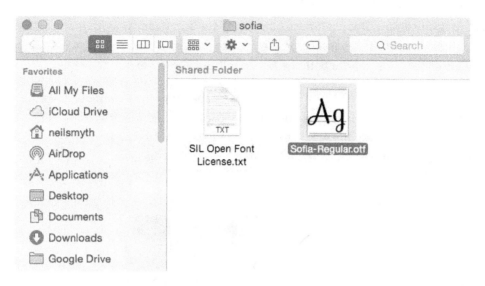

Figure 24-3

This font file will be added to the WatchKit app project later in this chapter so keep the Finder window open.

24.3 Creating the Custom Font Project

Start Xcode and create a new iOS project. On the template screen choose the *Application* option located under *iOS* in the left hand panel and select *Single View Application.* Click *Next,* set the product name to *CustomFont,* enter your organization identifier and make sure that the *Devices* menu is set to *Universal.* Before clicking *Next*, change the *Language* menu to Swift. On the final screen, choose a location in which to store the project files and click on *Create* to proceed to the main Xcode project window.

24.4 Adding the WatchKit App Target

For the purposes of this example we will, once again, assume that the iOS app has already been implemented. The next step, therefore, is to add the WatchKit app target to the project. Within Xcode, select the *File -> New -> Target...* menu option. In the target template dialog, select the *Apple Watch* option listed beneath the *iOS* heading. In the main panel, select the *WatchKit App* icon and click on *Next.* On the subsequent screen turn off the *Include Glance Scene* and *Include Notification Scene* options before clicking on the *Finish* button.

As soon as the extension target has been created, a new panel will appear requesting permission to activate the new scheme for the extension target. Activate this scheme now by clicking on the *Activate* button in the request panel.

24.5 Designing the WatchKit App Scene

Within the Project Navigator panel, locate and select the *Interface.storyboard* file located under the *CustomFont WatchKit App* folder so that it loads into the Interface Builder environment. From the Object

Library panel, drag and drop a Group interface object onto the scene canvas. With the Group object selected in the scene, display the Attributes Inspector and change the *Layout* property to *Vertical*. In the Position section of the attributes panel change both the *Horizontal* and *Vertical* menus to *Center*.

Drag and drop two Label objects from the Object Library panel onto the Group object in the scene layout. Double-click on the upper label and change the text so it reads "Hello". Shift-click on each Label object so that both are selected and, within the Attributes Inspector panel, change the *Horizontal* position property to *Center*. On completion of these steps, verify that the scene matches the layout shown in Figure 24-4:

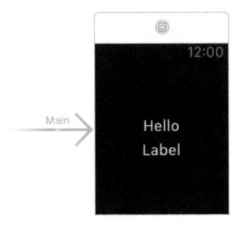

Figure 24-4

The last task to perform within Interface Builder is to establish an outlet connection on the second Label object. Display the Assistant Editor panel, verify that it is displaying the content of the *InterfaceController.swift* file and Ctrl-click and drag from the lower Label to a position immediately beneath the class declaration line in the editor panel. On releasing the line use the connection dialog to establish an outlet named *labelObject*.

24.6 Adding the Custom Font to the Project

There are two steps to integrating a custom font into a WatchKit app. The first step is to add the font file to the project. For the purposes of this example, the *Sofia-Regular* font will be used. Locate this font in the Finder window and drag and drop it onto the *Supporting Files* folder located beneath the *CustomFont WatchKit App* entry in the Xcode project navigator.

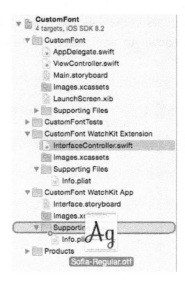

Figure 24-5

Since the font will need to be accessible to both the WatchKit App and the extension, make sure that both targets are selected in the options panel (Figure 24-6) before clicking on the *Finish* button:

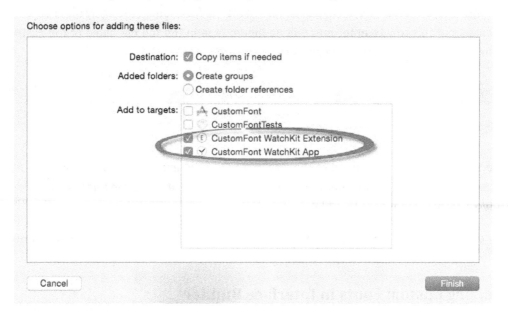

Figure 24-6

In addition to adding the font file to the project and configuring the targets, an entry for the font needs to be added to the *Info.plist* files for both the WatchKit app and extension targets. Begin by selecting the *Info.plist* file located in the *Supporting Files* section of the *CustomFont WatchKit App* folder in the Project Navigator panel. Once the file has loaded into the property list editor, select the last row in the list so that it highlights in blue. Click on the + button that appears in the selected row to add a new entry to the list. From the dropdown menu that appears, scroll down to and select the *Fonts provided by application* option as illustrated in Figure 24-7:

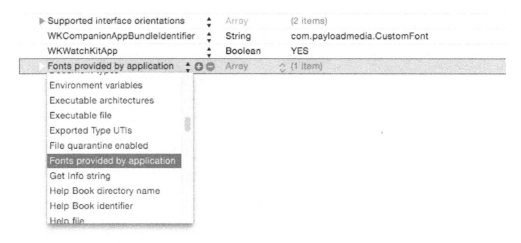

Figure 24-7

Click on the arrow to the left of the newly added row to list the first item in the array of fonts. Double click in the *Value* column of this row to enter into editing mode, type in the full file name of the custom font file including the .otf filename extension and press the keyboard Enter key:

Figure 24-8

The same entry also needs to be added to the *Info.plist* file of the extension target. Select the *Info.plist* file from the *Supporting Files* entry listed under the *CustomFont WatchKit Extension* folder and repeat the above steps to add an entry for the same font file.

With these steps completed it should now be possible to begin using the custom font within the WatchKit app.

24.7 Selecting Custom Fonts in Interface Builder

Once a custom font has been integrated into an Xcode project it should be listed as an option from within the Attributes Inspector panel. To verify this, open the *Interface.storyboard* file, select the upper Label object and display the Attributes Inspector. Click on the "T" icon in the Font field. In the resulting panel, click on the *Font* entry and select *Custom* from the popup menu. With the custom font option selected, the Sofia Regular font should be listed as outlined in Figure 24-9:

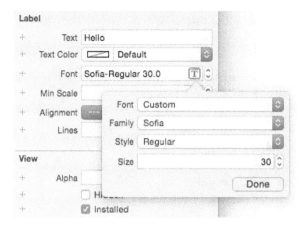

Figure 24-9

Set the *Size* property to 35 points and click on the *Done* button. Refer to the storyboard scene where the "Hello" text should now have been rendered using the custom font selection:

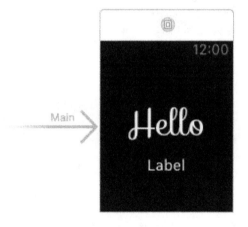

Figure 24-10

24.8 Using Custom Fonts in Code

Custom fonts can also be used in conjunction with attributed string objects to display text at run time from within the interface controller class of a storyboard scene. The technique will now be used to display some text on the second label using the same Sofia custom font.

As previously outlined in the chapter entitled *Working with Fonts and Attributed Strings in WatchKit*, attributed strings are represented using the NSAttributedString and NSMutableAttributedString classes and allow text to be combined with attributes such as fonts and colors. To begin with, a reference to the custom font needs to be obtained. This is achieved using the UIFont class and referencing the font name. Select the

InterfaceController.swift file and modify the *awakeWithContext* method as follows to create a UIFont object using the custom font:

```
override func awakeWithContext(context: AnyObject?) {
    super.awakeWithContext(context)

    if let customFont = UIFont(name:
            "Sofia-Regular", size: 22) {
    } else {
        println("Font not found")
    }
}
```

The above code attempts to create a font object using the custom Sofia font with a 22pt size and outputs a message in the event that the font could not be found.

The next task is to create a Dictionary object with a key set to *NSFontAttributeName* and the custom font object as the value. This dictionary is then used to specify the attributes for an NSAttributedString instance containing text which reads "Apple Watch". This string is then displayed on the Label object via the previously configured outlet connection:

```
override func awakeWithContext(context: AnyObject?) {
    super.awakeWithContext(context)

    if let customFont = UIFont(name:
            "Sofia-Regular", size: 22) {
        let fontAttributes = [NSFontAttributeName : customFont]

        let attributedText = NSAttributedString(string: "Apple Watch",
                attributes: fontAttributes)

        labelObject.setAttributedText(attributedText)
    } else {
        println("Font not found")
    }
}
```

Compile and run the WatchKit app at which point the second label should display the "Apple Watch" text using the custom font at the designated size:

Figure 24-11

24.9 **Summary**

WatchKit includes a set of system fonts which can be used when displaying text within a WatchKit app scene. Additional fonts may be added to a project as *custom fonts*. This is a process which involves the addition of the font file to the project and the configuration of the Info.plist property files for both the WatchKit app and the extension. Once a custom font has been incorporated into a project it is available both for selection within Interface Builder and as a rendering option from within the code of an interface controller.

When using custom fonts in code, it is necessary to use attributed strings to incorporate the font in the text string being displayed.

Chapter 25

25. Supporting Different Apple Watch Display Sizes

The Apple Watch family currently consists of two sizes of device in the form of 38mm and 42mm models. Although the difference in screen sizes between the two models is a mere 4mm, this is sufficient difference that a scene layout that fits perfectly on a 42mm Apple Watch may not fit on the 38mm model. It will frequently be necessary, therefore, to have different user interface layout attributes for each Apple Watch model. In addition to handling different screen sizes, a WatchKit app may also optionally display text using the user's preferred font size setting.

Fortunately both the WatchKit framework and Interface Builder tool make it relatively easy to adapt scene layouts to accommodate different screen sizes and font preference settings.

25.1 Screen Size Customization Attributes

Attributes are set on user interface objects within Interface Builder by selecting the object in the storyboard scene and making changes in the Attributes Inspector panel. By default, attributes set in this way are applied to the scene when running on both sizes of Apple Watch. While designing WatchKit app scenes it is quite common, however, to need to specify a different attribute value for the 38mm screen than for the 42mm screen. Fortunately, the Attributes Inspector panel provides a mechanism for configuring *screen size customization attributes*. These are attributes that will be applied to the selected interface object only when the app is run on a specific screen size.

Attributes that are eligible to have screen size customization values configured appear within the Attributes Inspector panel with a small "+" button positioned in the left margin as highlighted in Figure 25-1:

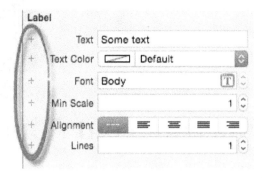

Figure 25-1

When clicked, these buttons display a menu (Figure 25-2) allowing a screen size to be selected:

Figure 25-2

Once a screen size customization attribute has been added to an interface object it appears as an additional option within the Attributes Inspector panel. Figure 25-3, for example, shows a font setting customization attribute that configures a label object to use a smaller font size when the app runs on a 38mm Apple Watch:

Figure 25-3

The general rule with customization attributes is that the default setting is applied on all screen sizes unless specifically overridden by a customization attribute. In the above figure, for example, the label will display text using the 16pt system font on the 42mm watch model. When running on the smaller 38mm watch model, however, the 14pt customization font attribute will be used. It is worth noting that it is not necessary to also add a customization attribute for the 42mm font setting since this is covered by the default value.

25.2 Working with Screen Sizes in Interface Builder

By default, the storyboard editor in Interface Builder displays storyboard scenes in *Any Screen Size* mode. When in this mode, interface objects are displayed using the default attributes. To see how the scenes within a storyboard will appear on different screen sizes, this mode can be changed using the selection at the bottom of the storyboard editor panel as shown in Figure 25-4:

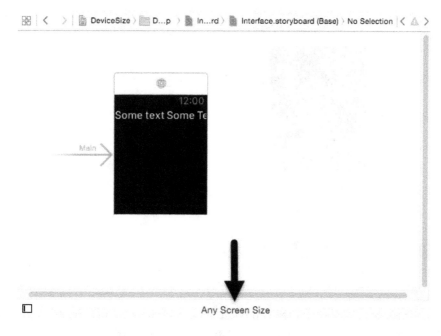

Figure 25-4

Clicking on the button displays a menu of screen size options which, when selected, change the mode of the storyboard canvas to match the chosen screen size.

When a specific screen size mode is selected in Interface Builder the scenes in the canvas will update to reflect the size of the screen. In addition, the interface objects within the scenes will change to reflect any customization attributes that have been set for the selected screen size. This allows you to review the user interface layout as it will appear when running on the designated Apple Watch model.

A more significant point to note about changing the storyboard screen size mode is that any changes made to the scene layout will apply only for the current screen size. Consider, for example, a scene containing a label. If the storyboard editor is in 38mm mode when the text of the label is changed within the scene then that change only applies to the layout when the app is running on a 38mm device. In other words, visually manipulating the objects and layout when the storyboard editor is set for a specific screen size essentially configures screen size customization attributes which also appear within the Attributes Inspector panel.

In Figure 25-5, for example, the text displayed on a label has been changed to read "My 42mm Text" from within the scene canvas while the storyboard editor is in 42mm mode. Note that as a result of this change a matching 42mm screen size customization attribute for the text property is now listed in the Attributes Inspector panel:

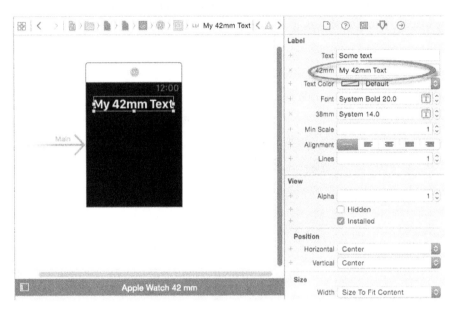

Figure 25-5

Clearly, screen size customization attributes can be configured both manually by adding custom attributes via the Attributes Inspector panel and visually from within the storyboard editor by changing the screen size mode and directly manipulating the interface objects.

When the storyboard editor is in any mode other than *Any Screen Size*, the toolbar at the bottom of the canvas is displayed in blue. This is intended as a subtle reminder that any changes made in this mode will apply only to the currently selected screen size. This includes the addition and deletion of interface objects from the canvas.

As a general rule, screen size customization attributes should be used only when a default setting will not work for both screen sizes. A useful approach is to choose a screen size as the baseline for the layout (for example the 42mm size) and design the user interface using default attributes. The layout can then be adapted for the smaller screen size by overriding the default settings only where necessary for the 38mm screen.

Apple also recommends changing the layout as little as possible between screen sizes to ensure a consistent look to the app on different devices. Drastic alterations that significantly change the appearance of the app user interface from one screen size to another should be avoided.

25.3 Identifying the Screen Size at Runtime

When developing WatchKit apps it is often necessary to make dynamic changes to the interface objects in a scene at runtime. Clearly such changes need to take into consideration the size of the screen on which the app is currently running. This can be achieved using the WKInterfaceDevice class. This class provides interface controllers with access to information about the watch device such as the size of the screen.

The first step in obtaining the current screen size is to get a reference to the current device object as follows:

```
let sharedDevice = WKInterfaceDevice.currentDevice()
```

Once a reference to the shared device object has been obtained the screen bounds property can be accessed:

```
let bounds = device.screenBounds
```

The bounds property is stored as a CGRect value from which the height and width dimensions of the screen can be accessed:

```
let height = bounds.height
let width = bounds.width
```

The screen dimension of the two Apple Watch models are as follows:

- Apple Watch 38mm – Height: 170 / Width: 136
- Apple Watch 42mm – Height: 195 / Width: 156

25.4 Summary

Although limited to two display sizes, steps will often still need to be taken to customize aspects of a scene layout to accommodate both the 38mm and 42mm Apple Watch models. This chapter has outlined the features of Interface Builder that are designed specifically for the purpose of creating scene layouts that adapt to the display size of the device on which the app is running.

Chapter 26

26. A WatchKit Map Tutorial

WatchKit currently provides limited support for displaying maps within an app running on an Apple Watch device. The features offered by the WKInterfaceMap class consist of the ability to display a designated map region and to add annotations in the form of colored pins or custom images at specified locations within the defined region. When tapped by the user, the Map object opens the built-in Apple Watch Map app configured to display the same region.

The remainder of this chapter will work through a basic tutorial designed to highlight some of the key features of the WKInterfaceMap class. The project will demonstrate the use of the parent iOS app to obtain current location information in the background and use it to display the current location within a WatchKit app.

26.1 Creating the Example Map Project

Start Xcode and create a new iOS project. On the template screen choose the *Application* option located under *iOS* in the left hand panel and select *Single View Application.* Click *Next,* set the product name to *MapDemoApp,* enter your organization identifier and make sure that the *Devices* menu is set to *Universal.* Before clicking *Next*, change the *Language* menu to Swift. On the final screen, choose a location in which to store the project files and click on *Create* to proceed to the main Xcode project window.

26.2 Adding the WatchKit App Target to the Project

Within Xcode, select the *File -> New -> Target...* menu option. In the target template dialog, select the *Apple Watch* option listed beneath the *iOS* heading. In the main panel, select the *WatchKit App* icon and click on *Next.* On the subsequent screen turn off the *Include Glance Scene* and *Include Notification Scene* options before clicking on the *Finish* button.

As soon as the extension target has been created, a new panel will appear requesting permission to activate the new scheme for the extension target. Activate this scheme now by clicking on the *Activate* button in the request panel.

26.3 Designing the WatchKit App User Interface

Select the *Interface.storyboard* file and drag and drop a Map and Slider object from the Object Library onto the scene canvas so that the layout matches that shown in Figure 26-1:

225

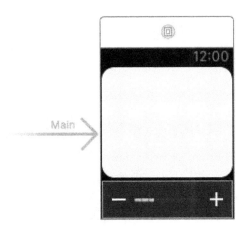

Figure 26-1

Select the Slider object, display the Attributes Inspector and configure the following property values:

- **Value:** 1
- **Minimum:** 1
- **Maximum:** 10
- **Steps:** 10

Display the Assistant Editor and establish an outlet connection from the Map object named *mapObject*. With the Assistant Editor still displayed, establish an action connection from the Slider object to a method named *changeMapRegion*.

26.4 **Configuring the Containing iOS App**

The rules of WatchKit app development dictate that tasks such as obtaining location information should be performed by the containing iOS app. In the case of this example, the containing iOS app will be required to identify the current location of the user and return that data to the WatchKit app extension. Before implementing this behavior, however, the iOS app target needs to be configured to enable access to location information.

Before any application can begin to track location information when running in the background it must first seek permission to do so from the user. This can be achieved by making a call to the *requestAlwaysAuthorization* method of the CLLocationManager instance. Since the iOS app will be launched in the background by the WatchKit app, it is essential that this method call be made within the iOS app.

Select the *AppDelegate.swift* file for the iOS app target and modify the code to import the CoreLocation framework, store a reference to the CLLocationManager instance and call the *requestAlwaysAuthorization* method within the *didFinishLaunchingWithOptions* method:

```
import UIKit
import CoreLocation

@UIApplicationMain
class AppDelegate: UIResponder, UIApplicationDelegate {

    var window: UIWindow?

    let locationManager = CLLocationManager()

    func application(application: UIApplication,
didFinishLaunchingWithOptions launchOptions: [NSObject: AnyObject]?) ->
Bool {

        locationManager.requestAlwaysAuthorization()
        return true
    }
    .
    .
}
```

The *requestAlwaysAuthorization* method call requires that a specific key-value pair be added to the Information Property List dictionary contained within the application's Info.plist file. The value takes the form of a string describing the reason why the application needs access to the user's current location. In the case of background access to location information, the *NSLocationAlwaysUsageDescription* key must be added to the property list.

Within the Project Navigator panel, load the *Info.plist* file (located under the *Supporting Files* section of the *MapDemoApp* iOS app target) into the editor. The key-value pair needs to be added to the *Information Property List* dictionary. Select this entry in the list and click on the + button to add a new entry to the dictionary. Within the new entry, enter *NSLocationAlwaysUsageDescription* into the key column and, once the key has been added, double-click in the corresponding value column and enter the following text:

```
This information is required to identify your current location
```

Once the entry has been added to the Info.plist file it should appear as illustrated in Figure 26-2:

Figure 26-2

The iOS app must now be run and the location tracking request approved. Select *MapDemoApp* in the Xcode run target menu and launch the iOS app on a device or simulator session. The first time that the app is launched, the system will request permission to track location information in the background (Figure 26-3). Tap the *Allow* button to enable this access.

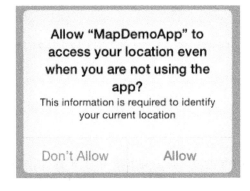

Figure 26-3

26.5 Enabling Background Location Updates

When it is opened by the WatchKit app, the containing iOS app will be launched in the background. The containing iOS app also needs to be configured, therefore, to allow background location updates to be received. To enable this mode, select the *MapDemoApp* target located at the top of the Project Navigator panel and make sure that the target menu in the settings panel is set to *MapDemoApp* as indicated in Figure 26-4:

Figure 26-4

Select the Capabilities tab and enable the *Background Modes* option. Once enabled, activate support for *Location updates* by selecting the corresponding checkbox:

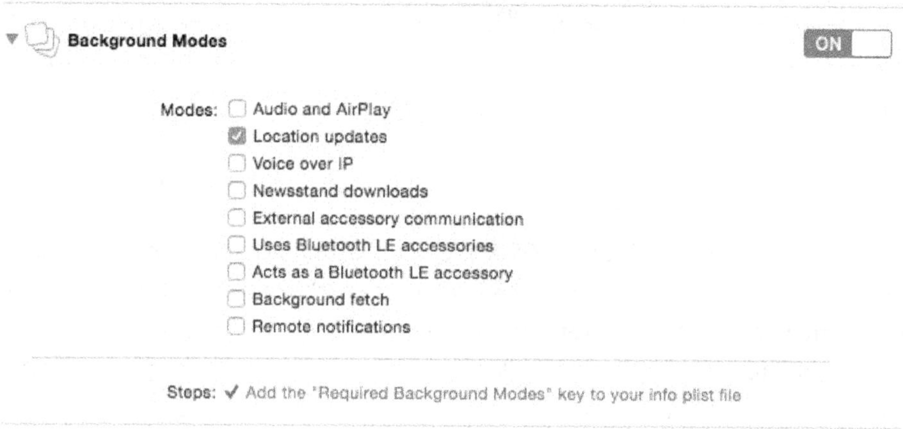

Figure 26-5

26.6 Handling the Open Parent App Request

The steps outlined in the chapter entitled *WatchKit App and Parent iOS App Communication* will now be used to launch the parent iOS app, obtain the user's current location and return that information to the WatchKit app extension.

The first step in this process is to implement the code in the app delegate of the iOS app to handle the launch request. Select the *AppDelegate.swift* file and begin by adding the *handleWatchKitExtensionRequest* method and declaring a variable in which to store the background request identifier value:

```
import UIKit
import CoreLocation

@UIApplicationMain
class AppDelegate: UIResponder, UIApplicationDelegate {

    var window: UIWindow?

    let locationManager = CLLocationManager()
    var bgIdentifier: UIBackgroundTaskIdentifier?

    func application(application: UIApplication,
            handleWatchKitExtensionRequest userInfo:
            [NSObject : AnyObject]?,
            reply: (([NSObject : AnyObject]!) -> Void)!) {
```

```
        bgIdentifier = application.beginBackgroundTaskWithName(
            "MyTask", expirationHandler: { () -> Void in
            println("Time expired")
        })
    }
    .
    .
    .
}
```

As discussed in the *WatchKit App and Parent iOS App Communication* chapter, one of the arguments passed through to the *handleWatchKitExtensionRequest* is a reference to the reply handler closure that is to be called in order to return data to the WatchKit extension. The mechanism for obtaining location data in iOS operates in a way that will require us to call the reply handler closure from within another method of the app delegate class. To make this possible, it will be necessary to store a reference to the closure handler reference in a variable where it can be accessed by other methods in the class. Remaining in the *AppDelegate.swift* file, therefore, add a variable configured with the signature of the closure and a line of code to store the reference as follows:

```
import UIKit
import CoreLocation

@UIApplicationMain
class AppDelegate: UIResponder, UIApplicationDelegate {

    var window: UIWindow?

    let locationManager = CLLocationManager()
    var bgIdentifier: UIBackgroundTaskIdentifier?
    var replyHandler: ([NSObject : AnyObject]!)->Void = {arg in}

    func application(application: UIApplication,
            handleWatchKitExtensionRequest userInfo:
            [NSObject : AnyObject]?,
            reply: (([NSObject : AnyObject]!) -> Void)!) {

        replyHandler = reply

        bgIdentifier = application.beginBackgroundTaskWithName(
            "MyTask", expirationHandler: { () -> Void in
            println("Time expired")
        })
```

```
        }
    .
    .
    .
}
```

26.7 Getting the Current Location

The next step is to instruct the location manager to begin receiving location updates. This involves declaring the AppDelegate class as implementing the CLLocationManagerDelegate protocol, assigning the class as the delegate for the location manager and starting the location update process:

```
    .
    .
    .
class AppDelegate: UIResponder, UIApplicationDelegate,
CLLocationManagerDelegate {

    var window: UIWindow?

    let locationManager = CLLocationManager()
    var bgIdentifier: UIBackgroundTaskIdentifier?
    var replyHandler:([NSObject : AnyObject]!)->Void = {arg in}

    func application(application: UIApplication,
            handleWatchKitExtensionRequest userInfo:
            [NSObject : AnyObject]?,
            reply: (([NSObject : AnyObject]!) -> Void)!) {

        replyHandler = reply

        bgIdentifier = application.beginBackgroundTaskWithName(
            "MyTask", expirationHandler: { () -> Void in
            println("Time expired")
        })
        locationManager.delegate = self
        locationManager.startUpdatingLocation()
    }
    .
    .
    .
}
```

Each time the location manager receives a location update, it will call the *didUpdateLocations* method on the delegate. This class now needs to be implemented in the *AppDelegate.swift* file as follows:

```
func locationManager(manager: CLLocationManager!, didUpdateLocations
locations: [AnyObject]!) {

    locationManager.stopUpdatingLocation()

    let currentLocation = locations[locations.count - 1]
                                    as? CLLocation

    var replyValues = Dictionary<String, AnyObject>()

    replyValues["latitude"] = currentLocation?.coordinate.latitude
    replyValues["longitude"] = currentLocation?.coordinate.longitude


    UIApplication.sharedApplication().endBackgroundTask(bgIdentifier!)

    replyHandler(replyValues)
}
```

The code begins by stopping location updates and accessing the most recent location data from the array of locations passed to the method. A Dictionary object is then created and entries added for the latitude and longitude of the current location. The system is then notified that the background task is complete before the reply handler is called via the previously declared reference variable passing through the dictionary containing the location data.

Work on the parent iOS app is now complete. All that remains is to add some code to the WatchKit extension to launch the parent app and display and manage the Map object based on the location data and the Slider object settings.

26.8 Implementing the WatchKit Extension Map Code

With the parent iOS app now adapted to handle an open request, the next step is to make a call to the *openParentApplication* method in the main interface controller class of the WatchKit app extension. Locate and select the *InterfaceController.swift* file and modify the *awakeWithContext* method to include a call to the *openParentApplication* method:

```
override func awakeWithContext(context: AnyObject?) {
    super.awakeWithContext(context)

    let parentValues = ["task" : "getLocation"]

    WKInterfaceController.openParentApplication(parentValues, reply: {
(replyValues, error) -> Void in
```

```
    })
}
```

Next, code needs to be added to the reply closure to extract the location data returned from the parent app and use it to configure the map object. This also requires the addition of a variable in which to store the user's current location information:

```
class InterfaceController: WKInterfaceController {

    @IBOutlet weak var mapObject: WKInterfaceMap!
    var mapLocation: CLLocationCoordinate2D?

    override func awakeWithContext(context: AnyObject?) {
        super.awakeWithContext(context)

        let parentValues = ["task" : "getLocation"]

        WKInterfaceController.openParentApplication(parentValues, reply: {
(replyValues, error) -> Void in

            let lat = replyValues["latitude"] as! Double
            let long = replyValues["longitude"] as! Double

            self.mapLocation = CLLocationCoordinate2DMake(lat, long)

            let span = MKCoordinateSpanMake(0.1, 0.1)
            let region = MKCoordinateRegionMake(self.mapLocation!,
                                                span)
            self.mapObject.setRegion(region)
            self.mapObject.addAnnotation(self.mapLocation!,
                    withPinColor: .Red)
        })

    }
    .
    .
}
```

The first task performed by the reply handler closure is to extract the latitude and longitude values from the reply dictionary object:

```
let lat = replyValues["latitude"] as! Double
```

```
let long = replyValues["longitude"] as! Double
```

These values are then used to create a CLLocationCoordinate2D object which is stored in the *mapLocation* variable:

```
self.mapLocation = CLLocationCoordinate2DMake(lat, long)
```

Next a span value is defined to dictate the area that will be covered by the map region. This is then used along with the current location to create the region that will be displayed by the map:

```
let span = MKCoordinateSpanMake(0.1, 0.1)
let region = MKCoordinateRegionMake(self.mapLocation!, span)
```

Finally, the map object is configured to display the region and a red pin added to mark the current location:

```
self.mapObject.setRegion(region)
self.mapObject.addAnnotation(self.mapLocation!, withPinColor: .Red)
```

The color of the pin is specified using the *WKInterfaceMapPinColor* constant which provides the following color options:

- WKInterfaceMapPinColor.Red
- WKInterfaceMapPinColor.Green
- WKInterfaceMapPinColor.Purple

With these changes made to the interface controller class, compile and run the WatchKit app which, when running, should display a map region centered around the user's current location as shown in Figure 26-6:

Figure 26-6

When running in the simulator, the location will be based on the current setting of the *Debug -> Location* menu.

26.9 Adding Zooming Support

A zooming effect can be added to a map by enlarging and reducing the currently displayed region. For the purposes of this example, the current region will be modified by the Slider object. Previously in this chapter the Slider object in the WatchKit app scene was connected to an action method named *changeMapRegion*. Edit the *InterfaceController.swift* file, locate this method and modify it as follows to change the region span based on the current slider setting:

```
@IBAction func changeMapRegion(value: Float) {

    let degrees:CLLocationDegrees = CLLocationDegrees(value) / 10

    let span = MKCoordinateSpanMake(degrees, degrees)
    let region = MKCoordinateRegionMake(mapLocation!, span)

    mapObject.setRegion(region)
}
```

Run the WatchKit app again and check that changes to the Slider object are reflected in the currently displayed map region giving the effect of zooming in and out of the map.

26.10 Summary

Maps are represented in WatchKit by the WKInterfaceMap class. This class is limited to displaying a static map region together with optional annotation markers in the form of pins or custom images. Tapping on the map launches the built-in Apple Watch Map app configured to display the same region where a wider range of options are available to the user.

This chapter has worked through the creation of an example project intended to highlight the basic features of the WKInterfaceMap class and to demonstrate the use of the parent iOS app in obtaining location data on behalf of the WatchKit app.

27. An Overview of Notifications in WatchKit

When an iOS app receives a notification, the operating system will decide whether the user should be notified of this event on the iPhone device or the paired Apple Watch device. If, for example, the iPhone is currently locked and the user has recently interacted with the Apple Watch, the notification will most likely be delivered to the watch.

Not all iOS apps receive notifications, of course, but for those that do it is important that the companion WatchKit app handle those notifications appropriately.

27.1 Default WatchKit Notification Handling

For many WatchKit apps it may not be necessary to make any changes to support notifications. In fact, the only step necessary to provide basic notification support for a WatchKit app is to add appropriately sized notification icons within the AppIcon image set of the WatchKit app bundle.

By default, if a notification arrives for an iOS app with a companion WatchKit app, the system will first decide whether to display the alert on the iPhone or the Apple Watch. In the event that the notification is delivered to the Apple Watch a "short-look" notification scene will first be displayed. This consists of the app icon, the title from the notification and the name of the WatchKit app.

A few seconds after the short-look notification has displayed, the long-look notification panel will appear. By default, this contains a smaller app icon, the name of the app, and the title and alert text from the notification. In addition, a Dismiss button is included which, when tapped, closes the notification and returns the user to the previous activity. Tapping anywhere else on the notification scene launches the WatchKit app associated with the notification. Figure 27-1, for example, shows a typical default long-look notification:

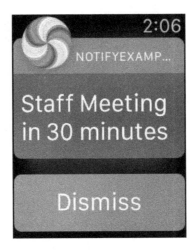

Figure 27-1

All of the default functionality outlined so far is provided without making any code changes to the WatchKit app. It is, however, possible to add additional capabilities to notification handling for the WatchKit app. Perhaps the most common requirement is the addition of *notification action* buttons.

27.2 Creating Notification Actions

Notifications within an iOS app can be configured to add action buttons which appear within the notification panel and, when tapped by the user, trigger application specific actions. If the iOS app has a companion WatchKit app, these same notification action buttons also appear within the long-look notification on the Apple Watch device. Figure 27-2, for example, shows a long-look notification which has been scrolled up to reveal two action buttons in addition to the default "Dismiss" button:

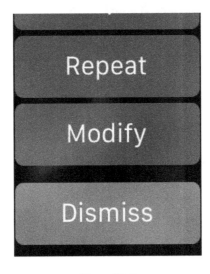

Figure 27-2

Notification actions are configured from within the code of the containing iOS app using a multi-step process. The code to configure the notification actions will need to be executed each time the iOS app runs, so is typically executed in the *didFinishLaunchingWithOptions* method of the application delegate class.

The first step in adding notification actions is to create a *notification action object* for each action to be added. Each notification action object is created as an instance of the UIMutableUserNotificationAction class which needs to be customized via a range of available properties:

- **identifier** – A string which uniquely identifies the action. This identifier will be referenced in the action handler code to ascertain which action was selected by the user.
- **title** – A string value containing the text that is to appear on the action button within the notification panel.
- **destructive** – A Boolean value indicating whether selection of the action will result in the loss of user data or input. When set to true, this causes the title string on the button to appear in red.
- **authentication** – A Boolean value indicating whether or not the user needs to unlock the device before the action can be performed.
- **activationMode** – Used to indicate whether the action should be performed in the foreground or background. In background mode the containing iOS app is launched in the background to perform the task. When a notification appears on the iPhone device, a foreground mode action causes the iOS app to be launched in the foreground. Selection of a foreground mode action when the notification is delivered to the Apple Watch causes the WatchKit app to be launched.

The following code demonstrates the creation of two notification actions, one configured for background mode and the other for foreground mode:

```
var repeatAction = UIMutableUserNotificationAction()
repeatAction.identifier = "REPEAT_IDENTIFIER"
repeatAction.title = "Repeat"
repeatAction.destructive = false
repeatAction.authenticationRequired = false
repeatAction.activationMode =
            UIUserNotificationActivationMode.Background

var modifyAction = UIMutableUserNotificationAction()
modifyAction.identifier = "MODIFY_IDENTIFIER"
modifyAction.title = "Modify"
modifyAction.destructive = false
modifyAction.authenticationRequired = false
modifyAction.activationMode =
        UIUserNotificationActivationMode.Foreground
```

Once the notification action objects have been created, they need to be packaged into a *notification category object* in the form of an instance of the UIMutableUserNotificationCategory class. As with the notification actions, the category object must have assigned to it a unique identifier string. The following code creates a new notification category containing the above notification action objects:

```
var notificationCategory = UIMutableUserNotificationCategory()

notificationCategory.identifier = "REMINDER_CATEGORY"
notificationCategory.setActions([repeatAction, modifyAction],
            forContext: UIUserNotificationActionContext.Default)
```

Finally, the notification category needs to be bundled into a UIUserNotificationSettings object along with any other required settings and registered with the notification system using the *registerUserNotificationSettings* method of the iOS application's UIApplication instance:

```
let settings = UIUserNotificationSettings(forTypes:
                UIUserNotificationType.Sound
            | UIUserNotificationType.Alert
            | UIUserNotificationType.Badge,
                categories: NSSet(array: [notificationCategory])
                    as Set<NSObject>)

application.registerUserNotificationSettings(settings)
```

27.3 Handling Notification Actions

Notifications are categorized as being either local or remote. A local notification is typically initiated from within the containing iOS app. A remote notification, on the other hand, is sent over the internet to the iPhone from a remote server.

As previously outlined, a notification can appear either on the iPhone device or the paired Apple Watch. When a notification action on an Apple Watch is selected by the user, the handler method that gets called will depend on whether the notification was remote or local in origin and whether the notification action was configured for background or foreground mode.

When a remote notification appears on the Apple Watch and the user selects a background notification action, the following method is called on the application delegate of the containing iOS app:

application:handleActionWithIdentifier:forRemoteNotification:completionHandler:

If the notification is local, however, the following method will be called on the app delegate of the containing iOS app when a background action is selected:

application:handleActionWithIdentifier:forLocalNotification:completionHandler:

When a remote notification appears on the Apple Watch and the user selects a foreground notification action, the WatchKit app will launch and the following method on the main interface controller will be called:

handleActionWithIdentifier:forRemoteNotification:

The same scenario involving a local notification on the Apple Watch will result in the following method being called on the main interface controller:

handleActionWithIdentifier:forLocalNotification:

The topics of WatchKit notification handling and action notifications will be covered in further detail in the next chapter (*A WatchKit Notification Tutorial*).

27.4 **Custom Notifications**

The previously outlined default notification handling within WatchKit is somewhat limited in terms of customization options. While it is possible to add action buttons to the notification when it is displayed to the user, there is no control of the layout and content that is presented within the notification scene. This shortcoming can be overcome, however, through the use of custom notifications.

Custom notifications allow the appearance of a notification category on the Apple Watch to be designed in terms of the interface objects that are presented to the user and the content that is displayed on those objects. In fact, a dynamic custom interface can contain any combination of non-interactive interface objects such as Label, Map and Image objects.

A custom notification is made up of two parts referred to as *static* and *dynamic* notifications.

27.5 **Dynamic and Static Notifications**

Custom notifications consist of a static and a dynamic notification. The static notification consists of a Label object which displays the content of the notification's alert body text. The static notification scene can be customized by adding additional non-interactive interface objects such as Labels and Images (note that any images displayed on the static notification scene must be bundled with the WatchKit app and not the extension), and the attributes of those objects can be customized at design time. Once those attributes have been set, however, there is no way to change the appearance or content displayed on the objects before the static notification appears (hence the term *static*).

An optional dynamic notification may also be added to the static notification. The dynamic notification scene may also be customized in terms of layout and the addition of non-interactive interface objects. The difference with the dynamic notification scene is that it has associated with it a *notification interface controller* (subclassed from WKUserNotificationInterfaceController).

As with a standard interface controller class, the notification interface controller can contain outlets connected to interface objects in the dynamic notification scene. When a notification arrives on the Apple Watch device, the dynamic notification interface controller is launched and passed via a handler method a notification object containing details of the alert.

The notification controller handler method is then given the opportunity to update the dynamic notification scene via outlet connections based on the details of the alert before it is presented to the user.

The decision at runtime as to whether the static or dynamic notification is used to deliver a notification on the Apple Watch is made by WatchKit based on a number of factors including the resources available on the watch device and the amount of time it takes the dynamic notification handler method to prepare the scene for display.

27.6 **Adding a Custom Notification to a WatchKit App**

A custom notification can be added to a WatchKit app at creation time by enabling the *Include Notification Scene* option in the new target options panel as highlighted in Figure 27-3:

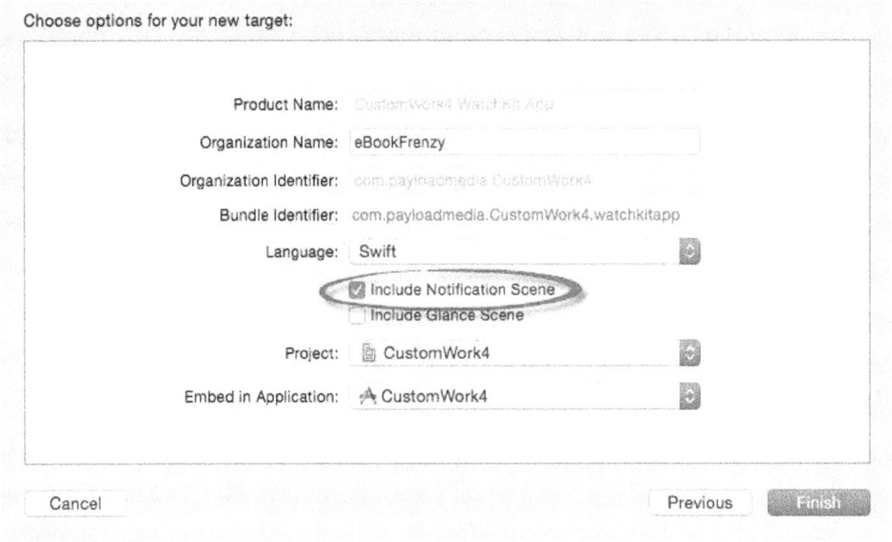

Figure 27-3

Alternatively, a custom notification may be added to an existing project using the following steps:

1. Drag and drop a *Notification Interface Controller* object from the Object Library onto the WatchKit App storyboard canvas.
2. Ctrl-click on the WatchKit Extension folder in the Project Navigator panel, select *New File...* and add a new Cocoa Touch Class to the project subclassed from WKUserNotificationInterfaceController.

3. Select the *Static Interface* scene within the storyboard, display the Attributes Inspector panel and enable the *Has Dynamic Interface* option. This will add the Dynamic Interface scene to the storyboard.

4. Select the newly added Dynamic Interface scene, display the Identity Inspector and change the Class menu to the class added in step 2 above.

Once a custom notification has been added with dynamic support, the scenes will appear in the storyboard as illustrated in Figure 27-4:

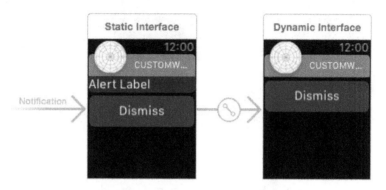

Figure 27-4

27.7 Configuring the Notification Category

As previously discussed, notifications have an associated category identifier that is used to differentiate one notification type from another within an app. Custom notifications also have a category identifier which can be specified from within the Document Outline panel. To access and modify the category identifier for a custom notification, select the static notification scene and display the Document Outline panel. Within the Document Outline panel, unfold the *Static Notification Interface Controller* section, select the *Notification Category* entry and, within the Attributes Inspector, change the Name field to the new identifier string:

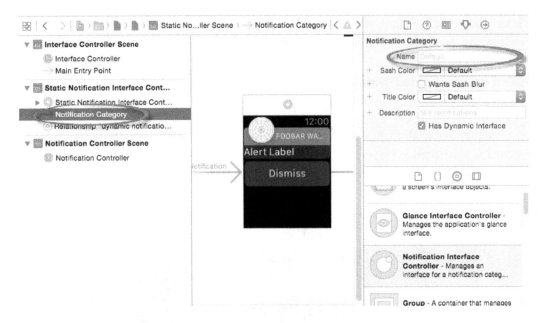

Figure 27-5

Once the custom notification has been assigned a category identifier, that identifier will need to be referenced whenever notification events are configured if those notifications are to be displayed using the custom notification.

27.8 Updating the Dynamic Notification Scene

In order for the notification interface controller to be able to dynamically update the interface objects in the dynamic scene, those objects must be connected to outlets. Once those outlets are configured, the code to update the interface needs to be placed in a handler method within the notification interface controller class. By default, Xcode will have placed templates for these methods within the notification interface controller class file. The choice of handler method to use depends on whether the notification is local or remote. For remote notifications the *didReceiveRemoteNotification* method is called by the system while local notifications result in a call to the *didReceiveLocalNotification* handler method.

Each method is passed a notification object from which can be obtained the details of the alert. For local notifications this takes the form of a UILocalNotification object. Remote notifications, on the other hand, receive a Dictionary object containing key-value pairs as defined by the remote notification server.

The handler methods are also passed a reference to a completion handler which must be called once the user interface updates are complete. If the completion handler is not called, or the user interface update takes too long to complete, the system will revert to the static notification.

The topic of custom notifications will be covered in further detail in the chapter entitled *A WatchKit Custom Notification Tutorial*.

27.9 **Summary**

Notifications are a common feature of many iOS applications and are often delivered to the paired Apple Watch, especially if the iPhone device is locked. A considerable amount of notification support is provided by default for WatchKit apps, including the appearance of both short and long-look notification scenes. Notifications can also be extended to include action buttons which can be configured to perform application specific tasks when selected by the user.

Custom notifications may also be used to provide a greater level of control over the layout and content of notifications when delivered to the Apple Watch device.

28. A WatchKit Notification Tutorial

This chapter will create an iOS project containing a WatchKit app that demonstrates the use of the iOS notification system. The example will make use of the standard WatchKit short-look and long-look notification interfaces and include the implementation of a notification action button within the long-look interface.

28.1 About the Example Project

The purpose of the project is to allow the user to specify a time delay before which a notification alert will be triggered. At the point that the notification appears, the user will be given the opportunity through a notification action button on both the iPhone or Apple Watch device to repeat the notification.

28.2 Creating the Xcode Project

Start Xcode and create a new iOS project. On the template screen choose the *Application* option located under *iOS* in the left hand panel and select *Single View Application.* Click *Next,* set the product name to *NotifyDemoApp,* enter your organization identifier and make sure that the *Devices* menu is set to *Universal.* Before clicking *Next*, change the *Language* menu to Swift. On the final screen, choose a location in which to store the project files and click on *Create* to proceed to the main Xcode project window.

28.3 Designing the iOS App User Interface

The user interface for the parent iOS app will consist of Label, Stepper and Button objects. Select the *Main.storyboard* file and add and configure these objects so that the layout matches that illustrated in Figure 28-1, making sure to position the objects in the horizontal center of the layout:

Figure 28-1

Display the *Resolve Auto Layout Issues* menu (Figure 28-2) and select the *Reset to Suggested Constraints* menu option listed under *All Views in View Controller* to establish sensible layout constraints on the view objects:

Figure 28-2

Select the Label object, display the Attributes Inspector panel and change the Alignment property so that the text is centered.

28.4 **Establishing Outlets and Actions**

With the *Main.storyboard* file still loaded into Interface Builder, display the Assistant Editor and establish an outlet connection from the Label object named *timeLabel* within the *ViewController.swift* file. Repeat this step to add an outlet connection from the Stepper object named *timeStepper*.

Next, establish action connections from the Stepper and Button objects to methods named *valueChanged* and *buttonPress* respectively. Review the code in the *ViewController.swift* file and verify that the actions and outlets match those included in the following code listing:

```
import UIKit

class ViewController: UIViewController {

    @IBOutlet weak var timeLabel: UILabel!
    @IBOutlet weak var timeStepper: UIStepper!

    override func viewDidLoad() {
        super.viewDidLoad()
    }

    @IBAction func valueChanged(sender: AnyObject) {
    }

    @IBAction func buttonPress(sender: AnyObject) {
    }
    .
    .
    .
}
```

28.5 **Creating and Joining an App Group**

Both the parent iOS app and the WatchKit app extension will need access to the current time delay setting. This shared access will be implemented using an app group and a shared user default setting key-value pair as covered in the chapter entitled *Sharing Data Between a WatchKit App and the Containing iOS App*.

Begin by selecting the *NotifyDemoApp* target located at the top of the Project Navigator panel and clicking on the *Capabilities* tab in the main panel. Within the Capabilities panel, locate the *App Groups* section and move the switch to the *On* position. When prompted, select an Apple Developer account to be associated with the app group.

When app groups have been enabled in the Capabilities screen, any existing app groups associated with your Apple developer account will be listed.

To add a new app group to your account, simply click on the + button and enter the new app group name, for example:

```
group.com.example.NotifyDemoApp
```

Add the current app to the newly added app group by enabling the checkbox next to the group name.

28.6 Initializing the iOS App

Each time the iOS app is launched it will need to check if the time delay value has been stored in the app group and, in the event that it has not, save a default value. Both the Label and Stepper objects will then need to be updated with the prevailing time delay value. Locate and select the *ViewController.swift* file and modify it to access the shared defaults and to add the initialization code to the *viewDidLoad* method, noting that the app group identifier will need to be changed to match the one you created in the previous section:

```
import UIKit

class ViewController: UIViewController {

    @IBOutlet weak var timeLabel: UILabel!
    @IBOutlet weak var timeStepper: UIStepper!

    let sharedDefaults =
            NSUserDefaults(suiteName: "<YOUR_APP_GROUP_ID_HERE>")

    override func viewDidLoad() {
        super.viewDidLoad()

        if let timeValue = sharedDefaults?.doubleForKey("timeDelay") {
            timeStepper.value = timeValue
        } else {
            sharedDefaults?.setDouble(10.0, forKey: "timeDelay")
            timeStepper.value = 10.0
        }

        timeLabel.text =
            sharedDefaults?.doubleForKey("timeDelay").description
    }
    .
    .
}
```

28.7 Updating the Time Delay

The Stepper object is the method by which the user adjusts the amount of time to delay before triggering the notification alert. This object was previously connected to an action method named *valueChanged*. When called, this method needs to obtain the current value of the Stepper object, display it on the Label object and store the value in shared defaults using a key set to "timeDelay". With these requirements in mind, locate and modify the *valueChanged* method in the *ViewController.swift* file so that it reads as follows:

```
@IBAction func valueChanged(sender: AnyObject) {
    timeLabel.text = timeStepper.value.description
    sharedDefaults?.setDouble(timeStepper.value, forKey: "timeDelay")
}
```

28.8 Setting the Notification

A method will now be added to the *ViewController.swift* file to configure the notification using the time delay value stored in the shared defaults with an alert title of "Reminder" and an alert body which reads "Wake Up!". In addition to these settings, the notification will be configured to play the default alert sound and assign a category identifier of "REMINDER_CATEGORY" (this category will need to be referenced again later in the chapter when action buttons are added to the notification). Remaining in the *ViewController.swift* file, implement this method as outlined in the following listing:

```
func setNotification() {

    if let timeValue = sharedDefaults?.doubleForKey("timeDelay") {
        var localNotification:UILocalNotification =
                            UILocalNotification()

        localNotification.alertTitle = "Reminder"

        localNotification.alertBody = "Wake Up!"

        localNotification.fireDate = NSDate(timeIntervalSinceNow:
                            timeValue)
        localNotification.soundName =
                    UILocalNotificationDefaultSoundName
        localNotification.category = "REMINDER_CATEGORY"


        UIApplication.sharedApplication().scheduleLocalNotification(
                    localNotification)
    }
}
```

The *setNotification* method will need to be called each time that the user taps the *Set Delay* button which is configured to call the *buttonPressed* method. Add the call to the *setNotification* method to the *buttonPressed* method:

```
@IBAction func buttonPress(sender: AnyObject) {
    setNotification()
}
```

28.9 Adding the Notification Action

When the notification is triggered, the user is to be given the option of repeating the notification using the same delay. This will involve the addition of a notification action to the notification using the "REMINDER_CATEGORY" identifier referenced each time the notification is set. The code to configure the action will be placed within the Application Delegate class within the *didFinishLaunchingWithOptions* method.

Begin by locating and selecting the *AppDelegate.swift* file and modifying the *didFinishLaunchingWithOptions* method to create the notification action as follows:

```
func application(application: UIApplication, didFinishLaunchingWithOptions
launchOptions:
[NSObject: AnyObject]?) -> Bool {

    var repeatAction: UIMutableUserNotificationAction =
            UIMutableUserNotificationAction()
    repeatAction.identifier = "REPEAT_IDENTIFIER"
    repeatAction.title = "Repeat"
    repeatAction.destructive = false
    repeatAction.authenticationRequired = false
    repeatAction.activationMode =
            UIUserNotificationActivationMode.Background

    return true
}
```

The above code creates a new notification action instance and configures it with an identifier string (this will be used to identify which action has been selected by the user later in the project). The action is also configured to display text which reads "Repeat" on the action button and to indicate that it is a non-destructive action (in other words it does not cause the loss of any data or information). In the event that the device is locked when the notification is triggered, the action is configured such that it is not necessary for the user to unlock the device for the action to be performed.

Finally, since the notification can be repeated without the need to display the iOS app, the activation mode is set to *Background* mode.

The next task is to create the notification category containing the action and register it with the notification system:

```
func application(application: UIApplication, didFinishLaunchingWithOptions
launchOptions: [NSObject: AnyObject]?) -> Bool {

    var repeatAction: UIMutableUserNotificationAction =
        UIMutableUserNotificationAction()
    repeatAction.identifier = "REPEAT_IDENTIFIER"
    repeatAction.title = "Repeat"
    repeatAction.destructive = false
    repeatAction.authenticationRequired = false
    repeatAction.activationMode =
        UIUserNotificationActivationMode.Background

    var notificationCategory:UIMutableUserNotificationCategory =
        UIMutableUserNotificationCategory()

    notificationCategory.identifier = "REMINDER_CATEGORY"

    notificationCategory.setActions([repeatAction],
        forContext: UIUserNotificationActionContext.Default)

    application.registerUserNotificationSettings(
        UIUserNotificationSettings(forTypes:
        UIUserNotificationType.Sound
            | UIUserNotificationType.Alert
            | UIUserNotificationType.Badge,
        categories: NSSet(array: [notificationCategory])
            as Set<NSObject>))

    return true
}
```

Compile and run the app and allow notification access when prompted by the operating system. Select a delay time and press the Set Delay button. Once the delay has been set, place the app into the background by pressing the Home button on the device (or selecting the *Hardware -> Home* menu option within the simulator). When the notification appears, swipe downward on the alert panel to display the action button as shown in Figure 28-3:

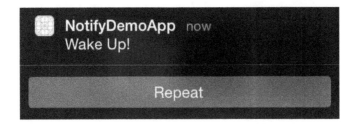

Figure 28-3

Assuming that the notification appears as expected, the next step is to handle the "Repeat" action.

28.10 Implementing the handleActionWithIdentifier Method

When a notification action button configured for background mode is tapped by the user, the *handleActionWithIdentifier* method of the app delegate class is called. Among the items passed to the method are a notification object from which both the action and category identifiers of the action that triggered the call can be obtained together with a completion handler to be called once the action has been handled. This method now needs to be added to the *AppDelegate.swift* file along with a variable in which to store a reference to the view controller instance as follows:

```swift
@UIApplicationMain
class AppDelegate: UIResponder, UIApplicationDelegate {

    var window: UIWindow?
    var viewController: ViewController?

    func application(application: UIApplication,
handleActionWithIdentifier identifier: String?, forLocalNotification
notification: UILocalNotification, completionHandler: () -> Void) {

        if identifier == "REPEAT_IDENTIFIER" && notification.category ==
"REMINDER_CATEGORY" {
            viewController = ViewController()
            viewController?.setNotification()
        }
        completionHandler()
    }
    .
    .
    .
}
```

The method begins by verifying that the category and action id match the repeat action. If this is a repeat action request, an instance of the ViewController class is created and the *setNotification* method of the instance called to repeat the notification. The completion handler block is then called to indicate that the action has been handled.

Re-run the app, set up a notification and place the app in the background. Display the action button in the notification panel when it appears and tap on the "Repeat" button. After the designated time has elapsed the notification should trigger a second time as requested.

28.11 Adding the WatchKit App to the Project

Now that work on the iOS app is complete, the next task is to add the WatchKit app to the project.

Within Xcode, select the *File -> New -> Target...* menu option. In the target template dialog, select the *Apple Watch* option listed beneath the *iOS* heading. In the main panel, select the *WatchKit App* icon and click on *Next*.

On the subsequent screen switch the *Include Notification Scene* and *Include Glance Scene* options off before clicking on the *Finish* button (the Notification Scene option is only required when working with custom notifications, a topic covered in the next chapter).

As soon as the extension target has been created, a new panel will appear requesting permission to activate the new scheme for the extension target. Activate this scheme now by clicking on the *Activate* button in the request panel.

28.12 Adding Notification Icons to the WatchKit App

The WatchKit app requires that six app icons be added to fully support notifications for the Notification Center, Short-Look and Long-Look views. For each icon category, images must be provided for both 38mm and 42mm Apple Watch models. The icons used in the example can be found in the *app_icons* folder of the sample code download available from the following URL:

http://www.ebookfrenzy.com/print/watchkit/index.php

Select the *Images.xcassets* entry located under *NotifyDemoApp WatchKit App* in the Project Navigator panel and select the *AppIcon* image set as outlined in Figure 28-4:

Figure 28-4

Open a Finder window and navigate to the *app_icons* folder. Once located, drag and drop the following icon image files to the corresponding locations in the image asset catalog:

- **HomeIcon@2x.png** -> Apple Watch Home Screen (All) Long Look (38mm)
- **Notification_Center_38mm.png** -> Apple Watch Notification Center 38mm
- **Notification_Center_42mm.png** -> Apple Watch Notification Center 42mm
- **Long_Look_42mm.png** -> Apple Watch Long Look
- **Short_Look_38mm.png** – Apple Watch Short Look 38mm
- **Short_Look_42mm.png** – Apple Watch Short Look 42mm

28.13 **Testing the Notification on the Apple Watch**

Make sure that the *NotifyDemoApp* target is still selected in the Xcode toolbar and run the iOS app on a physical iPhone device with which an Apple Watch is paired. This will launch the iOS app and install the WatchKit app on the Apple Watch device.

Configure a delay, tap the Set Delay button and lock the iPhone device. Pick up the Apple Watch device so that the screen activates. When the time delay has elapsed, the short look notification should appear on the screen using the designated icon. After a few seconds, the scrollable long look notification should appear including the alert title, alert body, the repeat action button and a Dismiss button:

Figure 28-5

Since the repeat action is already configured to launch the iOS app in the background and re-initiate the notification, tapping the Repeat button on the notification scene of the Apple Watch will cause the notification to repeat.

Make a swiping motion from the top of the watch display to view the Notification Center panel which should also include the notification as illustrated in Figure 28-6:

Figure 28-6

Tapping the app icon on the long-look notification button will launch the WatchKit app, where some work now needs to be performed to complete the project.

28.14 Adding the WatchKit App to the App Group

With the iOS app added to the app group, the WatchKit extension must also be added as a member of the same group in order to gain access to the shared container. To access the capability settings for the WatchKit extension, use the menu located in the top left-hand corner of the Capabilities panel as indicated in Figure 28-7:

Figure 28-7

When clicked, this menu will present a list of targets contained within the current project, one of which will be the *NotifyDemoApp WatchKit Extension*. Select this option and repeat the steps followed for the iOS app to enable membership in the same app group.

28.15 Designing the WatchKit App User Interface

The user interface for the WatchKit app main scene is going to consist of a Label, a Slider and a Button. Within the Project Navigator panel, locate and select the *Interface.storyboard* file to load it into the Interface Builder tool and design a layout that matches that of Figure 28-8 where both the *Alignment* and *Horizontal* position properties have been set to Center on the Label object:

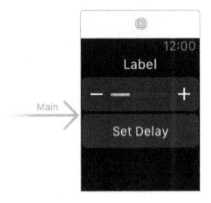

Figure 28-8

Select the Slider object and set the *Minimum* attribute to 0 and the *Maximum* and *Steps* values to 100 in the Attributes Inspector panel.

Display the Assistant Editor panel and establish outlet connections from the Label and Slider objects named *timeLabel* and *timeSlider*. Also establish action connections from the Slider and Button objects to methods named *sliderChange* and *setDelay* respectively.

Select the *InterfaceController.swift* file and modify it to declare a slider value variable, access the shared app group and to implement the code in the two action methods as follows:

```
import WatchKit
import Foundation


class InterfaceController: WKInterfaceController {

    @IBOutlet weak var timeLabel: WKInterfaceLabel!
    @IBOutlet weak var timeSlider: WKInterfaceSlider!
    var sliderValue: Double?
```

```
    let sharedDefaults =
        NSUserDefaults(suiteName: "<YOUR_APP_GROUP_ID_HERE>")

    override func awakeWithContext(context: AnyObject?) {
        super.awakeWithContext(context)

        // Configure interface objects here.
    }

    @IBAction func setDelay() {
        sharedDefaults?.setDouble(sliderValue!, forKey: "timeDelay")
    }

    @IBAction func sliderChange(value: Float) {
        sliderValue = Double(value)
        timeLabel.setText((value.description))
    }
    .
    .
    .
}
```

The *setDelay* method simply saves the current slider value to the app group shared defaults where it will be picked up by the containing iOS app next time it runs. The *sliderChange* method saves the current value to the *sliderValue* variable and displays it on the Label object.

28.16 **Testing the App**

Launch the iOS app on a physical iPhone device, configure a notification and then lock the device. Pick up the paired Apple Watch so that the screen activates and wait for the notification to appear. Tap the app icon in the long look notification scene and wait for the WatchKit app to appear. Change the delay value using the slider and tap the Set Delay button. Stop and restart the iOS app and verify that the new delay value is displayed.

28.17 **Summary**

This chapter has worked through the design and implementation of an example application intended to demonstrate the handling of notifications from within both a containing iOS app and the corresponding WatchKit app with a particular emphasis on the use of notification actions.

29. A WatchKit Custom Notification Tutorial

The previous chapter demonstrated the steps involved in adding action buttons to the default long-look notification scene within a WatchKit app. Although the addition of action notifications provided some additional functionality to the notification, the information displayed to the user was still limited to the alert title and body text. In order to provide a richer experience in terms of presenting information to the user in a notification it is necessary to use a custom notification. This chapter will add to the overview of custom notifications provided in the chapter entitled *An Overview of Notifications in WatchKit* by providing a tutorial based example of the implementation of a custom notification within a WatchKit app.

29.1 About the WatchKit Custom Notification Example

The project created in this chapter will consist of an iOS app with a companion WatchKit app. The iOS app will consist of two buttons which, when selected, will initiate local notifications configured to trigger after a 5 second delay. The WatchKit app that accompanies the iOS app will contain a custom notification which dynamically displays a different image depending on which of the two buttons was used to initiate the notification.

29.2 Creating the Custom Notification Project

Start Xcode and create a new iOS project. On the template screen choose the *Application* option located under *iOS* in the left hand panel and select *Single View Application*. Click *Next*, set the product name to *CustomNotifyApp*, enter your organization identifier and make sure that the *Devices* menu is set to *Universal*. Before clicking *Next*, change the *Language* menu to Swift. On the final screen, choose a location in which to store the project files and click on *Create* to proceed to the main Xcode project window.

29.3 Designing the iOS App User Interface

The user interface for the parent iOS app will consist of two Button objects. Select the *Main.Storyboard* file and add these objects to the storyboard canvas so that the layout matches that illustrated in Figure 29-1, making sure to position the objects in the horizontal center of the layout:

Figure 29-1

Display the *Resolve Auto Layout Issues* menu (Figure 29-2) and select the *Reset to Suggested Constraints* menu option listed under *All Views in View Controller* to establish sensible layout constraints on the view objects:

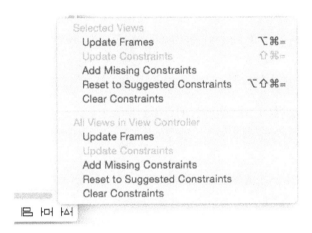

Figure 29-2

With the *Main.storyboard* file still loaded into Interface Builder, display the Assistant Editor and establish action connections from the Rain and Snow button objects to methods named *rainAlert* and *snowAlert* respectively.

29.4 Registering and Setting the Notifications

Select the *AppDelegate.swift* file and modify the *didFinishLaunchingWithOptions* method to register the notification settings for the app. These settings will ensure that the user is prompted by the app the first time it runs to enable access to the notifications system:

```
func application(application: UIApplication, didFinishLaunchingWithOptions
launchOptions: [NSObject: AnyObject]?)
-> Bool {
```

```
    let notificationSettings = UIUserNotificationSettings(forTypes:
        UIUserNotificationType.Alert |
        UIUserNotificationType.Sound,
        categories: nil)

    application.registerUserNotificationSettings(notificationSettings)
    return true
}
```

Next, select the *ViewController.swift* file and add a variable referencing the application context and the code for the two action methods to configure the notifications:

```
import UIKit

class ViewController: UIViewController {

    let app = UIApplication.sharedApplication()

    override func viewDidLoad() {
        super.viewDidLoad()
        // Do any additional setup after loading the view, typically from
a nib.
    }

    @IBAction func rainAlert(sender: AnyObject) {
        let alertTime = NSDate().dateByAddingTimeInterval(5)

        let notifyAlarm = UILocalNotification()

        notifyAlarm.fireDate = alertTime
        notifyAlarm.timeZone = NSTimeZone.defaultTimeZone()
        notifyAlarm.soundName = UILocalNotificationDefaultSoundName
        notifyAlarm.category = "WEATHER_CATEGORY"
        notifyAlarm.alertTitle = "Rain"
        notifyAlarm.alertBody = "It is going to rain"
        app.scheduleLocalNotification(notifyAlarm)
    }


    @IBAction func snowAlert(sender: AnyObject) {
        let alertTime = NSDate().dateByAddingTimeInterval(5)

        let notifyAlarm = UILocalNotification()
```

```
        notifyAlarm.fireDate = alertTime
        notifyAlarm.timeZone = NSTimeZone.defaultTimeZone()
        notifyAlarm.soundName = UILocalNotificationDefaultSoundName
        notifyAlarm.category = "WEATHER_CATEGORY"
        notifyAlarm.alertTitle = "Snow"
        notifyAlarm.alertBody = "It is going to snow"
        app.scheduleLocalNotification(notifyAlarm)
    }
    .
    .
    .
}
```

Note that both of the notifications have been configured with a category of "WEATHER_CATEGORY". It is essential that this category be referenced in the custom notification on the WatchKit app later in the tutorial.

Compile and run the app on an iPhone device and click on "Allow" when the system requests access to notifications. Once access has been allowed, tap on the Rain button and lock the device. After 5 seconds the alert should appear on the lock screen. Repeat these steps to test that the Snow button notification also works.

29.5 Adding the WatchKit App to the Project

Now that work on the iOS app is complete, the next task is to add the WatchKit app to the project.

Within Xcode, select the *File -> New -> Target...* menu option. In the target template dialog, select the *Apple Watch* option listed beneath the *iOS* heading. In the main panel, select the *WatchKit App* icon and click on *Next*.

On the subsequent screen switch the *Include Notification Scene* on and *Include Glance Scene* option off before clicking on the *Finish* button (the Notification Scene option is now required since we are working with custom notifications).

As soon as the extension target has been created, a new panel will appear requesting permission to activate the new scheme for the extension target. Activate this scheme now by clicking on the *Activate* button in the request panel.

29.6 Configuring the Custom Notification

Within the Project Navigator panel, select the *Interface.storyboard* file and locate the notification scenes as illustrated in Figure 29-3:

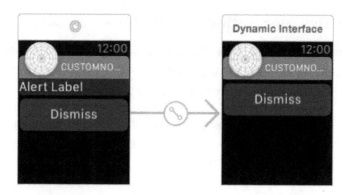

Figure 29-3

The left hand scene is the static scene. By default this is configured with a Label object which will display the content of the alert body text when a notification arrives. For the purposes of this example, no other static content is required on the static notification scene. Before designing the dynamic notification scene, the notification category for the custom notification needs to be changed to match that referenced when the notifications were setup in the iOS View Controller.

Display the Document Outline panel using the button indicated by the arrow in Figure 29-4 and unfold the section entitled *Static Notification Interface Controller*. Within this section of the panel select the *Notification Category* entry and, within the Attributes Inspector, change the Name field to *WEATHER_CATEGORY*:

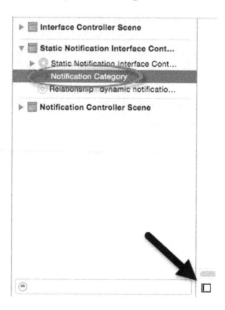

Figure 29-4

29.7 **Designing the Dynamic Notification Scene**

Remaining within the storyboard, drag a Label object from the Object Library and drop it above the Dismiss button in the Dynamic Interface scene. Select the Label object and, using the Attributes Inspector panel, set both the *Alignment* and *Horizontal* position properties to the center setting.

Drag and drop an Image object so that it is positioned beneath the Label object and set the Mode property to *Aspect Fit* and the *Horizontal* position property to *Center*. On completion of these steps the layout of the Dynamic Interface scene should match Figure 29-5:

Figure 29-5

Display the Assistant Editor, verify that it is displaying the *NotificationController.swift* file and establish an outlet connection from the Label object named *notificationAlertLabel*.

Establish a second outlet, this time connected to the Image object and named *notificationImage*. On completion of these steps the top of the *NotificationController.swift* file should read as follows:

```
class NotificationController: WKUserNotificationInterfaceController {

    @IBOutlet weak var notificationAlertLabel: WKInterfaceLabel!
    @IBOutlet weak var notificationImage: WKInterfaceImage!

    override init() {
        // Initialize variables here.
        super.init()

        // Configure interface objects here.
    }
```

.
.
.

```
}
```

29.8 Configuring the didReceiveLocalNotification method

When a notification alert arrives, the *didReceiveLocalNotification* method of the notification interface controller instance will be called and passed a UILocalNotification object containing details of the alert. A template for this method has already been added by Xcode to the *NotificationController.swift* file but is currently commented out. Open the *NotificationController.swift* file (located in the Project Navigator panel under *CustomNotifyApp WatchKit Extension*), locate this method and remove the /* and */ comment markers positioned before and after the method.

With the method uncommented, implement code as follows to identify whether a rain or snow alert has been triggered and to display a different image on the Image object depending on the alert type:

```
override func didReceiveLocalNotification(localNotification:
UILocalNotification, withCompletion completionHandler:
((WKUserNotificationInterfaceType) -> Void)) {

    if localNotification.alertTitle == "Rain" {
        notificationAlertLabel.setText("Rain")
        notificationImage.setImageNamed("rain_image")
    }

    if localNotification.alertTitle == "Snow" {
        notificationAlertLabel.setText("Snow")
        notificationImage.setImageNamed("snow_image")
    }

    completionHandler(.Custom)
}
```

Note the completion handler call at the end of the method. This notifies the system that the dynamic scene is ready to be displayed. If the completion handler does not get called or the code to configure the scene takes too long to complete, the system will revert to and display the static notification scene.

29.9 Adding the Images to the WatchKit App Bundle

The two images referenced in the *didReceiveLocalNotification* method now need to be added to the project. When configuring a dynamic notification scene, speed is essential to avoid the static notification scene appearing. In order to provide the app with quick access to the image files they will be added to the WatchKit app bundle as named images. The images used in this tutorial reside in the *weather_images* folder of the sample code download available from:

Within the Xcode Project Navigator panel locate the *Images.xcassets* entry listed under *CustomNotifyApp WatchKit App* so that the image catalog loads into the main panel. Ctrl-click in the left hand panel beneath the AppIcon entry and select *Import...* from the resulting menu. In the file selection panel, navigate to and select the *weather_images* folder before clicking on the *Open* button. Once imported, the images should appear in the image set as shown in Figure 29-6:

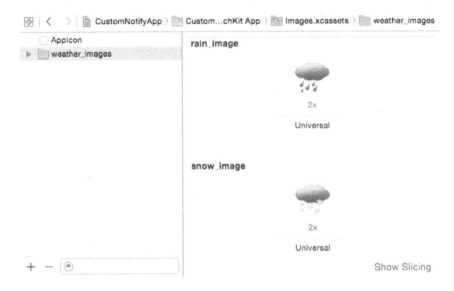

Figure 29-6

29.10 Testing the Custom Notification

If the run target in the Xcode toolbar is currently set to *CustomNotifyApp WatchKit App*, change it back to the *CustomNotifyApp* setting and run the iOS app on an iPhone device with which an Apple Watch is paired. When the iOS app main screen appears tap the Rain button and lock the device. Pick up the paired Apple Watch so that the screen activates and wait for the notification to appear, at which point it should display the rain cloud image as shown in Figure 29-7:

Figure 29-7

Scroll down within the notification scene and tap the Dismiss button to close the notification. Repeat the above steps, this time selecting the Snow button. This time the notification should appear on the Apple Watch using the snow cloud image. The app is now successfully using a dynamic custom notification.

29.11 Summary

Custom notifications provide a considerable amount of control over the content contained within a notification when it appears on an Apple Watch device. This chapter has worked through the creation of an example application that makes use of a custom notification to configure and present dynamic content to the user within a notification alert.

Index

A

Action Connections
    creating · 34
action methods · 22
addMenuItemWithIcon · 179
addMenuItemWithImage · 179
addMenuItemWithImageNamed · 179
Animated Image
    tutorial · 195
Animated Images · 191
Animation Sequence Images · 196
App Group
    creation · 123
    file sharing · 119
    suite name · 120
    user default sharing · 120
App Groups · 116
    adding apps and extensions · 116
App Icons
    adding to project · 17
    specifications · 17
AppIcon image set · 18
Apple Watch app · 1, 17, 18, 19, 39, 133, 134, 135, 136, 139, 140, 145, 148, 153, 154, 155, 201
Apple Watch Device
    running on · 14
ApplicationGroupContainerIdentifier key · 137, 150
Assistant Editor · 31
Attributed Strings · 201
    overview of · 203
Attributes Inspector · 12
Audio Background Mode
    enabling · 103
Audio Control Methods · 108

Audio Playback
    initialization · 106
AVAudioPlayer · 89
awakeWithContext() · *24*

B

Background Location Updates
    enabling · 228
backgroundTimeRemaining property · 99
becomeCurrentPage · 73, 76
becomeCurrentPage method · 73
beginBackgroundTaskWithName · 99
beginBackgroundTaskWithName Method · 99
Build Scheme
    adding to project · 160
    duplicating · 160

C

Capabilities tab · 100
Companion Settings Icon · 139
Container · 115
*container*URLForSecurityApplicationGroupIdentifier · 119
containing app · 4, 9, 119
Context Menus · 175
    creating in Interface Builder · 177
    example project · 180
    overview · 175
contextForSegueWithIdentifier · 75
contextsForSegueWithIdentifier · 75
Current Location · 231
Custom Font
    adding to project · 212

Index

Custom Fonts · 209
   in code · 215
Custom Notification
   adding to WatchKit app · 242
Custom Notification Tutorial · 261
Custom Notifications · 241

D

Data Sharing · 115
Default Preference Settings
   registering · 153
Default Preference Values · 138
Dictation Input · 93
didDeactivate() · *24*
didReceiveLocalNotification · 267
didSelectRow · 63, 68
dismissTextInputController · 92
Display Sizes
   handling · 219
Document Outline panel
   displaying · 43
Dynamic Notification Scene
   updating · 244
Dynamic Notifications · 241
Dynamic Text · 201

E

emoji · 91, 92, 93, 94, 95
entitlement file · 118
Errata · 2
Extension · 3
   structure · 5

F

File and Data Sharing
   tutorial · 121
File Sharing · 119
Font
   system · 28

Fonts · 201
   custom · 209

G

Glance
   adding to project · 158
   architecture · 157
   layout templates · 161
   passing context data · 163
   tutorial · 165
Glance Interface Controller · 159
Glances
   overview · 157
Global Tint attribute · 16

H

handleActionWithIdentifier · 240, 241, 254
handleWatchKitExtensionRequest method · 99, 100, 113, 114, 229
Hiding
   interface objects · 38

I

IBAction keyword · 22
IBOutlet · 23
IBOutlet keyword · 23
image asset catalog · 18
Image files
   importing · 56
Image Files
   adding to project · 56
Image.xcassets catalog · 187
Images · 185
   animating · 191
   Animation Sequence · 196
   caching · 189
   compression of · 190
   displaying · 185
   in extension · 185

named · 186
    template · 193
    tinting · 193
Images.xcassets file · 18
init() · 24
Interface Controller · 21, 30
    adjusting insets · 69
    modal presentation · 73
Interface Controllers
    adding to storyboard · 79
iOS Background Modes · 99
iOS Deployment Target · 15
iOS Extensions · 4

K

Key Color · 16

L

Lifecycle
    diagram · 24
Lifecycle methods · 24
long-look notification · 237

M

Map Tutorial · 225
Menu Item Images · 176
Menu Items
    adding and removing in code · 179
Modal Interface Controller · 71
modal option · 84
Modal Presentation · 73
    in code · 74
    using segues · 74
Modal Segue · 75
    passing context data · 75
Modal Segues
    adding · 84

N

Named Images · 186
next page segue · 72
Notification Action
    adding · 252
notification action object · 239
Notification Actions · 238
    handling · 240
Notification Category
    configuring · 243
Notification Handling
    default · 237
Notification Icons
    adding to asset catalog · 255
notification interface controller · 241, 242, 244, 267
Notification Tutorial · 247
Notifications · 237
    custom · 241
    Dynamic · 241
    Static · 241
NSAttributedString · 151, 152, 203, 204, 215, 216
NSDate object · 87
NSFileManager · 119
NSFontAttributesName · 151
NSObject · 41
NSTimer object · 88

O

Object Library · 11
openParentApplication method · 98, 99, 103, 111, 113, 114, 232
OpenType · 210
Outlet Connections
    creating · 31
outlets · 22

P

Page Scenes · 72
Page-based User Interface · 71
parent app · 4, 98, 116, 120, 232, 233

Parent iOS App Communication · 97
popController method · 63
popToRootController method · 64
Preferences · 133
presentControllerWithNames method · 74
presentTextInputControllerWithSuggestions method · 92, 93, 95
pushControllerWithName method · 64, 68

R

registerDefaults method · 138
reloadRootControllersWithNames · 73, 76
root interface controller · 64
Root.plist file · 136, 137, 138, 143, 150
    editing · 143
Row Controller Class
    creation · 51
Row Controller Type · 42
rowControllerAtIndex · 45

S

Sandbox · 115
Scene Title · 16
Scene Transition · 63
Screen Size
    runtime identification · 223
Screen Size Customization Attributes · 219
Screen Sizes
    in Interface Builder · 221
Segues · 72
    establishing · 80
setBackgroundImageNamed · 186
setImage · 192
setImageNamed · 186, 192
setNumberOfRows · 45
setRowTypes · 45
Settings Bundle · 17, 133, 134, 141, 142, 144, 145, 146, 150, 154
    add to project · 134
    code access · 137
    controls · 135

Settings Bundle Controls · 135
short-look notification · 237
Simulator · 13
Slider object · 29
    Continuous checkbox · 29
Sound
    playing · 88
Source Code
    download · 1
startAnimating · 192
Static Notifications · 241
stopAnimating · 192
Supporting Files · 106
System Fonts · 205

T

Table
    add title row · 58
Table Navigation · 63
Table Row
    deletion · 47
    insertion · 46
    scroll to · 47
Table Row Controller · 41
Table Row Controller Class
    adding to extension · 44
Table Row Initialization · 42
Table Rows
    runtime creation · 45
Tables
    overview · 41
Template Images · 193
Text Input Controller · 92
Text Style Fonts · 201, 203
Timer · 82
Timer object
    configuration · 87
TrueType · 210

U

UIBackgroundModes key · 100

updateUserActivity method · 163
User Default Sharing · 120
User Defaults · 115
User Input · 91
  obtaining · 94
User Interface
  designing · 28

V

voice dictation · 91

W

WatchKit app
  extension · 3
  running · 13
  scene · 11
WatchKit App
  adding to App Group · 127
  adding to project · 9
  architecture · 21
  entry points · 5
  lifecycle · 24
  overview · 3

project creation · 7
  removal · 39
  storyboard · 10
WatchKit Extension
  guidelines · 25
WatchKit framework · 21
WatchKit Framework · 4
WatchKit Settings Bundle · 133
WatchKit Table
  tutorial · 49
WatchKit Tables · 41
willActivate() · 24
WKInterfaceController · 21, 66, 73, 84, 98, 157, 160, 166, 185, 233
WKInterfaceGroup · 186
WKInterfaceImage · 53, 185, 189, 191, 192, 194, 266
WKInterfaceMap · 225, 235
WKInterfaceMapPinColor · 234
WKInterfaceMenu · 175
WKInterfaceMenuItem · 175
WKInterfaceTable · 41, 45, 47, 54, 67, 68, 171
WKInterfaceTimer · 82
WKMenuItemIcon values · 179
WKTextInputMode.AllowAnimatedEmoji · 92
WKTextInputMode.AllowEmoji · 92
WKTextInputMode.Plain · 92
WKUserNotificationInterfaceController · 241, 242, 266

www.ingramcontent.com/pod-product-compliance
Lightning Source LLC
Chambersburg PA
CBHW080357060326
40689CB00019B/4045